NIPPER

NIPPER

The Story of Leonard 'Nipper' Read

LEONARD READ
AND
JAMES MORTON

Macdonald

A Macdonald Book

First published in Great Britain in 1991 by
Macdonald & Co (Publishers) Ltd
London & Sydney

British Library Cataloguing in Publication Data
Read, Leonard
The "Nipper" Read story.
1. England. Police – Biographies
I. Title II. Morton, James
363.2092

ISBN 0–356–19749–2
Typeset by Selectmove Ltd, London
Printed and bound in Great Britain by
BPCC Hazell Books
Aylesbury, Bucks, England
Member of BPCC Ltd

Macdonald & Co (Publishers) Ltd
165 Great Dover Street,
London SE1 4YA

A member of Maxwell Macmillan Publishing Corporation

This book is dedicated with my grateful thanks to all those men and women who worked on the two Kray investigations

INTRODUCTION

When I was first approached by James Morton to do this book I refused.

It was too late. The whole Kray thing had been done to distraction. There had been a very successful film. I was convinced that the public had been saturated and in any event my memory of some of the events of twenty and more years ago was unreliable. I did not want to jeopardize the validity of a book by falling down on detail. James Morton, however, was persistent, not to say cunning. His next approach was to my wife, Pat.

After the release of the film *The Krays* I had done two very long interviews for television companies. This convinced Pat that my memory was better than I suggested and she insisted James and I should meet again. After a series of talks I surrendered – but I wanted to skip my early life in the police and concentrate on the two Kray investigations and the following trials. Unfortunately I was overruled on this point and it was explained that an outline of my career was essential. For this reason many of the twists and turns of both cases involving the Krays have been omitted and for this I apologize.

The day to day hunt for evidence is a fascinating business and one to which I am devoted. To have tried to condense this into a book of reasonable length would have been impossible and, I am almost persuaded, finally uninteresting. While we were working on the second Kray case I used to tell Frank Cater, my right hand man, that there was one story we could tell to the public, one to the lawyers and one we could only tell each other, simply because we had so many setbacks, so many disappointments, so many side tracks at the end of which we found ourselves in cul-de-sacs that only a detective would be remotely interested. Each has a story and, when we had a drink together, it was about those incidents we invariably spoke. Not the tracing of a particular witness, not the tip that led us to housing another suspect, but those stories that started off with such promise and then led nowhere. The times we spent chasing a lead we knew was kosher only to run into the same brick wall. I have managed to sneak in one or two of these, but there were many more.

I have not mentioned many of my squad in the second case by name. It would be an impossible task to pay credit to so many individuals. They know who they are and how much they contributed to make the inquiry so successful. For all this they have my thanks and great respect. Being in charge of this case was a great privilege and I was always conscious of the outstanding workrate of My Firm.

The Kray case wasn't the biggest case of all time nor, perhaps, the most important. It did however signal the end of an era. With the convictions in the case organized crime in London on the scale on which they operated was ended. Of their time, however, photographed by the fashionable, mixing with the stars, they were as much part of the sixties as Twiggy, the Mini car and the mini skirt. Perhaps the way the Krays were regarded in the East End is summed up by the attitude of a man I interviewed. He had been a prosperous businessman in good health and socially secure. Now, as a result of persistent pressure from The Firm, he was a sick, penniless outcast. I pointed out to him he had been ruined physically, socially, and financially by the Twins and he agreed.

'But, Mr Read.' he said, 'they're such nice fellas.'

PROLOGUE

BACK IN THE 1960s there was no such thing as privacy at the Old Bailey. Jurors, police, solicitors, counsel, witnesses (if they were still around), defendants in the next case milled around in the hallway; friends and relatives mostly waited downstairs in the canteen for the verdict. All through the trial the matron had let us use her room, which was off the main hall almost opposite the No. 2 Court, for a bit of privacy. A big Scots woman with ginger hair showing a bit grey at the roots, Mrs Hamlin stood no nonsense from anyone. That day she made endless cups of tea. The jury had been sent out shortly after midday and it was now early evening. Again, those days were different. Now a jury on anything a bit more serious than a shoplifting case can look forward to at least one night in a hotel, but in the 1960s a retirement anything longer than two hours was rare. It was said that a verdict in the first hour meant a conviction, in the second hour an acquittal and after that it swung back and forth. There were no majority verdicts. One person, stubborn, unconvinced, got-at, could force a re-trial.

It was just after 7 p.m. on that evening of Tuesday 4 March 1969 when a City of London copper put his head around the door. 'They're back, Guv'nor.'

You get so many false alarms. Sometimes 'they're back' means everyone goes back into court and the atmosphere becomes electric until the foreman of the jury stands up and asks 'Can we see Exhibit 6 again please?' or 'What is the burden of proof?' which means they haven't understood anything that has gone on for the past week. The jury had not done this the whole afternoon and we had the nod they had reached verdicts.

'This is it,' I said to Frank Cater who had been with me throughout the long afternoon. He took a last drag at his cigarette, stubbed it in the overloaded ashtray, and together we walked across the hallway and turned right towards No. 1 Court.

We sat in our usual places underneath the jury box, itself at right angles to the dock. No question in those days of the jury being out of sight from the public gallery. Anxiously we scanned the jurors' faces.

There's a theory, or more properly a superstition, that if there is to be an acquittal, particularly in a serious case, then, as they file back into court, the jurors will look at the defendants. This time it was different. The judge, Melford Stevenson, had decided that, to prevent any outburst, the defendants should be brought up one at a time. Counsel and solicitors fiddled with their papers, trying to appear calm; but there is no calm at the end of an important trial, just a feeling of an incipient panic which has to be shut down. As the judge came into court there was a buzz in the public gallery, quelled immediately by one of the policemen ushers.

My mouth was dry and I knew that if I put out my hand I wouldn't be able to stop my fingers shaking. All we had done, all we had worked for, would be made useless by one single word.

The Clerk of the Court was Leslie Boyd, a tall, elegant man who read out the first counts on the indictment, asking the jury if they had reached their verdicts.

'Would the foreman please stand? Mr Foreman, would you answer me first of all just yes or no. Members of the jury, with regard to Ronald Kray, have you reached a verdict upon which you are all agreed?'

'Yes, sir,' replied the foreman, now for a few brief moments the single most important person in the court. He seemed a little taken aback at the echo of his voice.

'Do you find the prisoner Ronald Kray guilty or not guilty on the first count of murder?'

'Guilty.'

I can't say the rest didn't matter. Of course they did, but that was the one that really counted. Cater put his hand on my shoulder to murmur congratulations. Boyd and the foreman continued their dialogue through the counts on the indictment and through the defendants one by one. I only half heard them as I thought of the long hours my team had put in over the months, the careful compilation of evidence, the watching, the waiting, the planning, the persuading and the pleading with witnesses to come forward and tell the court what had really happened in the London underworld of the 1960s. All of it seemed so long ago, so remote, but although it was then the longest murder trial in legal history, it was only 38 days since the trial had started. It seemed a lifetime.

I didn't look up in response to Frank's touch. I was afraid people would see the tears in my eyes.

CHAPTER ONE

PEOPLE SAY THE KRAYS had a deprived upbringing and that this could have been what turned them to crime, but I reckon there was more money coming into their house than into ours. Their father seems to have been something of a wanderer but, overall, they were a close-knit family.

My early life was a bit different. I was born in 1925 in Nottingham, the third in line after my two older sisters, Ida May – named after my mother – and Dorothy; my brother Eric was the youngest. Four years later my mother died. It was a tragedy which we young children didn't really understand. All we knew was that our mother had gone and was never coming back. When my father died many years later I found the bill for my mother's funeral amongst his possessions. It had cost £29 and there had been four black plumed horses. It must have been some sight, but I don't remember it or even whether I was taken to the cemetery.

It was then that the family was split up for a time. My father had no way of coping with us and we had to be farmed out to various relatives. The only alternative was a children's home and no one wanted that. The thought of being parted terrified us. My father's brothers had a number of children and we would have been too much of a burden, so I was sent to an uncle and aunt on my mother's side. I barely knew them because I had hardly seen them. They were strict Catholics and very religious. He was in insurance and was considered to be the wealthy side of the family. I was named after him, in the hope, I suppose, that eventually I would benefit from his will, but I never did. In fact I don't remember seeing them again after the family got back together.

They lived in Bobbers Mill, which at that time was a fairly wealthy part of Nottingham. As a kid, I thought the house was far too big for just two people. It was dark and there were religious objects on the wall in every room. I'd always been to a Methodist Sunday School and, of course, I had learned about gentle Jesus meek and mild, but here on the wall of my room was a harsh frightening face which terrified me. I remember lying awake at night, frightened to look, and then pulling the covers over my head to sleep.

My uncle and aunt were kind enough and looked after me, but they were very strict and far more religious than I was used to. Fortunately my stay with them did not last long. Just about all I remember apart from the pictures is a bus ride I took with my aunt, but where we went or why I can't say now.

As soon as convention allowed my father remarried and the family was reunited. My stepmother was called Doris and she was a very beautiful woman. She and my father had known each other before he married my mother and she was obviously very much in love with him. At the same time it was an enormous undertaking to marry into a ready-made family. You have to admire her taking on a man with four young children, but we, her stepchildren, never did. I think all of us resented the fact that she had taken our mother's place and found it difficult to accept her. She was very strict with us and, looking back, I suppose we all rebelled because she was not our real mother. However, we also understood that the alternative for us would have been far less acceptable. Later we came to realise the problems she had made for herself in marrying my father.

When my father was in work it was as a hand frame knitter. He worked a large, cumbersome machine which produced elasticised garments. From time to time he would take me to work and I was allowed to sit on a box beside him whilst he moved the levers and trod the foot pedals which made the machine work. I would watch, fascinated. It was like seeing a cinema organist.

During the First World War he had falsified his age and joined the Scots Guards. He survived Gallipoli, but he was always most reticent about his experiences. He kept his medals in the little box in which they had been sent to him, and would never wear them on Remembrance or Empire Days. He had also kept his heavy khaki greatcoat and when, in winter, Eric and I complained of the cold he would fetch it and throw it over the bed.

His hobby was breeding birds and he won prizes with them all over the country. He was a fine gardener and when, later in his life, he developed heart trouble he took up breeding cacti, at which he was equally successful.

At the end of his life he became an avid follower of the wrestling on television on a Saturday. I used to scold him for getting too excited, but one afternoon he became so involved in a bout he had the heart attack which killed him. I suppose if he'd been asked he might well have chosen that as the best way to go.

We children had flown the nest years earlier. Ida May married when she was 20. Dorothy joined the Land Army, married and moved to Stamford. I went into the Navy and then down South into the police. Eric followed me into the Navy a year later. After service he returned to Nottingham and worked alongside my father in a clothing factory before, eventually, he became a postman.

School for me was bliss. I enjoyed everything about it, and it gave me the opportunity to extend my greatest love: reading. I was never out of the top three in either junior or senior school. At senior school I had my first taste of both boxing and acting. Chosen for a lack of height rather than any ability, I was David Copperfield in the school play. The part of the waiter in the chop house went to a much taller beefier boy for, I suspect, probably the same reasons. Years later, when I was appointed as Superintendent to the Murder Squad, I was being introduced to the rest of my squad by the Chief Inspector who said, 'And this is Sergeant Chapman.'

He put out his hand and said, 'Welcome to the Yard, sir.'

'What you should have said is, "There's half a pint of ale for you, sir, will you have it now?"' I replied. Those were the opening lines Alan Chapman had had to say 34 years previously in *David Copperfield*.

I won my first medal for boxing at school when I weighed something like four stone seven. I can't remember much about the contest – it couldn't have been a crowd puller at that weight. I do know my father was very proud when I brought home the medal, and even more so that I had my picture in the *Nottingham Evening Post*. Many years later I asked him where the medal was but he said he didn't know. It was only after his death, going through his possessions, that I found it carefully wrapped in tissue paper in a little box marked 'Len's first medal 1937'.

I joined the Grundy Boxing Club, later to become the rather grander sounding Nottingham School of Boxing, which spawned such great champions as Herol Graham and Kirkland Laing. It was there I got the nickname 'Nipper'.

I left school at 14, although I had had hopes that I might go on to Nottingham High School. I passed all the examinations, but there was a penalty involved: my father would have had to pay certain fees for books, a uniform and so on, and that was impossible. I knew there was no possibility really, but later in life I began to resent the fact that I had never been given the opportunity to stretch myself scholastically. My father felt this, and for years afterwards when we spoke of it he would go to great lengths apologising, making the point that, in the circumstances, it would have been impossible to support me. He lived to see me become the Assistant Chief Constable of Nottingham and he was inordinately proud of my appointment. I am glad he had that satisfaction.

He was a lovely man. When he was out of work during the depression years it had wounded him deeply. He had spent days tramping round Nottingham looking for work to support his young family and he never forgot it. His philosophy was that you must never be out of work, and he drummed that message into all his children. He must have been impressive because none of us ever were.

When I left school my good leaving report made it easy for me to find a job. Dated 30 March 1939 it read:

> Leonard Read leaves this school on April 5th. The fact that he has been in the top form and that he is a school prefect is eloquent testimony to his intelligence and to his reliability and excellent behaviour. He is a keen mathematician, gets thoroughly interested in his work and is most industrious. He gives most willing service, never hangs about and is absolutely trustworthy. I recommend him confidently.

The job was in a wholesale tobacconist's warehouse. I was paid the princely sum of 10 shillings a week, gave eight to my stepmother and kept two.

At that time Nottingham was a Mecca for major industrial concerns. There was Player's tobacco factory, Raleigh Cycles, Boots the Chemist, Bairns-Wear, Viyella and a host of other textile companies. But Player's was the big attraction. Most young people in Nottingham set their sights on getting a job with them. Here I was lucky.

My two sisters worked at Player's and this gave me an entrée, as family connections such as this were encouraged. The wages were good and they paid a lump sum bonus. This made it a most attractive proposition. If you stayed there until you were 40, you were assured of a nice home and a small car. It was that kind of job: safe, sound and well paid.

I worked in the basement of No. 1 factory as a feeder. It was my job to feed the raw leaf tobacco into the back of a machine which turned it into cigarette tobacco. The machines had enormous blades which cut through the leaf at high speed and the resulting noise, heat, dust and stench were unbearable. The conditions were really horrific and yet as a young lad I didn't seem to mind it much. There was a good spirit amongst the employees and we had fun. I don't think I ever contemplated it as a career, however.

Some years later I met one of the chaps who had worked with me. He had become a manager of a number of the factories. He had a large house in the poshest part of Nottingham and he drove a Mercedes. As I said, the rewards were good if you stuck at it.

I was there just on two years, until in April 1943 I was called up for service in the Royal Navy and posted to the stone frigate HMS *Ganges*, the naval training base at Harwich. I had never been outside Nottingham and for a time the dialects defeated me. I could not work out how a man who insisted he was a cockney could come from 'Oban' which I knew perfectly well was in Scotland. Of course, he meant 'Holborn' in central London.

My paybook photograph shows me as a frightened-looking young man with close-cropped hair and wide staring eyes. It must have shown something about me because in the early summer I went before a naval psychologist who decided I could do better than swabbing decks, and I was packed off to the naval college to be an engineer. It may sound grand but it wasn't. At that time the college was in Harrods' warehouse in Fulham, not in Greenwich. From there I qualified as a mechanic, was promoted leading seaman and, in early 1944, equipped with all the right gear – thick woollen stockings, heavy arctic underwear, duffel coats and thick sea-boots – I was on my way to the heat and humidity of the Far East.

Whilst I was in the Navy I was determined that on my demob I wouldn't go back to Player's, amongst all that dirt and tannin. By law my job was still open to me but I had no intention of returning. My life in the Navy had given me freedom. My education had been broadened. I had met a delightful man, Eric Stealey, a well-spoken and intelligent man who had worked as a shipping clerk in the docks in the East End. We had discussed what future we contemplated after the war and he said that on his discharge he was going to join the police. When I asked him why he said it was an outdoor life, with a certain amount of freedom to make decisions and, of course, it was a career with a pension at the end of it. This was something that was always in my mind. To me there was never the possibility of doing my own thing – starting my own business. I was born and educated in a period when it was drummed into you that you should have a career, perhaps in the post office, the railways, the forces, something that was totally secure. That was the thing to aim for. My father had been unemployed; I'd seen unemployment. He'd always said there must never be a day when you are out of work. After all, the day after I left school I had started work. My friend Eric's words made a considerable impression on me. At the time he said them a career in the police was possibly the last thing I would have considered.

I was demobbed in December 1946 with the rank of petty officer and I had a month's leave. My father was nagging me to get a job. He was then a senior foreman in a clothing factory and he urged me to go down there with him. I'd come out of the Navy with another man who lived locally and my father suggested we should both go down to his factory 'to look the place over'. We said we would. My father started this other fellow and was furious when I wouldn't join the firm. 'You've got to get started again. You don't want to be idle.' It was a sin, especially when there was work being offered.

I looked around – with my father getting to be a pain, nagging me to get a job – and I decided I had two options. Either go back in the Navy or join the police force. I knew I could get back in the Navy as a chief petty officer or something of that kind, but I didn't have much hope for the police because I was too small. It was a wild card. No way could I join the Nottingham force because there was a minimum six-foot requirement. It could only be the Metropolitan Police in London whose minimum was four inches shorter.

So off I wrote and got an interview, with a Civil Service examination, a medical and an interview on the one day at Beak Street just off Regent Street. I knew I'd romped through the Civil Service exam – there wasn't any question about that; but as for the medical, I must have weighed under ten stone and I was certainly under five foot eight. The bloke who was doing the business was a Sergeant who, after he'd looked me over, said, 'Good God son, if you're accepted you'll have to take some stretching exercises because you don't really qualify.'

'Of course,' I said, adding hopefully, 'I'm still growing.'

Then I went before the Board and was asked why I wanted to join the police. I said I'd done over three years in the Navy which was such a difference from working in a factory. I said I saw the police as a career and that it was an open air life. Then when I was asked about sport, off I went – football, boxing, and I'd played hockey and cricket for the Royal Navy. I told them about the time I took ten wickets for 11 runs for the Navy against the Royal Indian Navy. I could see in my mind their marking this down as a plus, because the Metropolitan Police (the Met) had always had a very good sporting record. The fact that I'd been in the forces was also a plus because I knew what discipline was, and that would not present problems. The other thing in my favour was that there had been no recruiting during the war years and they were desperate for men. Perhaps, when it came to it, they were taking almost anyone.

I came to London as a police probationer in the bitterly cold February of 1947. The Thames was frozen over, snow was thick on the streets for almost the whole month, and over London there was the noise of bursting pipes and an air of depression and despair. Rationing was still in force. We all still carried identity cards; bomb damage was visible in every borough if not in every street. Emergency air-raid shelters and water tanks lined those streets and ex-army surplus was as much standard clothing as jeans are today.

Training was a twelve-week stint at the old Hendon Police College. There was drilling and lectures on public order, diseases of animals, child neglect, company fraud, incest, rape, bigamy, sodomy, helping children at school crossings, suicide, infanticide, drunks, down-and-outs, prostitutes, ponces and traffic control. Everything which made a policeman's life worth living. The discipline was by no means as strict as the Royal Navy's version, and so it was fun. Fun but still frightening, because as the weeks went by I realised that what was theory was soon going to be practice. Everything was taught in the school. We did not go outside the walls for experience. Accidents were staged for us, and we had to report on them. I felt terribly inferior when I was picked on to make the report. Even today I hate making speeches.

I've never really kept in contact with the others who were at college with me. One, Dickie Day, was posted with me and I still see him, but the others were scattered far and wide. Some of them certainly became middle-ranking officers, but none exactly hit the heights.

Apart from passing the written and oral examinations at the end of the course, speculation grew amongst us on our posting. Some areas were more highly sought than others. At least I knew I would not be sent to 'A' Division which covered the City of Westminster. Officers there were on duty at the Palace and the Houses of Parliament. They were seen as setting an example of the Metropolitan Police and had to be at least six feet tall. Otherwise it depended on your attitude because 'good' was generally considered as far away from the centre as possible – Ealing or Esher were thought to be marvellous. They were nice quiet areas with no problems. The 'grotty' areas were the East End and Kentish Town and West End Central.

I became a member of the boxing team at the training school and won, for the first time, a major competition: the Lafone Cup. I was also in training for the police championships. Certain Divisions were known for their boxing teams. In the late 1940s it was 'G', whose area was Hoxton, and 'N', who covered Kentish Town, who had the best teams, and it was possible I would be sent to join one of them. In fact when the announcement came on our passing out parade I was told I was going to 'D' Division, which then comprised the areas of Regent's Park, Marylebone, Paddington and Camden Town. So much for their belief in my boxing ability. But I was delighted at the time and, with hindsight, it could not have been better for me.

CHAPTER TWO

I NEVER LIKED BEING in uniform. In those spring days of 1947 we still wore the high choke collar left over from pre-war policing, and I was far too small and skinny to fill out the uniform. Particularly, I didn't like the big helmet. In it I thought I looked an idiot and, it turned out, so did the Sub Divisional Inspector.

Shift work meant I had to leave the section house by 5.15 a.m., fully kitted out, and walk from Camden Town to Albany Street. Again in those days the general public was pleased to see us, pass the time of day with us and step out with us. Most mornings my colleagues and I would walk along Albany Street with a smartly dressed man who, he said, worked at a bakery in Kentish Town and lived over a shop opposite the police station. His routine was working in the bakery at night, sleeping most of the morning and then sitting during the afternoon in Regent's Park reading philosophy. I think most of us enjoyed his company. Certainly I looked out for him every morning.

We young postwar blokes were very much dominated by the prewar officers. At first they resented us and this was quite noticeable. Unlike normal recruiting times, where new faces would appear at regular intervals throughout the year, there had been a tremendous gap during the war, and suddenly here was an influx of young but mainly experienced fellows who had served in one or other of the armed forces. We had the menial tasks, and such perks as there were were jealously reserved for the more senior constables who were given work in the station; wireless duties and such transport as there was went to them. They had the more favoured beats whilst we found ourselves on the less attractive ones. Their beats were smaller and busier where you got to talk to people. One I was on was Albany Street to Baker Street, right the way up through the park, then round Prince Albert Road, and all I ever saw were the animals in the zoo.

We seemed to be outrageous to the older officers. We were the new breed who were coming in. They looked on us, at first, with horror and resentment, but this quickly wore off. We had about a week what we called 'learning beats' and, depending on the quality and attitude of the man to whom you were attached, he might show you one or two wrinkles. On the other hand he might as easily say, 'Right, you walk with me,' and that would be it. I was sent round with a man who seemed to me to be quite a nice old boy. There was a regulation pace of two miles an hour over the beat. I've always had an inclination to walk quickly and he said, 'Wait a minute, son, wait a minute. This is your first lesson and it's something you'd better remember if you're going to do your thirty years. Never walk if you can stand, never stand if you can sit down, never sit down if you can lie down. Now you'd better learn not to run if you can walk, so slow down to my pace.'

After the week I was on my own. It was a disciplinary offence to walk with another officer, although of course we did arrange to meet up just to get a bit of company for a few minutes.

Music hall comedians had it right when they imitated police officers. Officers invariably stood with their hands behind their backs, and they did bend their knees, because they were getting a bit tired standing up after eight hours which was the shift then. The only relief was if the officer had a hidey hole. I remember walking with an old officer, when we passed a little alley and suddenly he was gone. I trotted after him and we went into the back door of a little Greek restaurant which fronted on to Euston Road. Off came the helmets and, without a nod, there on the table were two cups of coffee. This was the sort of hideaway that every beat officer had in some fashion. Even if it was a residential area, in those days, there were maids and serving staff who would give you tea or coffee where you could have five minutes' rest.

The older officers could also get away with things we newcomers could not – not only did they know all the places where you could drop in for a cup of tea, they knew the kind of thing that could take them back to the nick, which was the real haven. The only other resting place was the police box, but generally they could find an excuse to get back to the nick and have a smoke and a chat. If we did that the station officer would immediately say, 'What the hell are you doing here? You're supposed to be on your beat.' The Section Sergeant, Station Sergeant, and especially the Inspectors would come down much harder on us youngsters for even the most minor breach of regulations.

There was a famous story about one night duty officer who was on the beat at Euston Station. Now although that was policed by railway police it was always possible to call in to their office for a cup of tea and a smoke, and this was accepted practice. One night this officer wandered through the station, by-passed the railway police room, got into a carriage which in those days had a full length banquette, lay down and off he went. He was halfway to the North when he awoke. You can imagine the panic which ensued, because you had to ring in to book off, either from a public phone or preferably from a police box.

We were taught the perimeters of the beat but not how we were to deal with the public. That was something you were supposed to acquire with time. In those days we still had War Reserve policemen. They didn't conform to the usual discipline. I remember we had one who, when we lined up for inspection, was always drunk, and as soon as the parade was over he was off onto his beat all right but straight into the pub.

We had one pocket book and we had to report everything in it, so in one book you could have details of property found in the street, a murder, a traffic accident, every single thing. It had to be done in a particular fashion called the 'box method' of reporting. It always started off 'On day date time place'. The idea was that you missed nothing.

If you did something wrong you had a station officer, a Sergeant with three stripes and a crown – a position of great authority – to contend with. Ordinary Sergeants were bad enough even if some were just about friendly. Station Sergeants as a breed were an incredibly officious bunch. My memory is of a Station Sergeant sitting there with an old-fashioned nibbed pen, writing in copperplate in the occurrence book, an enormous ledger. They had to put every event of any moment into this book. Then the Superintendent would come round and initial it in green ink. Station Sergeants were in charge of the station. One of the first times I put in a report was when someone had handed me a parcel he had found in the street. The Station Sergeant, without moving his eyes from the desk, flung the book back at me. There was no question of my picking it up and saying 'What's wrong with it, Sergeant?' I had to scurry into the Reserve Room which was always manned by a senior PC on the switchboard. He was the buffer to stop any enquiries going to the station officer. He was the one who taught me how to do it. I took it back and the Sergeant said 'That's better, son.' It was a funny way of teaching people.

The older officers had their own methods of observation on premises. In Camden High Street, for example, there were a number of small shops – electrical goods, tailors, ladies' dress shops and so on. The backs of these premises were very vulnerable because there were few alarm systems. Older officers would mark premises with a couple of pins and a bit of black cotton. That would be on the door, and then further back something might be draped over an entrance so that if anybody had got in they would know. If an officer found his thread had been broken he would have to run to the police phone to call for help. Things weren't as violent then, but he would not be expected to go in on his own. If he couldn't get to a police post all he had was a whistle. As youngsters, we thought that was quite hilarious. Once one officer had marked out a wall with a piece of cotton so that if anyone had jumped over the wall the thread would be broken and he could then raise the alarm. One of the younger officers had found the cotton and had put a cigarette packet propped up on the wall on which he had written, 'You should be more careful. You'll break somebody's neck with this.'

In Hampstead Road there was a tailor's shop which was the first premises I saw that had a rudimentary silent alarm linked to Scotland Yard. It was a sort of record in a biscuit tin, and if anyone entered the premises and broke a circuit this set off a message saying, 'This is 79 Hampstead Road. Thieves have broken in. . . .' The number of people who were arrested as a result was incredible. For a period of time, once a fortnight someone broke in and was arrested. Nowadays, of course, it would be sussed out immediately. You could actually hear it whirring round, it was so unsophisticated. But then there was no back-up alarm to serve as a warning, and so thieves would be loading up when there was a thunder of hooves on the stairs and up came the Bill.

My very first arrest was supervised by a Station Sergeant at Albany Street called Handley, obviously known as Tommy. You looked for someone to nick. This was how you gained experience. This way you got to court and court was where the policeman's final training came. I was down around Euston Station and a bloke came staggering out of a pub shouting and swearing. I arrested him for being drunk and disorderly. He was no trouble at all and I walked him back to Albany Street because vehicles were at a premium. There was one van which was used for everything. So we got back to the nick together and I reported to the station officer who used to charge the defendant after writing everything down in longhand. Fingerprints weren't taken for a drunk-and-disorderly, and after the Sergeant read out the charge he just said, 'Put him down'.

The senior PC in the Reserve Room doubled as gaoler and had the keys. I had to get them from him, and then walk my prisoner down the long corridor at Albany Street to the cell.

Everything had gone beautifully. Old Tommy had patted me on the back and said, 'Well done, son, you've got your first arrest.' Then, just outside the cell, the man went into a spasm. At first I thought he was going to kill me. I had hold of him and he grabbed my arm. I didn't realise that he was having an epileptic fit. Then I thought that he wasn't going to kill me, but that he was dying. He was thrashing about like a shark. No one seemed to know what to do except Tommy who, hearing the commotion, came walking in saying, 'Leave him alone, leave him alone.' The man was still thrashing around on the floor and Tommy said, 'Get the van and take him to University College and don't leave him. He's your prisoner. Understand, boy?'

I took the man to University College Hospital and they ran some tests on him, with me just hanging around. They must have identified what was wrong with him because he was put to bed in a small ward. I stood at the door with my helmet under my arm until the Sister came up and asked what I was waiting for.

'I've got to watch the prisoner,' I replied.

'He's not your prisoner any more,' she replied, 'He's my patient. You can leave.'

I considered that as he was safely tucked up in a hospital ward it would be perfectly all right for me to do just that and I went back on foot down Tottenham Court Road to Albany Street. I went in to the front desk to report to Tommy.

'Where's your prisoner, boy?'

'He's at University College Hospital, Sergeant.'

'He's bleeding not. Five minutes ago he belted the night Sister and escaped. Tomorrow morning, Clerkenwell Court, warrant.' Everything Tommy said was in a kind of shorthand. There was no 'you will have to . . .'. So it was back into the Reserve Room again to speak to the senior Constable.

It was good experience. Compressed into that one little incident was: going to court, seeing the warrant officer, making an application to the magistrate, obtaining a warrant and recording it in the book. As far as I know the man was never nicked. If he was, no one ever told me.

Not that we didn't have some guidance. When we left the station to go on our beats the Station Sergeant would always call out, 'Remember lads, you can always ring the station for help – if it's a murder.' I did ring in once. I had been on my first spot of traffic point duty when I had taken over from an officer who had gone to relieve himself. I didn't at first believe the traffic would stop when I waved a white gauntlet at it, but when I found it did I began to enjoy myself. That is, until a coal lorry drew up alongside me and the driver shouted, 'Jump in, Guv.' Although I had no idea what it was about, I did so without hesitation. The driver then explained that a bull had escaped from Caledonian Road cattle market and was rampaging down Eversholt Street. When we got there he managed to force the beast into a cul-de-sac, and position his lorry so its escape was blocked. I decided I should play my trump card and call the station. After I had explained the position the Sergeant asked, 'Where exactly is it now?' When I told him he replied tersely, 'It's not on our manor, lad.' And the line went dead. Fortunately by the time I got back to the scene a vet had arrived and put the poor thing out of its misery.

There is a similar story told about the great detective Reggie Spooner, a wonderful man who was never without a cigarette. Spooner went to investigate the body of a taxi driver found in his cab just at the top of Notting Hill. The car was on an incline and would run down Holland Park Avenue into another Division quite nicely. 'What do you think, Guv?' asked the aide who was with him.

'Release the fucking handbrake,' replied Reggie, lighting up.

I had not been on beat duty for more than a few weeks before I was told to appear before the Sub Divisional Inspector (today his equivalent rank would be that of Commander). Senior officers were god-like figures. They were also invisible. I'd never seen him, let alone spoken to him. I wondered what on earth he wanted to see me about. I hadn't done anything wrong to my knowledge. I hadn't been in the job long enough to learn any of the tricks and dodges more experienced officers could get up to. I wasn't helped by the Divisional Sergeant who saw me standing outside the Sub's office.

'What you been up to, then, boy?'

I shook my head and mumbled that I didn't know.

'Must have been up to something, lad. He doesn't see you just to pass the time of day.'

But inside the door things were very different. Here was a tall gentlemanly officer who greeted me pleasantly.

'Well, young man, I've got a job for you. I want you to be working for me in plain clothes. You will be working with one of my special Sergeants and will be reporting directly to me. Now, how do you fancy that?'

And, of course, I did fancy it a great deal. Even if I hadn't, it wouldn't have made much difference. Outside, the Sergeant told me what had happened. The Superintendent had been making a tour of the Division when he had seen me in Camden High Street – it then had two-way traffic – and he watched me walking along, with the costermongers making only the token gesture of picking up the handles of their barrows and doing a couple of shuffles to indicate they were aware of the presence of the law.

'Who the hell is that?' he had asked his driver, and when told it was '241 Read' had replied, 'He'll have to come off the bloody streets. He'll get the Force a bad name.'

This led to my working under the Station Inspector, Richard Mathews, who went on to be Chief Constable of Devon. He was a lovely, lovely man who stood about six foot five. He never used to call me Nipper – always 'Tich'. He was known as 'Gosh' because he would say 'Gosh, look at that. Oh my Gosh.' He never realised he was saying it, because one day he asked, 'Oh, Tich, why does everyone call me Gosh?'

He placed me with a big fat Sergeant, Ivor Hatchard, a Welshman, who was everyone's idea of what a police sergeant looked like in those days – very short back and sides, big red cheeks and a big big belly. It was no use his being in plain clothes because he still looked like everyone's idea of an off-duty policeman. He had had an accident to his right hand

and taught himself to write left-handed in a beautiful script. He had good information and he would then put me in at ground level to get the evidence, rather as a poacher works a ferret.

So bookies' runners, betting shops and brothels which had previously been untouched all fell victim to what was a new and winning team.

One of the first times I was put in disguise was when a pub was being used as a betting shop, in a sense that suggested the landlord was only too well aware of what was happening. As the pub was near Euston Station I got myself a British Railways waistcoat – they were black with stripes – and a railway cap. With no trouble at all I could watch what was going on, logging the people coming in to lay their bets, and watching the landlord turn a blind eye. On the final day of observation I was sitting reading a paper, trying to be inconspicuous, and suddenly there was a tap on my shoulder and there was the railway foreman.

'What are you doing here?' he asked.

I said, 'I was just going, Guv'nor, I was just going, actually.'

'Where are you?'

I said 'No. 4 platform, sir,' and before he could answer I'd shot out. That was the narrowest squeak I had, because if I had been exposed as not being a railwayman I could have expected a hiding. Subsequently the pub was raided by Inspector Mathews and the Sergeant, and the landlord was prosecuted. They tried to avoid my having to give evidence to preserve my anonymity, but the case was fought by the landlord – a conviction would mean the loss of his licence – and so I had to be called, and had my first experience of having my evidence challenged – by Henry Elam who went on to be Chairman of Inner London Sessions. The landlord was horrified to hear me give the details of my period of observation. He had not even recognised me as a *habitué* of his pub. He was even more horrified when he was convicted.

There was a bookie's runner they had been after for years. He collected slips and money from all the local public houses for a bookmaker who had an office in Albany Street. They'd tried to use women police, but in those days women police were great strapping wenches bigger than me and they were spotted right away. So they tried me, because in ex-army surplus clothes no one would ever believe I was a policeman.

I remember nicking him as he came out of a pub in Hampstead Road. I let him turn right because I knew he was on the way to Albany Street. I'd been told that all I had to do was go up to this guy, make sure he had the bets on him and that he didn't throw them away. I said, 'Right, you're nicked.' I must have shown him my warrant card because he wouldn't have believed me otherwise. I told him to put his hands in his trouser pockets and keep them there.

'Don't worry, son,' he said, 'I've got them all on me. Can I have a fag?'

'No,' I said, 'no.' I was terrified there'd be betting slips all over the place.

Then we did the betting office itself, which was opposite the barracks in Albany Street. The betting offices then weren't the grand places with colour television they are today – just a room with a ticker-tape machine giving the results, and a few telephones. Observation was set up with Hatchard, 'Gosh' Mathews and me. We had to get in the premises. It was suggested that when the runner came up I would leave the observation post and go behind him, and as he went in I would open the door to let the others in. The only problem about this was that the office was in a mews and so I had to wait until the runner was actually inside the door before I could go into the mews itself. Mathews gave me the signal: 'Right ho, Tich, off you go and for Christ's sake don't miss it.' I watched as the man opened the door and then I sped down the mews. I was on him before he could get the door closed, and shortly afterwards Mathews and Hatchard arrived at a leisurely pace.

'Gosh, Tich, you cut that fine,' said Mathews as we climbed the stairs to confront the surprised bookmaker and his staff. It was a perfect collar, but whilst we were in there the phone went and I recognised the voice of a local Detective Sergeant ringing up to place a bet.

'Sorry, Sid,' I said, 'the office is closed today.'

The brothels in the 1940s were not just a couple of girls working together from the same premises, but actually 'Houses' with a Madam. The girls would pick up the clients down Euston Station and Hampstead Road way and bring them back to the big old houses in Eversholt Street. The neighbours would complain, and then observation was kept on a number of girls who frequented the premises regularly and who would be identified at the time as 'tall, black-haired' and referred to as 'A', 'short and blonde,' referred to as 'B' and so on.

I remember when we went into one with 'Gosh' Mathews who had obtained the warrant, we saw the Madam. Raids were not something they resented unduly and so there was never any bad feeling when we went in at two in the morning. Once inside the premises it was my job to go from room to room identifying the girls I had designated as 'A', 'B' and so on to Mr Mathews. We went into a ground floor room and much to the consternation of the client I said, 'Sir, this is the woman identified in my report as 'C'. We then left and explored the other rooms. I then had to go back and take full particulars. I went back to the ground floor room and found the client had recovered his composure. Looking over his heaving back, Miss 'C' said, 'Well, he's got to get his two quid's worth, hasn't he?'

For me, then, this was a kind of a fun thing, after just a few weeks on the beat which I had found boring. In fact Hatchard and I had such a run of successes that by the end of the year I collected my first Commissioner's Commendation which was quite an achievement for a young copper still serving a probationary period.

I was still playing football for the Division and, of course, boxing. I won my first Police Boxing Championship at Manor Place Baths down near the Elephant and Castle. I stood holding what was an enormous silver trophy and basking in glory when the Superintendent, who would be the equivalent now of Commander, took it from me telling me to get back on brothel observation and saying, 'I'll look after this for you. Back to work.' The cup joined the others in the station's trophy room and I did not see it again until I had to return it for the next year's tournament.

At that time the way to join the CID was to put your name down in a book. Then when there was a vacancy as an aide, applicants would be considered. When I entered my details I noticed I was the first applicant since before the war.

A few months later I was called to see the Divisional Detective Inspector (now the equivalent of a Chief Superintendent) who asked whether I still wanted to join the CID. For a moment I was uncertain. I was doing well with Ivor Hatchard, and 'Gosh' Mathews had more or less promised that I would make rapid progress in the uniformed division. He was pleased with the work Hatchard and I were doing and, when we had a raid, he was there to lead it, and so went on the score sheet, so to speak. The better I did, the better he did. But I knew that soon my small successes as an undercover man would come to an end. I would begin to get known and then I would have to be taken off the streets. The CID was where I really wanted to be.

'Yes, please,' I said.

CHAPTER THREE

I WAS SENT TO St John's Wood Police Station, a few hundred yards from Lord's Cricket Ground, to serve what turned out to be a four-year apprenticeship as an aide to CID. This was the turning point of my career because I was put under the wing of one of the best detectives I have ever met, although he never rose beyond the rank of aide to CID. His name was Martin Walsh. It is perhaps trite to say that I owe him the credit for any success I have had, but it is true. He was an older man, then in his late forties, who was used as a 'tutor' aide. He taught me what investigating was all about.

He was, without doubt, the most dedicated man I have ever met. Everyone knew his qualities. He was tenacious and persistent. The words could almost have been coined to describe him. He would sit, and have me sit with him, for hours on end observing a suspect. He would watch someone leave a building and say, 'He'll be back.' When after a few hours I would say, as an impatient 22-year-old, that we had blown it, he would reply, 'Give it a bit longer' and I would grudgingly accept the long and dreary hours. Sure enough, the man would return. Nor was there any question of spelling each other by taking turns to keep watch. Four eyes were better than two. The difference between him and Flying Squad detectives, who sit four in a car with the windows up and fogged up with cigarette smoke, was amazing. They just don't know what an observation is. He did. He (and I) would sit and sit and wait and wait, and more often than not something came from our patience. He was a Birmingham man, and once when the City was in a cup tie being broadcast on the wireless, I suggested he might want to listen to it whilst on duty. He absolutely slated me for the suggestion.

He had a sixth sense of what was going wrong. Just after the war stealing lead from churches – blue-flying it was called – was the rage and there was good money to be made. Martin would sit and watch people go in and out of disused or bombed churches, just waiting for the moment to make an arrest. There was no point in doing it before they came out because there was always the excuse, 'I'm only here for a piss.' So he would wait until the thieves had loaded up their prams or handcarts before he made his move. One man he knew, George O'Brien, was a regular, and we watched him one day go into an old convent on the borders of St John's Wood and Kilburn. This time, unusually, he was without his handcart. He came out, seemingly empty handed, but Martin had the feeling we should pull him. As we followed him he looked over his shoulder, saw us, and began to run. I chased after him and was surprised how quickly I was catching up with him when he fell over. He tried to get up, but he couldn't, and I thought he might have hurt himself. Martin didn't. He looked down and said, 'You see, George, you will try and take too much. This should be a lesson to you not to be so greedy.' George had wrapped sheets of lead around his body, and so when he had overbalanced could not pick himself up.

Martin was not much taller than I was and together we would bicycle round the beat. We had a basic signalling system when Martin, who usually led, smelled something wrong and would peel off into a side street, leaving me to go on to the next turning. It was a simple but incredibly successful ploy and we would be able to approach and make the arrest before the suspects knew we were there.

I wish I could say I had been with him in early 1949 when, after another long and patient observation, he arrested a loiterer. We had what for us was an early night, packing it in about 5 p.m. Martin lived in Scott Ellis Gardens at the side of Lord's Cricket Ground, and he walked to the corner to get himself an evening paper. There he watched a man behaving suspiciously and eventually arrested him. I was with him when the next morning the man was taken to Marylebone Court. Before the case was called there was a great commotion in the gaoler's office and a Detective Inspector appearing saying he was taking over the case. We had no idea why and we were not told but we stayed at court. The reason for the interest in and hijacking of the case was that the man was Harry Lewis and he was charged with the murder of a lightning cartoonist, Harry Michaelson.

Michaelson was living alone in a basement flat in Marylebone when, on Boxing Day 1948, Lewis, then aged 21, got in through an open window. At the time Michaelson was asleep in the bedroom and woke to find Lewis on his way out, having picked up what cash there was in Michaelson's pockets. Michaelson called out; Lewis turned, picked up a chair, and battered him with it. Michaelson was taken to hospital where he died following a brain operation. It was after Martin had had Lewis's fingerprints sent to the Fingerprint Department at Scotland Yard to discover if he had a criminal record that these were matched with those on the chair.

It was argued on Lewis's behalf that the real cause of death was the brain operation and that the verdict should be one of manslaughter, but the then Lord Chief Justice Lord Goddard would have none of it, telling the jury that if they found that this was the case of a burglar killing a householder to avoid arrest it must be one of murder. The jury in fact added a recommendation of mercy, possibly because of Lewis's age. A reprieve was refused and he was hanged on 21 April 1949. Cases were heard more quickly in those days.

I never met Michaelson, but he was well known at police functions where he would draw cartoons of the guests. It was always said he was such a kindly man that if Lewis had only asked for the money in all probability he would have given it to him. As for the chair, that stayed in the Detective Inspector's office at Paddington for years. The last time I saw it, there was still the exhibit number stuck to it with an arrow showing where the fingerprint officer had found the give-away print. Then one day the Deputy Detective Inspector, Jock Jamieson, took it away to use in a lecture and it never came back.

After his arrest of Lewis, Martin was offered the opportunity to become a Detective Constable in the CID, but he turned it down flat. 'This is what I do best,' he said.

During the time we were together we were posted to various murder enquiries. The first of them was of an old lady who had been found strangled in the grounds of Winfield House, then the home of the Woolworth heiress, Barbara Hutton, and now the official residence of the American Ambassador. Not much was known about the poor woman. Indeed for a long time she was not identified and Martin and I were sent round the area to try to make some sort of identification. One of the calls we made was to the Princess Alice, a pub in Acacia Road, and there the landlord, Dave Kleinfield, told us the description sounded like that of one of his public bar regulars whom he had not seen for some time.

Martin sent me down to the police station to collect her clothes and when we put them on the floor the landlord was immediately able to identify them as belonging to a woman he knew as Kate Higgins who lived in a mews, Townshend Cottages – they were not so fashionable then – near by, and from Kleinfield's directions we found the house. It turned out that Kate was known as Irish Kit and, aged over 70, was still working as a prostitute.

We reported back to the Detective Inspector, John Bliss, who later became the National Co-ordinator of the Regional Crime Squads. He organised the opening-up of her house, and there on the kitchen table was a pair of kippers. Now as the house hadn't been open for at least two weeks the smell was unimaginable.

It was decided that a crucial help in the investigation would be to discover where she had bought the fish, and I was detailed to go with a Detective Sergeant Joe Pratley from another Station who had been drafted into the enquiry, a little tiny fellow who looked like the actor Gordon Harker. He spoke a bit like him too. He always wore a trilby hat at a jaunty angle. 'Right, son,' he said, 'how many bleeding fishmongers are there in St John's Wood?'

When you were talking about St John's Wood then you were talking about the High Street and nothing else. I told him there were three. We set off at 10.30 in the morning and came to the first pub, and knocked on the side door. Down came the landlady, who saw him and said, 'Joe, Joe, come on in! What are you drinking?' Bass was the answer. Turning to me he said, 'Pop over the road to the fishmonger's, son.' They knew nothing about the kippers, and I came back and sat sipping a Guinness whilst Joe was drinking Bass until it was coming out of his ears. Then, all of a sudden, he said 'Thanks very much, off we go.' We walked round the corner, came to the next pub and it was exactly the same: 'Come on in, Joe.' Off I went to the second fishmonger's and again they said no, so I went back and reported. 'Right, that's it,' Joe said, 'she must have bought them at the other one.' So we stayed there for nearly an hour and then he said, 'Lunchtime,' and off we went to a third pub where they gave us fish and chips.

We got back to the station about 2.30 p.m. and, to general acclaim, Joe announced that the kippers had come from the third shop. If this is conducting a murder enquiry, no wonder there are no arrests, I thought.

No one was ever charged with Kit's murder. There was a strong suspicion that it was someone from the RAF, who were stationed in Viceroy Court near by, but it was no more than suspicion.

I enjoyed being involved in the murder squads, mainly because it meant I could watch how senior detectives worked, but one disappointment was that it meant long hours just hanging around waiting to be sent off on some errand or another. And these generally turned out to be proving a negative rather than having a material bearing on the case. I vowed to myself that if ever I achieved senior status I would organise the enquiry in such a way as to limit or even eliminate the need for men to be left waiting around for dispersal.

The other thing I resented, and it was a common failing amongst senior officers at the time, was that we were not told of the progress that was being made. In fact we weren't told anything at all. We operated in a vacuum. This was also something I changed when I was in a position to do so. In serious cases I always kept my team up to date with a series of conferences, when we discussed progress and tactics generally.

Then, on 19 May 1949, I returned to the station and was told I was to be on guard duty. In those days young officers were put in the cells with people arrested for serious crimes such as murder. On this occasion an escaped murderer had been recaptured after a raid on a house in Albany Street and I was detailed to sit in the cell with him. The cell door was opened by the Station Sergeant and there sitting quietly was my friend the Kentish Town baker.

At the age of 25, John Edward Allen had been the assistant chef of the Lamb Hotel at Burford in Oxfordshire and had killed Kathleen Woodward, the 17-month-old daughter of two other workers in the hotel. Before the killing he had apparently been devoted to the child and had taken her for rides on his bicycle. On 19 June 1937 he went to the Woodwards' room and asked to take the child 'for an airing', and he gave her two pennies. Later her body was found by the roadside in nearby Fulbrook with the coins still in her hand. She had been strangled with a clothes-line. Allen had disappeared, but he gave himself up to Southwark police two days later. He had twice been in mental institutions and, when in October of that year he was found guilty of Kathleen's murder, the jury recommended an inquiry be carried out into his mental state. Mrs Woodward believed he had killed her daughter through jealousy because she – Mrs Woodward – had been put in charge of making cakes for a banquet.

Allen was sent to Broadmoor where he had stayed for nearly ten years when on 20 July 1947, wearing a parson's collar which he had as a prop for the 'Broadhumoorists', the institution's concert party, he escaped. The press called him the 'Mad

Parson'. Later he described his escape as 'incredibly simple and about as risky as walking carefully across Piccadilly during the rush hour'.

That day we had long discussions. He was, of course, a prime suspect for a number of murders which had occurred locally, including those of Gladys Hanrahan,[1] a prostitute Russian Dora, and frail bespectacled 69-year-old Emily Armstrong,[2] beaten to death in a St John's Wood cleaners, something which he vigorously denied to me. The thinking ran that he had killed these women whilst suffering a mental blackout. When, next day, he was placed on identification parades he was not picked out, and so he was returned to Broadmoor. It was quite true he had been working during the years he was on the run because he obtained a tax rebate of £6 10s. while back inside. Allen was released in September 1951 and later wrote a book, *Inside Broadmoor*, which described his experiences both inside and out.

Another man with whom I sat on guard duty was one of the most engaging confidence tricksters I have ever come across. In fact he was the best in the world – he told me so himself. When I first saw him he was lying in bed in a private room in the

---

[1] Gladys Hanrahan was found bound and strangled on Cumberland Green. Enquiries were led by Jock Jamieson and centred on a male friend of hers with whom she had been seen drinking that morning and rowing on previous occasions. At the inquest, at which he was represented by F. Elwyn Jones who later became Lord Chancellor, the man gave an alibi that he had gone on impulse to Brighton on the day of the killing. This alibi was at least partly broken by witnesses who said he had been in London. The Coroner told the jury that even if they disbelieved the man there was still nothing to connect him to Miss Hanrahan's death, and a verdict of murder by person(s) unknown was returned.

[2] Emily Armstrong was beaten to death with a weapon which resembled a claw-hammer in her small dry-cleaning shop in the High Street, St John's Wood, then no more than a few shops. The attack took place during the lunch hour when, at that time, shops closed, and although the killer must have been covered in blood there was never a sighting of him. No one was ever charged with the offence.

National Temperance Hospital in Hampstead Road. William Wakeham was very tall, aged 35, and he looked rather like the young Duke of Edinburgh. He had all the charm in the world – he had to, for it was his stock in trade. He had swallowed a razor blade to get to a hospital rather than spend a remand period in a police cell, after his arrest for stealing a suitcase. He would be there until the blade passed its way through his system. When Detective Sergeant Sid Ray appeared at Clerkenwell Court to explain the defendant's absence he euphemistically described the incident as one where Wakeham had tried to cut his wrists.

He operated in the years, long before credit and cheque cards, when a gentlemen's cheque was accepted on its face value and without any need for additional identification. Wakeham was a notorious and successful kiter. 'All I need is a cheque book,' he told me. 'Once I've got that I'm in business.' It was his proud boast that he could no longer walk down Bond Street. 'I've done just about every jeweller's shop in the street.'

His 'scam' went like this. First, he would either steal a cheque book or buy one from a thief, and then go, expensively dressed and with the best of accents, into a top class jeweller's and propose to buy various very expensive pieces. He would explain to the assistant that he wanted to buy 'a little something' for his wife or girlfriend. The purchase always took a long time, as he asked for advice on the merits of pieces and drew the assistant into discussing which of them he thought would appeal more as a present. It was all part of the process of slowly gaining the assistant's confidence. Then, when he was ready, out came the stolen cheque book and he would write out a cheque, signing it with a flourish.

Now came the next stage in the con. He would explain that he had no wish to take the jewellery with him but asked instead that it be sent to the Waldorf, the Ritz, the Mayfair or whichever luxury hotel he had chosen at the beginning of the particular caper.

And finally the sting. He began querying the time it would take to deliver the pieces and then, apparently shrugging aside the assistant when he asked if there was a problem, he would grudgingly admit that it would, in fact, be a disappointment for the wife/girlfriend, as that night there was to be a special celebration dinner. It would have been delightful if he could then give her the present – still, no matter. It almost invariably worked. His manner had so impressed the assistant by this time that he understood how disappointed the lady would be and certainly sir must take the goods with him. Wakeham would make a token protest, insisting that he did not want the man to break the shop's rules, and then off he would go triumphantly clutching his haul.

It was simplicity itself to turn the jewellery into cash either by pawning it 'only temporarily, you understand – had a bad run on the gee-gees' or selling it to a 'fence'. On the rare occasions when his charm failed him he would not be too disappointed: there was always another time and another shop.

He explained to me that the real pleasure was in the sting element of the operation, in using his wit and guile to persuade the mark to part with the goods. One of his operations epitomised this. He was staying at the Strand Palace Hotel – on somebody else's cheque book, of course – where a short time earlier Neville Heath, the handsome but sadistic RAF officer, had been discovered with the wife of an army officer and had been asked to leave. Wandering fairly aimlessly along the Strand, Wakeham had gone into a stamp dealer's.

Wakeham, merely for something to do, or so he said, began by asking to be shown an album worth several thousand pounds. He had, he told me, no real interest in the stamps, nor anywhere ready to sell them, but it was an interesting work-out. He played the assistant carefully, pretending to be only mildly interested and asking to see stamps of lesser value. The more Wakeham dropped his sights the keener the assistant became to sell the quality album. Eventually, after Wakeham had seemed about to leave, a price was struck; out came the cheque book and an arrangement made to send the stamps to the Strand Palace. He and the assistant were chatting about the wisdom of the purchase when Wakeham recalled an avid stamp collector colleague who was returning to the States that very day. Wouldn't it be wonderful for him to share the beauty of this latest acquisition before he left?

Wakeham walked out of the shop, straight across the road to Charing Cross Station and stuffed the wretched album in the first litter bin he saw.

Like Heath, it was inevitable he would attract the ladies, but in his case, whilst they almost invariably ended in tears, at least they did not end up dead. He had no compunction about stealing from them. The best scam he had played, so he said, involved a titled lady who had fallen madly in love with him and with whom he soon became bored. For him the chase was far more interesting than the capture, and so was his escape. He took her to a luxurious country hotel for the weekend, something she could arrange only after the most careful deception of her husband. After a candlelit dinner and a night of passion he left at first light, taking with him all her cash, jewellery and cheque book. 'How she paid the bill wasn't my problem,' he told me, 'nor how she squared it up with his lordship.'

His latest escapade had gone horribly wrong and that was how he came to be in hospital. One of his regular methods of operating was to go onto the departure platform of a main line station – all that was needed then was a one penny platform ticket – and get into a first class compartment to wait for the arrival of a suitable victim. Usually it would be a man, but the principal requirement was luggage. It would then be only a matter of time before victim and his baggage were parted.

Now, however, he had come unstuck. The latest mark was a man named Greenlees from the Atomic Research Division of the Ministry of Supply who carried both a suitcase and a briefcase. Wakeham chatted with him and then, looking at his watch, suggested a drink in the Euston station bar before the train left. Greenlees's bags would be perfectly safe with all the porters about (and anyway sneak thefts from railway carriages were not nearly as common as now).

Down to the bar they went. Wakeham ordered and paid for the drinks, said 'Cheers' and that he had to go to the lavatory.

Then he went back to the platform, ordered a porter to collect the bags, telling him he had changed his mind, called a taxi and went to the Aldwych Hotel to count the takings. He was all right. There was a cheque book. That evening he dined well in the hotel's restaurant, ordered the morning papers to be sent to his room and had his last good sleep for some time.

It was all there in the headlines: 'Atom Secrets Stolen from Euston Station'. The bag had contained important papers. Wakeham, his nerve gone, left within minutes and, taking only the cheque book, headed for the South Coast. He was easily traced because of the cheques he was cashing. The affair was a great *cause célèbre*. The town where he stayed was for a time sealed off, until his capture. Back he was brought to Albany Street.

He was, of course, a model prisoner. He insisted, rightly, that he was a mere con-man and not an atomic spy. His record bore this out and fairly soon the investigating officer accepted that he had not even looked at the secret papers. Nevertheless Wakeham's record was a bad one. Six months from a magistrates' court would not be sufficient and it would be 'up the steps' to the Old Bailey where a much longer sentence could be imposed. Wakeham did not fancy this. He swallowed the razor blade. Whoever had looked at Wakeham's record had not studied it carefully. He had done this before to delay the exchange of the comfort of the best hotels for a prison cell.

'In every CID office,' he told me, 'where they take your prints there is always a black inkwell holder with pens and paper clips. And there's always a razor blade to sharpen your pencils.' He was right, there always was.

'Well, I just take the razor blade back to my cell, ask for a drink of water and swallow it.' I looked sceptical. 'No bother,' he said, 'It just goes down like aspirin. Once I've done that I call the Sergeant and tell him I've swallowed a razor blade and he'd better get an ambulance. I've never met one once that would take the risk of not calling one. Once

I'm in hospital it only needs one X-ray to show I'm telling the truth.'

He was completely unrepentant. 'I don't mind doing the bird. As a matter of fact I don't mind it at all because as soon as I've been registered you can bet your life I'll be working in the library. I've done it before everywhere I've been and *they know they can trust me*. No, it's just that I like to spend about two weeks nice and comfortable in hospital before I have to start the porridge. It sort of eases my way in.'

Then one day he greeted me cheerily with the news. 'Hi, Nipper, they say "Good mornings begin with Gillette" – well this morning I gave birth to a razor blade.'

Before he left to go to Clerkenwell Magistrates' Court on his way to the Old Bailey where he received four years' corrective training from the Common Sergeant H. E. Beazley, he told me he looked forward to the day when he was a little older and with greying hair. 'Then I'll put on the old dog collar and, with that, I'll get away with murder.'

I've no idea whether he achieved his ambition. I always intended to look up his file, but I never did.

Aides were considered to be the lowest of the low in the CID hierarchy and really we were encouraged to dress as we wished, provided that we didn't look like policemen. There was no clothing allowance and so we wore our everyday clothes. At the time I had a rather dashing green shooting jacket and a pair of corduroy trousers. It was outrageous for the time but it went unremarked by the bosses. Not so if you were a CID officer proper. They almost had a regimental uniform of suit, trenchcoat and trilby hat. Peter Beveridge, one of the 'Big Five', was the Detective Chief Superintendent at Paddington at the time and he insisted on his men wearing hats. He had in mind the image of an officer approaching a man and taking off his hat saying, 'Good morning, sir. I'm DS Read. I've come to investigate . . .' This was epitomised by the picture of Beveridge raising his hat to Mrs Florence Ransom in Holborn as he arrested her for the murders of Mrs

Dorothy Fisher, her daughter Freda and her maid Charlotte Saunders.[3]

There was one man I remember at Albany Street. He had a very fine head of dark wavy hair of which he was very proud, and he would never wear a hat. Beveridge warned him once, saying if he wanted to be a detective he must wear a hat.

'I never wear a hat,' the man replied.

'You will if you want to be a detective,' replied Beveridge. The next time he saw the man he still had no hat, so he said, 'If you can't get yourself a hat, I can get you one.' Two days later the officer, who was really quite a good detective, was back in uniform wearing a helmet.

Ken Jones, who ended his career as a Detective Chief Superintendent with the Murder Squad, was luckier. He and I had been out patrolling St John's Wood and came back to find Beveridge on a spot check sitting at the desk in the CID room. Quick as a flash Ken made a gesture towards the hatstand inside the door as though he was hanging his hat up.

'You'll have to be quicker than that, Mr Jones,' said Beveridge. 'Where's your hat?' And when Ken admitted he did not have this essential piece of equipment he was sent straight on a bus to Selfridges to buy one.

Meanwhile, as an aide, my social and sporting life was suffering. Then there were fewer opportunities for time away from duties. This applied particularly to the CID and even more to the lowest in the pecking order, the aide. The life of an aide was one of continual patrolling of the streets for lengthy periods, keeping observation on premises from exposed positions in all kinds of weather, standing by waiting to be sent on what was often a fruitless errand and

---

[3] Mrs Ransom, jealous of her lover's good relationship with his estranged wife, shot her and the others on 9 July 1940. She was traced through a white hogskin glove left at the scene of the crime. On 8 November she was convicted at the Old Bailey but the following month was sent to Broadmoor after being pronounced insane.

trying to keep up an arrest record that would impress senior officers. This meant giving up all semblance of a social life, so the maximum possible time could be given over to 'the job'. There was no reporting sick for anything that required less than a spell in hospital and, much to my chagrin, there was no real time for sport except darts, cards and snooker, none of which was I interested in. There were boards and tables in almost all police canteens, and senior CID officers could be seen screwing the cue ball back onto the black or fifteen-twoing during most meal breaks.

Nor was there any question of overtime for aides. If you wanted to get into the CID proper, and that was the hope of all aides, you also knew that if anyone was going to be inconvenienced it would be you. An aide in those days worked a twelve-hour tour at least four days a week.

However, somehow I still managed to be active in the police athletics team, a keen footballer, and remain in the boxing championships. Unfortunately I was the only boxer at that level in the Division and so I had to train alone. And that, as anyone who knows anything about boxing will agree, is disastrous.

I used to train early in the morning – three miles round Regent's Park, finishing with sprints and a work-out in the gym in the police section house where I lived – before reporting for duty. I couldn't wait until the evening as I never knew when I would finish work.

I won the championship again in 1949, but I was finding it more and more difficult because of a lack of training facilities. I was also playing regularly for the station football team as well as for the Division but this meant that invariably I had to work a split shift, coming on in the morning, taking the afternoon off and reporting back for duty in the evening. It all blew up one afternoon when I asked the First Class Sergeant to be allowed to play in an important match. He was a man weighing about 18 stone, keen on a pint and cribbage. What he was not keen on was my taking the afternoon off.

'It's about time you made your mind up, Nipper,' he said, 'Do you want to be a professional footballer or a CID officer?'

I was young and perhaps a bit cheeky.

'Well, really I'd prefer to be a professional footballer, but as there's no hope of that I think I'd rather be a detective.'

He did not like my reply one little bit and I had a severe dressing down in which he outlined my career prospects if I continued the way I was going, ending with the warning 'you can always go back to wearing a big hat, you know'.

Fortunately for me he moved soon afterwards and I kept playing football. Boxing was a different matter. I could no longer give it the systematic and disciplined training needed. One problem was that even without me Martin insisted on keeping up the patrols, and one afternoon he tackled a man leaving a derelict building who turned on him and beat him up with a three-foot piece of wood. It was not until the man was arrested a few days later that it was discovered he had already done time for the manslaughter of a prison officer. He could not face another stretch, and hanged himself whilst on remand. Nevertheless I felt very badly about Martin.

Eventually the time came for me to appear before the selection board which would confirm me as a fully fledged Detective Constable. We candidates all sat together outside the interview room, chatting and waiting for the fearful summons before the Board. One of my colleagues said, 'Nipper, if I don't get through this today, I'm going to pack it in and go back into uniform and take my chances.'

He did fail and he kept his promise. Later, he became Sir Stanley Bailey, Chief Constable of Northumberland, and is now one of Her Majesty's Inspectors of Constabulary.

I passed and was sent to Harlesden where I started my career as a detective by almost burning down the CID office.

CHAPTER FOUR

At the time, the Harlesden CID office was a shed with a high-pitched wooden roof in the station yard, heated by an old fashioned pot-bellied coke-fed type of stove. On Sunday duty it was my job to feed it. Sunday was a split shift day – on from nine until one, when I had to bank up the stove to make sure it was burning when I returned at six. I then had to bank it again and pull the damper in, leaving it to slow burn until I could tend to it again.

One Sunday I came on at 6 p.m., pushed the damper out and opened the trap at the bottom. There was no reaction and I cursed because the shed was freezing cold. I thought I would make sure I got it going and I picked up a whisky bottle now filled with petrol which was then always kept handy in CID offices to clean off the fingerprint ink when dabs were taken.

I pushed the bottle inside the top of the stove and tipped some petrol on the coke. There was no reaction and so I held it there, pouring in a good dose. Suddenly, with an enormous roar, flames leaped from the bottom of thc stove into the room. I pulled the bottle out but it was ablaze and now so was my coat sleeve. Instinctively I threw the bottle onto the floor and watched transfixed as it rolled and smashed, spreading nearly a pint of blazing petrol onto the furniture which also quickly caught fire. Then I reacted. I dashed to the main building and grabbed a fire extinguisher from the wall. This did little good, mainly because it was empty – no one had ever needed it and as time had gone by nobody had bothered to check it – and so I ran back into the yard and dragged the water hose into the room. Training should have told me that this was the worst possible way of dealing with a petrol fire but I was in a state of panic. Fortunately it worked rather better and I got the blaze under control. Looking round, the place was a mess. Desks were charred, a typist's chair reduced to a metal skeleton. Fortunately there were no calls for me that night, and paper work was put to one side as I spent the next three hours cleaning the place up as best I could. Next day I confessed to the rest of my colleagues who had a whip round, and with one of them, Bill Brittain, I had to go to a second-hand shop down the Harlesden Road to replace the typist's chair. It was a good example of pulling together.

General orders, the big black book which controlled and authorised every minute of an officer's life from getting married to receiving a pension, had been completely ignored. By the book I should have called the fire brigade, but I never reported the fire and although I spoke informally to the Station Sergeant it can never have been discovered because otherwise I would have been on a report. The Station Sergeant agreed to do nothing about the empty fire extinguisher and let someone else discover it was out of use. The only one who suffered was the CID typist who did not like the replacement chair I had obtained from the second-hand shop and who could not understand where her proper chair had gone to and why she had to have such an uncomfortable replacement.

When I first became a detective we had no means of identifying latent fingerprints. When we visited the scene of a crime, after looking at windows, or doors, the probable point of entry, to see if there were any obvious fingermarks, we used to breathe on any object we thought might be useful, such as a cigarette box, to see if there was a positive result. If so, and the crime was sufficiently serious, we then had to call a photographer and a fingerprint man from the Yard. It was a long and complicated process.

Then around that time we were given a short course in fingerprinting and each station was given a fingerprint box containing camel hair brushes, black graphite and grey powder. This was a great novelty at first and it became fashionable for detectives to leave the nick armed with a little wooden box to examine a reported housebreaking. Dusting for prints is really a very skilled science. Inexpertly applied graphite powder takes some removing, and we young lads often left a trail of damage in our wake.

One officer who qualified as a fingerprint man was an old prewar man, Arthur Mizon, who wore his very dark hair in the fashion of a centre-forward, smarmed back with a parting straight down the middle. He had reached his ceiling as a Detective Sergeant Second Class and was proud of his new qualification. One day he went to a housebreaking in the Bayswater Road and began patiently and very professionally to 'dust' all the windows and doors. He was followed round by the householder, an obviously well-to-do gentleman who persisted in asking questions about when the burglars would be apprehended and when he would get his property back.

It got to the point that he was telling Arthur where to dust, and when there was no reaction or compliance with his instructions he became more persistent. 'Look there, officer, I'm sure that's a print on the window.' Arthur went along with this for a while until he could stand no more. He put down his camel hair brush and said, 'Look sir, I was chosen by the Commissioner to attend a course which has qualified me as an expert in identifying latent fingerprints. Now, this being so, I would be grateful if you would allow me to employ this expertise. Now I would not presume for one moment to tell you how to do your job . . . what is your work, incidentally?'

The man replied that as a matter of fact he was a ship broker.

'Yes,' said Arthur, 'well there we are. You can probably go down to the dock, look at a ship and say, right – break it here and break it there. Now that's your job, so please don't tell me how to do mine.'

Rather more constructive was the time I spent with one of the great detectives, H. W. 'Bert' Hannam, known, amongst other things, as 'Suits' because he was always immaculately dressed. At that time he was an Inspector and he could not have been more helpful to me as a newly appointed Detective Constable. A lot of people didn't like Bert. They thought he was too flash. He didn't fit into the mould of the popular guv'nor who could outdrink his oldest sergeant or tell the raciest story, but as far as I was concerned I could not have had a better leader. He was kindness itself to me. He took me to my first post-mortem, explaining what was required of a CID officer at such a time, and whenever there was a serious crime which needed his personal attention he would co-opt me and have me along as his bag-carrier. He made sure I went with him to Quarter Sessions and to the Old Bailey so that I became aware of the routine of attending and giving evidence before a judge and jury. He was extremely patient with me and made sure I knew exactly what was going on and, more importantly, the reason why.

He was an actor and a poseur and, wearing his wonderfully well-fitting suits, he looked more like a banker at a time when Ernie Millen, on his appointment as Head of the Flying Squad, had been photographed on the beach wearing flannel trousers and braces.

To see Hannam giving evidence was an education. He had an almost photographic memory and, if need be, would demonstrate this by quoting extensively without referring to documents in front of him. He was actually able to recite pages and pages of statements, and he taught me how to do it as well, so that in the future if notes weren't taken by one of my Sergeants, I was able to recall great passages. It wasn't a question of being selective: you wrote down what you remembered and Hannam was brilliant at this.

The other thing he had was an ability, in one sentence, to create a situation which made things seem very sinister and totally detrimental to the defence. But he did this in such a way that there could be no grounds for a re-trial. In one case, a corruption trial involving a solicitor and a Detective Sergeant, when he was giving evidence before the Lord Chief

Justice, Hannam handed him a file saying that it contained a report to the Home Office which 'I do not want to let out of my hands' and adding, 'The report is highly confidential.' It was immediately obvious to everybody in the court, including the jury, that the report had gone all the way up to the top, and that the corruption it concerned was the subject of interest at Cabinet level. This situation had been created by just one sentence. A lot of officers would have missed the opportunity, but not Bert.

Perhaps his greatest success was when he had been promoted and had joined the Murder Squad. It followed his investigation of the Towpath Murder of 18-year-old Barbara Songhurst, who was stabbed on the towpath at Teddington at the end of May 1953. She had gone cycling with her friend, Christine Reed, whose body was found a week later. She had been raped and stabbed. A witness said he remembered seeing a man riding a woman's bike along the towpath late on the night of the girls' disappearance. One problem for Bert was that he could not find the murder weapon, thought to be an axe. In his usual flamboyant way, he therefore announced that he intended to dam part of the Thames. Despite cries from certain quarters that this was impossible, he went ahead and did it – but he did not find the weapon. Then on 17 June a labourer, Alfred Whiteway, arrested for assault and the rape of a 14-year-old girl, was driven to Kingston Police Station sitting in the rear of the police car. The next day a Constable found an axe under the car's rear seat, but foolishly took it home and used it for chopping wood. It was almost a month before he realised its importance and then handed it to a colleague. The axe exactly fitted an injury in Christine Reed's skull. Whiteway was questioned by Hannam on and off over a period of six weeks, finally saying, 'It's all up. You know bloody well I done it, eh! I'm mental.' At his trial he alleged that Bert had fabricated his confession, a claim which the trial judge, Mr Justice Hilbery, dismissed almost contemptuously. 'Look at the statement . . .' he told the jury. 'Do you think that an experienced novelist, a writer of fiction could have done much better that that? It is said to have been done by a police officer.'

Rather less successful was Bert Hannam's investigation in 1956 into the deaths of elderly ladies in Eastbourne which resulted in the prosecution of local doctor John Bodkin Adams. Hannam had previously upset the chief crime reporter of the *Daily Express*, Percy Hoskins, over his handling of the Whiteway investigation. Hoskins had worked with Sir Peter Rawlinson, counsel for Whiteway, in the Towpath case when Rawlinson, as young counsel, had read the papers for libel on behalf of Beaverbrook newspapers and believed that Hannam's investigation was 'at best, unsavoury'.[1] Now, backed by the *Express*, Hoskins took up Adams's cause with relish. Years later, when I was a senior officer and Percy had become a good friend of mine, I found time had not mellowed him on the subject of Bert. When I sang his praises, saying he was one of the truly great detectives, Hoskins was scathing in his denunciation. 'He was like a big chocolate Easter egg,' he said, 'Beautiful on the outside but fuck all inside.'

The allegation against Adams was that he had administered fatal doses of morphine to elderly patients who had left him money or gifts in their wills. One difficulty faced by Hannam was that he had failed to find the medical records of the woman with whose death Adams was charged, and these were produced in a spectacular manner by the defence, changing the whole complexion of the case. Adams, who did not give evidence and was brilliantly defended by Geoffrey Lawrence, was acquitted, much to Hoskins' delight. Later Percy told me that he was the only crime reporter supporting Adams's cause and that he had been personally seen by Lord Beaverbrook who had warned him that he had better be right or both he and the paper would be the laughing stock of Fleet Street. When the jury found Adams not guilty Beaverbrook sent Hoskins a telegram reading 'Two were acquitted'. Adams remained

---

[1] Hoskins, P. *Two Men Were Acquitted*, Martin Secker and Warburg (1984).

grateful to Hoskins for his support and left him £1,000 in his will, noting that he was one of the few people who had had faith in him.

Hannam also seems to have upset the judge, Lord Devlin, who later wrote in his account of the trial[2] that 'Suits' had proved an adept manipulator of the press, 'apparently for his own glorification rather than for any assistance which it could give to the investigation'.

So far as I am concerned Bert Hannam was a gentleman. I am grateful to him for his attitude towards me when, as a fledgling CID officer, he taught me much that stood me in good stead throughout my career. That said, certainly Bert was not everyone's cup of tea. He smoked expensive cigars, and spoke in a precise way with an affected accent. He also cultivated the acquaintanceship of the upper strata of society. These traits, coupled with his rather superior manner, did not endear him to his colleagues or find favour with senior officers, and throughout his later career there was much jibing and sniping at him by people who were, in one way or another, jealous of him. Another thing which did not help his popularity was his investigation into corruption in the Met in 1955 which arose following allegations that a solicitor and a Police Sergeant from Savile Row had conspired to pervert the course of justice. Bert conducted the inquiry with the thoroughness and diligence which he brought to all his cases. In doing this he did himself no favours and earned the contempt of some junior officers but, more tragically, the distrust of some senior ones.

This attitude, held especially by some of the top brass in the CID at the Yard, was a serious lack of judgement. I have long held the view that the troubles of the 1970s and 80s could have been avoided if complaints of corruption made in the 1950s had been more thoroughly examined. An investigation into corruption was almost universally resented and there was a widely held view at senior level that the name of the Force

---

2 Devlin, P. *Easing the Passing*, The Bodley Head (1985).

had to be protected and that this was best done by having as little publicity as possible about such matters.

Of course, the opposite was the case. The reputation of the Force and the manner in which it was regarded by the public would have been much better served if corruption had been ruthlessly investigated and the offenders identified at the earliest possible stage. Instead there was a pervading sense that the name of the Force had to be protected at all costs. The officer who undertook the enquiry was immediately looked upon as an intruder – a rubberheeler – and this, coupled with a policy of self-protection, served to colour the attitude of some investigating officers.

It was an unfortunate attitude which still persisted into the 1970s. In a blaze of publicity following allegations of corruption in *The Times*, Frank Williamson, Her Majesty's Inspector of Constabulary for crime, was appointed as adviser to oversee the enquiry. Williamson, who had a reputation as an honest and painstaking detective, was seen as an intruder who, it was feared, would ensure that a positive rather than an inconsequential report was produced. His views on police corruption were well known and he had stated at many detective training schools that until the words 'except police officers' were written into certain statutes, they must be dealt with in just the same way as any other offender.

At the time of the inquiry I was a Chief Superintendent at Scotland Yard and Frank, a good friend of mine, would confide in me both the difficulties he was experiencing and the attitude of some of the top brass of the CID. It can be summed up quite neatly. One day he asked to see me and I said, 'I'll meet you at the Yard.'

'Good God,' he said, 'We can't do that, Nipper.' And when asked why ever not, he said, 'I'm *persona non grata* at the Yard.' I was dumbfounded. Here was a man who had been a provincial Chief Constable and who was now an Inspector of Constabulary whose presence in the Yard was being questioned.

We had to meet in a pub and there he expressed his concern at the quality and ability of officers seconded to his inquiry from the Yard, giving as an example Detective Chief Superintendent Bill Moody.[3]

As a result of this attitude, investigations were normally little more than a whitewash. As far as the top brass was concerned, if one officer got into trouble he was just a rotten apple who had already been picked out of the barrel, but any suggestion of widespread corruption was resisted because of the effect it would have on the Force and public confidence. They wouldn't accept that there was deep-seated corruption or that it should be investigated properly. For a long time the investigation was held in check on those grounds, which was ludicrous. It was only with the inquiries into the Porn Squad that it was finally accepted that corruption was established and had been going on for a long, long time. The production of these whitewash reports was the reason that the then Deputy Commissioner Sir Robert Mark was finally given the authority to create A10.[4]

During the Kray inquiry I was approached by a Detective Inspector from the Porn Squad. It had become semi-public knowledge at the Yard that I was busy in the West End. He came to me and said, 'Guv, if any of my lads' names comes up, you'll let me know, won't you?' It was absolutely incredible that these people had come to believe they could walk on water.

I didn't stay at Harlesden long, but the experience I gained was invaluable. I learned from all the CID officers there. Sid Coomber was 'my' Sergeant and he, too, was a patient tutor. He taught me how to compile my reports, and generally made sure I was pointed in the right direction. A self-effacing man, he had won a George Medal during the war but never mentioned

---

3 Williamson's fears were fully justified. Even whilst engaged on the *Times* inquiry, Moody was taking vast sums of money from pornographers in the West End. He later received a sentence of 12 years' imprisonment for his part in an extensive corruption racket.

4 The body which would investigate all allegations of crime and corruption and report directly to the Deputy Commissioner. It meant that responsibility was finally removed from the C1 department.

it. I only learned of it at his retirement party. Both Charlie Braybrook, the other Detective Constable, and Bill Brittain who had gone with me to buy furniture, were real characters. Bill was fond of a glass or two of gin and pep, and one morning after several too many glasses he was at his desk, his head on his clenched fists, demanding perfect silence. When Hannam came in and asked if he was all right, Bill gave us all a lesson in quick thinking. 'Perfectly sir,' he replied, 'just doing a yoga exercise.'

After some 15 months I was moved to Paddington where I stayed for the next seven years. It was an area of contrasts. There was a fairly big Irish element who lived in the little streets off the Harrow Road up towards Willesden and Harlesden, where there were one or two identifiable Irish pubs; but towards the south side it bordered on Hyde Park and so you had luxurious flats and lovely squares such as Sussex Square. Sussex Gardens was a kind of dividing line. Eastbourne Terrace, Porchester Terrace and so on were where the prostitutes were working round the station. And there was always the scandal that the Church owned the property and, so it was considered, tacitly encouraged prostitution.

It was always busy because there was a permanent, definite, criminal element in the area. Activity was generated by Paddington Station: there were always parcels and cases being nicked, and nearby Praed Street was famous for being a place where one was able to hock bent gear. There were one or two shops known throughout the locality and by the broader criminal underworld where you could get rid of a radio set or the new toy of the time, the tape-recorder, or things that had been nicked from cars. Then there was a famous place, the Cider House on the corner of the Edgware Road and the Harrow Road, which sold nothing but raw cider. It was frequented by a predominantly Irish element and their girls. You would get the occasional stranger who wandered in there and who, not knowing the score, would be picked up by one of the girls, taken round the corner into a quiet back alley, clobbered by the men and thus lose his wallet. This was a scam known as 'the Murphy game'. The police station was past Paddington Green where there was a statue of the actress Sarah Siddons. The station was almost on the corner of the Bishops Bridge Road. There were a couple of pubs opposite, one of which was one of the quaintest places you've ever seen, and looked like an ordinary house. It might have had an indication in a window that it was a pub, but that was all. When you walked in there was a series of doors leading to a tiny little bar and then a sitting room. As you looked through there would be a man who seemed always to be eating something. His standard greeting was, 'What do you want?' We, the police, chose that pub because we could be entirely on our own. He didn't even bother to draw the beer: we had to do that. If you called the landlord for a drink, he would reply, 'I'm not getting up, serve your bloody self.' It became almost like a club. If someone whom he didn't know came in, he would refuse to serve them. In a curious way it was the same as the Krays when they took over pubs and would have only their friends in. How he existed I'll never know. We used to joke that he only needed one barrel a year.

Paddington was a good training ground. It was a real working police station. In a league table I suppose it would have been on a par with Leman Street and then the next down would be West End Central, in terms of activity if not quality of crime. Paddington was always regarded as a stepping-off station. If you worked there you were almost certain to get a promotion from whatever rank you were in. It was that sort of station. You were only sent there if it was thought you could do it and, in turn, you knew that having got there you could guarantee promotion provided you didn't blot your copy-book. When it came to it, in all I served eleven years there – seven as a Detective Constable and four as a First Class Sergeant. It was an area I came to like because of the variety. There was St Mary's Hospital, the canal, the station, two Underground stations, and then there were people like Jack Spot living on the manor. It was a cosmopolitan area I found attractive.

When I was first posted to Paddington, the Detective Inspector was a big Scotsman and former schoolmaster, John

McIver, who years later said to me in his piping Highland twang, 'Yes, young Nipper, I may not have taught you much but at least I taught you how to do a decent report.' I am not sure he did. All our reports were vetted by the Detective Inspector, and John still kept his schoolmasterly habit of going through them with a red pen. Once the report was slung back at us we would have to retype it with the corrections and re-submit it. By the afternoon, when John had had a substantial and almost invariably liquid lunch, the report would come back once again with more red highlights. John had revised his revision.

Ian 'Jock' Forbes,[5] who later became one of the best investigators on the Murder Squad and also the second National Co-ordinator of the Regional Crime Squads, was a Sergeant there. He had an incredible memory, or at least gave the impression he had. When he went into an office he would say 'Hello, Read,' or 'That's Jones, isn't it. How's your wife?' This was very impressive. Of course, he may have been cheating. John Bliss, who was the first Co-ordinator, did. He told me he kept a little book and if he was going to, say, Manchester he would look at all the names and when he arrived would speak to the Chief Inspector who would mark his card. Jock Forbes was a master at it and he developed a wonderful rapport with his men. He was enormously helpful to me and other young officers. If you were in doubt about a case you could go to him for help and guidance, which is so important for a young bloke. You can make some incredible boobs if you are left on your own. A lot of senior officers then

[5] He successfully investigated a number of provincial murders including the case of a woman and her lover who set up a car crash to make it appear her husband had died in an accident and the dreadful killing in 1967 of little Christine Darby in Cannock Chase. For her murder Raymond Morris, a foreman in an engineering factory who lived close to Walsall police station, received a sentence of life imprisonment.

assumed you knew what you were doing and didn't care if you didn't.

In those days investigations were much more difficult. I saw a programme on television recently about an investigation – not a particularly big one – where a Holmes computer was in use. In those days you did not have the benefit of a computer which you could ask, 'How many people named Smith have been interrogated?' or 'How many boats were coloured blue?' You had lists of people, descriptions, cars, car numbers, locations, and who had been seen in a location. The drill was that you, as the officer in the case, had to go through all these and either memorise or note that certain people were at certain places at certain times, extracting all the material you thought was important. In a big case you would have a second or even third reader to extract information they thought was important, so there was a kind of fail-safe, but basically the task of extracting all that information was yours.

Tommy Butler, who later led the London end of the Great Train Robbery investigation and who had a great reputation as a detective, was also at Paddington as a senior First Class Sergeant. People had enormous affection for Tommy because, on the face of it, he was such a lovely man. He had a good sense of humour and a nice attitude. The police and detection were his only obsessions. As a detective he was good, but he was also most frustrating. He was always helpful if your report was ill defined or directed. In the old-fashioned way he would say 'what a lot of bollocks', but he would then sit down and go through it with you, sentence by sentence, helping you put it in order. But in one way Tommy Butler was the worst detective I've ever come across. He was so secretive. He was a great investigator and plotted things up beautifully, but really opening up and having a conference saying, 'Listen, chaps, this is what it's all about,' would have been as alien as cutting his throat. He was obsessed by security. He would never tell his men what was happening where or when. He would say, 'Come with me,' rather than, 'Come with me, I'm going to interrogate three blokes they've got at Paddington Station.' If he was going to organise a raid he would assemble his forces in the police station at, say, 6 a.m., but it would not be until they arrived at the actual house or premises that they discovered where they were going.

Sometimes, over the years, I have wondered whether it was I alone who thought this a failing, but I have asked around and all have been in agreement that this was his great fault. Occasionally he would join his team for a drink, but it was only occasionally. He was a very private man and no one was ever really close to him. Unmarried, he lived with his mother, but home was really the CID office, and when those of us who could tried to slope off at half past six or seven in the evening Tommy, a workaholic, would say derisorily, 'Another early night then?' He spent every evening typing in his room upstairs at Paddington. Downstairs we could hear the tapping of the machine. No one knew what he was doing. It may have been that he was rewriting poorly compiled reports by the rest of us, but this can't have been every night. The only other thing I can think of is that he was putting together a diary with a view to compiling his memoirs. But none was ever published.

On the other hand the other First Class Sergeant, Frank Gloyne, a good solid detective, was everything a senior officer should have been towards a young detective. He showed me how to fill out reports, prepare case papers for court and to interrogate suspects. As a First Class Sergeant at Paddington he was assured of further promotion until, that is, he became involved defending a fellow officer in disciplinary proceedings. It did for his career.

Curiously, the case also involved Bert Hannam. Hannam had it in for a Sergeant at Harrow Road with whom he had had a row and eventually charged him with the disciplinary offence of unlawfully consorting with criminals. He was, under police regulations, entitled to have a 'friend' appear with him at the inquiry. Now in those days it was just about impossible for a CID officer not to consort with criminals. They were your eyes and ears for what jobs might be going off and, when they had gone off, who might be involved. The officer went to Frank and asked him if he would 'be his friend' and appear for him at the disciplinary hearing. As was customary, Frank checked out with his superiors that it would not be held against him in his career, and was assured it would not have any effect on his promotion prospects. The officer was found guilty and required to resign, but Frank appealed the case to the Home Secretary and the man was reinstated. From then on Frank's possibilities of promotion were zero. He was moved almost immediately from Paddington, not even sideways but downwards to Highbury Vale, then something of a backwater, and there he stagnated whilst junior officers were promoted over him. Eventually he handed in his papers before completing his full tour; a scandalous waste.

I did not hear of him for some years until I was appointed National Co-ordinator of the Regional Crime Squads. One day my staff officer met him and Frank asked to be remembered to me. After he left the job he had set up a firm of builders and was, by then, a millionaire driving a smart new Rolls Royce. I was not surprised, since without the prejudice and venom which had been directed at him he would have gone to the top in the Force. Quite by chance I spoke to him in December 1990 and asked him what he thought he would have achieved had he stayed on.

'Well,' he replied, 'it's difficult to tell. I may have got to be Chief Inspector, or maybe Superintendent, but I'll tell you this, Nipper, I wouldn't have got a Roller, would I?'

As for the officer he defended, Hannam had been right, because later the man ended up with a prison sentence after being found guilty of conspiracy to pervert the course of justice. Hannam gave evidence in that trial as well. Curiously, and sadly, when the man was released some officers regarded him as something of a hero and Hannam as the villain.

At the time, the police station was very different from the modern block it is today. It was a very old-fashioned red brick Victorian building in the Edgware Road at the junction with Bishops Bridge Road. The station fronted on to the street but down the side was a passageway and you went into a big yard which was all stables. One part had been designed as the ostler's quarters and this was now the CID office. The mounted branch still occupied one upstairs room and the others were for the DI and the DS. Downstairs was an office we, the DCs, all shared. The conditions were really terrible. It was one big room with one little office which the First Class Sergeant had, and we sat all the way round the other. It was always filthy with dust and dirt from the horses who were exercised in the yard outside. It really wasn't workable and I don't suppose the unions would accept it nowadays. It was a station long overdue for reconstruction, but it was, by far, the busiest on the Division.

We also policed a very different type of area from today. It was cosmopolitan but it was an Italian and Irish area rather than the Arab quarter it has become. Halfway down the Harrow Road was the old Metropolitan Music Hall where I would pop in the stalls bar for a drink with Mr Vasco the manager, who was always immaculately dressed in stiff white collar and tie. He was a most polite man and good company. Together we would have a tot and watch Carol Levis's *Discoveries* with Violet Pretty and Ronnie Carol, Paul Raymond's *Soldiers in Skirts* with Larry Grayson and, best of all, Max Miller. It wasn't time wasted. You could never tell which of the faces from the 'wanted' posters on the station walls might be there, and I was lucky enough to bag three of them. One was a man wanted for an extensive series of frauds who, even then, tried to explain to me that an arrest inside a music hall was illegal.

Another was a man whom I had seen at Paddington Police Station where he had been arrested for stealing a wallet from a chauffeur's pocket whilst he was cleaning a car. There was his picture on the wall with the caption that he was wanted for stealing a typewriter. Not many days later I found him in the stalls at the Metropolitan. He was sent for sentence at the old Inner London Sessions where, because of his record, he received 14 years' imprisonment under the Preventive Detention Act which was still in force.

The third was a Glasgow hard man wanted in Scotland for his part in a protection racket. Because of pressure from the local bobbies he had decided to hide away in London for a while. He was just having a night out at the Metropolitan when I ran into him.

All in all, Paddington had a better class of crime than Harlesden, but there were still some amusing incidents. One of them involved a prostitute, an olive-skinned beauty who whizzed a lorry driver out of his wallet with about £40 in it. He came in to tell a fairly familiar story that he had met this girl in the Bayswater Road which in those days was lined with prostitutes. She had taken him to a place in Lancaster Mews and, 'I can't believe it,' he said, 'she was such a nice girl and the best screw I ever had.' There was no difficulty in finding the girl. She was very attractive, slim figure, small, beautiful features, who looked part Asian and made no protest when I took her back to the nick and said she had to be charged. I don't really know what made me question the sex. There was nothing to go on at all, I just had a feeling all was not quite right. Eventually I said I would call the matron to search her and she said, lowering big brown eyes, 'I think you'd better do it yourself.' It was then the thing became unstuck and I realised he was a fellow, known as Saul.

The lorry driver was dumbfounded. 'If you hadn't told me, I wouldn't believe it now,' he said.

Months later I met Saul again. I was in Marylebone Court and there was an Inspector who had charged him with soliciting. I said, 'Hello, Sam, what have you nicked him for?'

He said, 'What are you talking about?'

I said, 'He's a fellow, you should do him for importuning not soliciting.'

'Bollocks,' he said.

'Yes,' I said, 'that's what you'll find if you make him drop his panties.'

It was at Paddington that I first met Jack Comer, also known as Jack Spot because he was always on the spot when he was needed to prevent trouble. The year 1956 saw the end of him as a major force in London's underworld. Known then as a hard man, he had been around since before the war. During the time of Sir Oswald Mosley's fascist marches throughout the East End, Spot had been employed by the wealthy Jewish element to provide resistance, and in his memoirs he wrote proudly of the battles he had waged with the blackshirts. One bloody encounter known as the 'Battle of Cable Street' convinced the authorities they had to take some action, and further marches by the fascists were banned. Spot became the hero of the East End, turning his popularity to good advantage by offering Jewish shopkeepers and clubs his protection. He also ran 'spielers', and after the war became controller of the bookmaking pitches on the 'free side' of many point-to-point meetings and race courses. These he let off to bookmakers who wanted to set up a stand. It was a lucrative business and he became a wealthy man.

By the 1950s he was one of the two self-styled 'Kings of the Underworld' – the other was Billy Hill – and was something of a grand old man. He had mellowed since his early days, had married a beautiful Irish girl, Rita, and now was well groomed with well-tailored – usually brown – suits, a brown fedora hat and handmade shoes. He would leave his flat, walk across the road to his barber's and then down to the Cumberland Hotel where, at a corner table in the Bear Garden, he would hold court, offering advice and wisdom to anyone who sought it. He looked like a successful businessman. He seemed to have modelled himself on the American mafioso, Frank Costello, but he had neither that man's intellectual power nor his political connections.

In August 1955 he had been involved in the celebrated knife fight in Soho with Albert Dimes, Hill's right-hand man. Hill was tired of Spot's control of the bookmaking pitches and this was a direct challenge for them. It was a fight which 'never was'. Both men were charged with affray and were acquitted following the perjured testimony of an old and senile vicar, Basil Andrews. He said by chance he had been passing and had witnessed the whole incident. He gave evidence which favoured Spot who was acquitted. The Crown felt it could not continue with the case against Dimes. Later Andrews admitted he had been given £14 for his perjured evidence. He again appeared at the Old Bailey, this time giving evidence for the Crown against his bribers.

Now Billy Hill had more or less retired and was about to head for Tangier. He wrote his memoirs, entitled *King of the Underworld*, and Spot was foolish enough to do the same, giving his preferred version of life in Soho to the *Daily Mirror* and also having it published by the Olympia Press in Paris with an introduction by Hank Janson.

Outside his own little empire, Spot had not been a popular man for some years and now he had annoyed even more people. It was also thought that he should be sharing some of his spoils from bookmakers' pitches with other deserving enterprises. Indeed he had hired the Krays for a day at the Epsom Spring Meeting when, it was rumoured, Billy Hill had been lining others up for an on-course battle. In the spring of 1956 Spot had known he was in trouble, because he had been coming to the Paddington Police Station asking to see Peter Beveridge to give him police protection. But the rumours were vague, and Beveridge was unable to act unless there was more concrete information. In fact he told Spot to stay away until he had evidence and was prepared to share it with him. When he got nowhere with Beveridge he would come to me saying, 'Nipper, they're definitely going to get me.' I would listen and indeed sympathise, but there was really no way I could help him. If the Chief Super had turned him away there was nothing a Detective Constable could do. As a betting man he must have known it was 6–4 on that he would eventually become a victim, but it was impossible to offer him protection in a situation which he had manufactured for himself.

But Jack was right. He had been so worried he had thought of retiring and buying a small pub. Around 9.30 p.m. on 2 May 1956, when he returned with Rita from looking at a possible purchase, The Little Weston off Praed Street, to his flat in Hyde Park Mansions, he was attacked by a group of men and was badly slashed. Spot was hit with a shillalegh and knocked to the ground. As he fell, one of his attackers stepped in and gave him a final slash across the face which caused the worst of his wounds. True to tradition, by the time he had been given over a hundred stitches at St Mary's Hospital, he was able to say, 'It was all over in seconds. I couldn't recognise a soul.' Rita was made of sterner stuff. She was prepared to name names and she did so. Billy Hill had wielded the shillalegh, ironically given to him by Spot in happier days. The other attackers she said included Albert Dimes, Bobby Warren and Frank Fraser. Jock McIver sent me with another Sergeant, Fred Byers, to make the arrests.

Billy Hill, short, slim, and with his hair greased and pasted back, looking every inch a spiv of the 1950s, was unconcerned. It was just as if he had expected a pull. He took his tiiime getting dressed and smartening himself up even more. Just before we left his small flat in a nondescript block in Moscow Road, Bayswater, he went to a sideboard, opened a cupboard and took out a roll of notes which would have choked a pig. 'I suppose I'd better bring a few quid, just in case,' he said as we took him away.

Albert Dimes, who lived in Clerkenwell, was equally unconcerned and rightly so. Both he and Hill had alibis and were never charged. Frankie Fraser had left for Ireland until the trouble died down, and so McIver set a trap. He let it be known that the heat was off and Fraser was not amongst the men wanted. Sure enough, within a few days we had word Frankie was on his way back. We went in three cars – two of which broke down on the way – to London Airport, and by the time we arrived the passengers had disembarked. We looked around desperately and I saw him, suitcase in hand, at the bottom of an escalator. His face was livid when it dawned upon him that he had been duped.

Bobby Warren was arrested a short time later and he and Fraser appeared at the Old Bailey in June. Spot refused to give evidence and was merely produced as an exhibit to show the scars resulting from his 180 stitches. Rita was the main prosecution witness and did her stuff. She coolly faced

Patrick Marrinan,[6] an Irishman who had a boxing blue, parrying his questions. She stuck by her story, denying that she had named Hill merely to get rid of him and leave the 'Crown of the Underword' on her husband's head. Fraser and Warren were each sentenced to seven years' imprisonment.

It was my job to get Spot and Rita back to the safety of their flat because Billy Hill, who had been watching the trial, was not pleased. He believed the law should not intervene in these domestic disputes. It was the first time I had the experience of driving in a police car through London at top speed, blue light flashing and headlights on. Three more of Spot's attackers were subsequently arrested, including Billy Blythe who refused to stand on an identification parade. On conviction on 16 October he was sentenced to five years and later died in prison. His funeral was one of the most spectacular of gangland funerals.

Meanwhile McIver thought there would be reprisals and so had Spot's flat watched, but when the counter-attack came it was in a very different way. On 20 June Tommy Falco, a close friend of Hill and Dimes, alleged that Spot had attacked him outside Bertie Green's Astor Club, a smart night spot just off Berkeley Square. He had received wounds requiring 47 stitches in his arm. The police had been outside Spot's flat that night and had not seen him leave, but when another man, Johnny Rice, went to the police station to corroborate Falco's story, Jack was arrested. The trial was one of the more interesting of the time because Victor 'Scarface Jock' Russo came forward to say he had been offered the then considerable sum of £500 to allow himself to be slashed and to say Spot was responsible. Hill himself gave evidence to say this allegation was ridiculous, but Mr Justice Streatfield, summing up to the jury, commented: 'Among these gentry, if they can be called that, they appear to have their own methods of dealing with those who displease them . . . It might afford a background for what has been called a

---

6 Marrinan was later disbarred because of his association with Hill.

"frame-up".' Spot, ably defended by Victor Durand, was acquitted.

Shortly after that, a club Jack owned in partnership in Bayswater was fire-bombed and he drifted away from the scene, taking work in a meat-packing factory. Years later, in the second Kray enquiry, I was to see Spot to try to get some piece of concrete evidence on which I could work. By now he had split with Rita and had clearly been on hard times. Otherwise he hadn't changed that much. There was still the well-cut suit and the smart brown fedora. He could still talk a good fight, asserting he had taught the twins 'all they know'. 'You know what did me, Nipper?' he asked. 'The papers. All that "King of the Underworld" thing. It was the worst day's work I ever did. Nobody even knew me before that and then suddenly everybody's trying to put one on me. That was my mistake, Nipper, publicity.'

Before my promotion there was one last arrest which was to anticipate the second Kray trial. I had just finished a tour of night duty one evening when an Inspector rushed in and said 'Everybody out'. We all poured into a van and went to the Westminster Bank on Praed Street at the junction with Eastbourne Terrace, answering a 'suspects on premises' call. We did the usual bit of circling the bank and then went in to search. At first we found nothing and we went down into the basement. For a moment it seemed everything was in order until I noticed a small movement in the pile of coke. In a loud voice I said, 'Well it doesn't look as though we're going to find anybody, perhaps we should call in the dogs.'

The effect was immediate. A man rose, phoenix-like, from the pile and shouted, 'No, it's all right, no dogs.'

We knew there must be others involved and so began the job of finding them. I decided to go to the house next door as I could see the roofs were adjoining ones. I went to the top of the building and could see how easy it was to get into the next one. I climbed through the window and into a tiny bedroom. There, a man in bed demanded to know who I was and how I dared burst into his room. I was about to retreat as gracefully as

I could when I noticed he had smudges on his face. I whipped back the bedclothes and Jimmy, a good old-fashioned villain, was lying there fully dressed. He gave up like the good 'un he was and asked if we had arrested anyone else. When I told him yes, he replied, 'That fucking Frankie. Every time I go on a job with him I'm nicked. He's just bad luck for me.' They had gone into the bank over the weekend and had worked away. Just as they were leaving in the early hours of Monday morning they triggered the alarm. Years later Jimmy was to contact me when I was investigating the disappearance of Frank Mitchell, the Dartmoor escapee.

CHAPTER FIVE

I LEFT PADDINGTON IN June 1958 when I was promoted to Detective Sergeant and sent back to St John's Wood. From that quiet station I plodded away for a year investigating a round of housebreakings, small robberies and blackmail, the diet of the Divisional detective. During this time I had appeared before a selection board for promotion to First Class Sergeant, and as the weeks went by I anxiously watched for details of my confirmation and posting.

When it came it was in tragic circumstances. I was moved to Chelsea following the shooting of Detective Sergeant Ray Purdy by a German named Gunther Podola. It was a crime which at the time caused a great outcry, first over the shooting of a police officer and then over the circumstances surrounding the arrest of Podola.

He had been born in Berlin in 1929, the son of a barber. A petty thief and blackmailer, after the war he emigrated to Canada, was deported and then turned up in Soho where he used the name Mike Colato. He returned to Germany and then came back to England in June 1959. In early July he broke into the South Kensington flat of a model, Mrs Vera Schiffman, and stole jewellery and furs worth some £2,000. More importantly, he took letters which he thought he might use to blackmail her.

Using the name of Fisher and calling himself a private detective, he telephoned Mrs Schiffman and invited her to buy back the letters and some tape-recordings. In turn, she telephoned the police. On the afternoon of 13 July he called her again, but the call was traced to a telephone kiosk at South Kensington Underground station. Purdy and another officer, John Sandford, went to the station and when Podola ran, chased him and caught him in a block of flats in Onslow Square. Whilst Sandford went to get help, Purdy was left guarding him. For an instant Purdy looked away and Podola shot him at point-blank range. He then ran back to his room at the Claremont House Hotel in nearby Queen's Gate.

It was there he was captured on 16 July when the police broke down the door of his room. Podola, standing behind the door, apparently about to open it, received a blow to the head as the door fell. Unconscious, he was taken to the police station where he was examined by the Divisional Surgeon and then sent to St Stephen's Hospital.

The public thought the worst, believing that the arresting officers had beaten up Podola, and, as so often happens, opinion swung sharply against the police. Questions were asked in the House of Commons about his arrest and for assurances that he was not chained to his bed. A fund had been set up for Ray Purdy's widow, but contributions now dried up and a rival fund was begun for Podola's defence.

The solicitor who appeared for him at West London Magistrates' Court faced a problem. Podola, he said, could not give him instructions because he could not remember anything prior to the blow. This became the central point of the trial. Was he unfit to plead or was he malingering?

At the trial four doctors called by the defence thought his amnesia was genuine, as did Mr Frederick Lawton[1] who defended him and who later presided at the second Kray trial. Two doctors called by the prosecution thought he was faking.

In the end it all turned on his answer to a letter written to him in Brixton by an old shipmate of his who said how sorry he was to hear of his troubles and asking whether Podola wanted some cigarettes sent to him. He wrote back, 'Dear Ron . . .'

---

[1] Later Lord Justice Lawton.

and the prosecution made much of that letter. If he genuinely had no idea who the man was, surely he would have written back, 'Dear Mr . . .' The jury decided he was fit to plead, and with the evidence against him overwhelming he was hanged in the November of that year.

I was posted to replace Ray Purdy at Chelsea and found it a difficult task trying to live up to the reputation of a man who had become a police hero. I stayed only a matter of months before I was sent back to Paddington.

It was there in 1960, now a First Class Sergeant, that I became involved in the arrest of Niven Craig, the brother of Christopher who was detained for life for his part in the murder of PC Miles in the celebrated Craig and Bentley case.[2] One of the arguments put forward on behalf of Christopher in that trial had been that the sentence of 12 years' imprisonment that Niven had received for an armed robbery had turned his younger brother to crime.

About 3 o'clock on the morning of Sunday 30 October 1960 Liam Gillespie, then a young Police Constable, was patrolling with another officer, P C Bennett, and as they walked along the Edgware Road they saw a young woman standing next to a parked Volkswagen car on the corner of Penfold Street and Church Street. She seemed nervous and was looking about her as though keeping watch. They were on their way to speak to her when suddenly there was an almighty explosion from a nearby shop and sheets of flame and smoke billowed out from what had been the premises of West's the butcher. The officers ran towards the shop and, as they did so, four men hurtled out and jumped into the waiting car. Off they went, leaving the poor girl running along beside it trying to get on board. She failed, fell in a heap on the pavement and was arrested.

When I saw her later that morning, a tall good-looking blonde with a nice figure and a Welsh accent, she denied all knowledge of doing anything wrong. She maintained that she

---

[2] Wilkinson, L. *Behind the Face of Crime*, Muller (1957).

had been for a ride with a couple of guys and was waiting for one of them, a man called Reg, to take her home to a flat in Leinster Gardens. Fortunately the officers had managed to get part of the number of the car and when I spoke to the owner he confirmed he had lent it to a man called Reg.

It paid to be patient. The girl wasn't going anywhere; it was a fine clear day and traffic was light; there was no pressure on the records department at the Yard. For a time the car owner stuck to his story and, to a certain extent, I believed him. He then told me that Reg had a girlfriend who lived in Leinster Gardens. I thought the coincidence too much and down I went to see if, by any chance, Reg might be waiting for her. He wasn't but there were some photographs of a good-looking man and some letters stamped HM Prison Wormwood Scrubs, marked N. Craig and signed Niv. Well, that was no problem. He was still serving, and a call to the prison confirmed this was the case. I did have a run through his record and it turned up that he was now on the hostel scheme. Could he possibly have been out? Another call to the prison. Yes, he was on weekend leave, due back on Monday morning.

The hostel scheme was the Home Office policy to assist prisoners to rehabilitate themselves into normal society and was, I believe, the biggest load of rubbish that could ever have been devised. So far as Niven Craig was concerned the idea was that he worked in an Islington garage during the day and returned each evening to the prison. In fact he never went to the workshop; nor was it the garage owner's duty to report back to the parole officer to say he'd never turned up. I went to see him in Wormwood Scrubs the next morning and, old hand that he was, there was no chance of a sudden confession. 'I've been with my parents all weekend at Caterham,' he told me. The answer was an identification parade to see if the owner of the car and the police officer picked him out. When they did he was nonchalant about it. He shrugged his shoulders and grinned wryly, 'Well, that's the way it goes.'

He drew five years when he appeared at Inner London Sessions before Reggie Seaton, the Chairman. He admitted he had had the car that evening but said he had returned it and once more told the story that he had been with his parents, but the jury didn't believe him.

'There are, unfortunately, people like you, Craig, who appear in the dock from time to time and who have made up their minds they are going to commit crime,' said Seaton, adding, 'You will find yourself qualifying for preventative detention.' The total haul from the butcher's shop had been just £26 16s. 11d.

Liam Gillespie and the other officer with him were given commendations over the case and so was I. I met Liam last year at a celebration party, when he retired with the rank of Detective Chief Superintendent, and we chatted about the case. 'You know Bennett really deserved the commendation more than we did,' he said. 'We were just young officers and he wanted to have a cigarette. I said that if the Sergeant caught him, there would be hell to pay and that if he really must he should go down this alleyway into Church Street. That's the only reason we were there. But you really set me off on my career. Do you remember, after the case, telling me I should join the CID?'

One problem for police officers is to disguise themselves so they don't stick out every time they go into a pub. I've been in pubs and clubs and restaurants with either an informer or a friend when someone has walked in, given me a tap on the arm and said, 'Who's your friend, Guv'nor?' I've looked round and seen that a very obvious copper, often a brand-new detective, full of his own importance, had just walked in. 'Some of these Old Bill might as well be wearing the helmet,' the informant would grumble. Still fresh out of uniform and not yet over the transition period, this sort think the fact they no longer wear a uniform makes them invisible. It's the same when keeping observation in the street, where the whole idea is to be noticed as little as possible. It infuriates me when I've often been driving along and seen the big Rover or Zephyr parked at the kerb, four up, sitting well down in the seats, all smoking and looking bored as hell. With the windows steamed up, all they really need is the blue light flashing on top of the motor.

Disguise conjures up the image of grease-paint, false beards, toupees and elaborate clothing, but in fact a simple pair of horn-rimmed glasses, a tee-shirt, a dirty overcoat, walking a dog on a lead, or being seen with a girl on your arm is just as effective cover, if not more so. From Day One I also had the distinct advantage over my colleagues in that I didn't look like a copper because I was so small. I could get into places and close up to people without being 'sussed out'.

As for observations on premises, I was always one for 'getting up'. Have you ever realised how often you look up when you are walking along a street? Hardly ever. How many times have you walked down a particular street day after day for years and then one day have taken a bus down that same street and, looking down from the upper deck, have realised you have only been seeing half the picture? Everything above eye level has been blacked out to you. It is the same with villains. They may look each way down the street and clock all the motor cars and wonder about the roadsweeper, but they don't look up. Their business is on the ground. What's upstairs but the sky? Well, if a detective has any sense at all that is where *he* is. He should be on the stairs of a block of flats, on the balcony, on the roof. Better still, he should be in a first floor flat where comfort makes the tedium of watching bearable, anywhere that is a few feet off the ground, so he may watch his quarry, keep in touch with his colleagues, and get back down to earth quickly.

If foot surveillance is necessary, then it has to be carefully arranged with a number of officers, men and women in radio communication or with an agreed set of signals to do the job properly. Crime dramas on television, with the officer fifteen feet behind the suspect, make me angry.

A good villain expects to be followed. He will go down the Tube, turn and come out again, get on a train and get out of the doors as they close, take a bus and drop off at traffic lights, go in a store with a number of exits by one door and leave by a different one. Suddenly he will jump into a cab. In a pub he will leave his drink and go to the lavatory. Five minutes later you realise there is an exit into another bar. He is following his profession, and self-preservation comes high on the list of his priorities.

If you have to stay on the ground, then blend in with the background. Talk to the barman, the man sitting next to you, pat his dog, play the video game, be anonymous, so that afterwards if the suspect is asked about observation he will swear no one else was in the pub. From my early days with 'Gosh' Mathews I was always being dressed up to keep observation on suspects. Often all I needed was a pair of overalls with some paint spots and plimsolls and there I was, a young chap just out of the army, working on a decorating job round the corner. As an aide in St John's Wood I rode a racing cycle. I've had dozens of trades and professions: a GPO telephone linesman, a naval petty officer (wearing my own uniform to follow a ponce in the West End), a roadsweeper, delivery boy, and a Hertz chauffeur at London Airport when I went to arrest a man on a drug smuggling charge.

It was as a milkman that I made one arrest as a DI. A man named McGelligot had escaped from Pentonville Prison where he was serving a substantial sentence for a variety of offences including armed robbery and shooting at a police officer. We received information from a local constable that two escapees were holed up in a house in Tower Hamlets. We kept observation on the house for a couple of days with nothing to show for our time, and I went back to the young copper to double check his information was correct. He was adamant the man was in the house; and so we decided to give the place a spin, early the next morning. We arrived just after dawn when the only person in the street was the milkman. Somehow we had to get into the house without arousing McGelligot's suspicions and so creating a potentially dangerous situation both for him and ourselves. We could, of course, have broken down the door and for a time, short of that, I could see no way in. Then I thought about the milkman. Supposing he knocked . . . if someone looked out, would he take any notice?

A few doors down the road I stopped the man and borrowed his coat, cap and bottle carrier. 'Only a few minutes . . .' Off I went whistling as milkmen did then, rattling the bottles and putting the carrier down on the step with a clatter I tapped on the door. No answer. Everyone was dead to the world. After all, it was still around 6 a.m. I knocked louder and louder and then rapped on the front ground-floor window. That roused someone because a man pulled aside the curtain and I could see him mouthing a string of curses through the glass. What the – hell did I want?

We knew that no one on the ground floor had anything to do with McGelligot and so I took out my warrant card and, pressing it close to the window, I put my finger to my lips and indicated to him to open the door. As he did so, the lads were in like a pack of foxhounds. By the time I had put the milk down, given the cap back to the milkman and followed them in, McGelligot and his mate were sitting on his bed, hands firmly handcuffed behind their backs, looking amazed.

Later in my career for a short while I became a man of the cloth, but perhaps one of my most successful appearances in Paddington days was as a clerk in a betting shop.

It was over a betting shop protection racket directed at Nathan Mercado who, as Sid Kiki, ran a chain of betting shops. He was a man who had one foot on the pavement and one in the gutter because he was always said to be the man – something he denied to me – who fingered Jackie Spot outside his flat off the Edgware Road for the slashing which finally ended his career as one of the two 'Kings of the Underworld'. He was also a good informer.

In the summer of 1963 there were threats to petrol-bomb his shop and those of other north-west London bookmakers. The team was headed by a man, Patrick Ball, who was known as 'The Professor' because he was always smartly dressed and carried a rolled umbrella and briefcase. Twice they set fire to the shops of James Burge, a bookmaker from Acton who was then in his sixties. Looking back now it seems incredible that the going rate for 'protection' was £10 a week, and sometimes the price was open for negotiation. In fact they were a small team operating on their own without any back-up from bigger organisations such as Billy Hill's. The Professor spoke to Burge and said he was taking over the manor and wanted a weekly payment. Burge asked, 'What will you get out of a dump like this?'

'Surely you can afford a fiver,' was the reply. Burge said he did not want to know, and a fortnight later his shop was petrol-bombed during the night. Sid Kiki and another bookmaker, Leslie Potter, were also being threatened. Both men resisted the pressure and came to see me separately, saying the man had a 'bleeding cheek' by implying that he represented an element of organised crime. It was arranged that I should spend a few days in Kiki's shop at Shepherd's Bush as a clerk. I had on spectacles and ticker tape wound round my neck. The trouble was that it was a bit much for me. I was never very keen on racing itself, let alone betting, and that day was a Saturday when the Northumberland Plate – the Pitman's Derby – a handicap which attracted a lot of betting, was run. There were also meetings at Newmarket, Windsor and Worcester. Twenty-four races in all. It was a nightmare. Kiki was very good, keeping up the pretence that I knew what I was doing and not complaining when I pulled too hard and broke the ticker tape.

The Professor came into the shop after the last race. Kiki was a little Jewish fellow with a good deal of bottle. He was all ready for this man. Remember, he'd more or less thrown out The Professor, and now with me he had the back-up. Instead of doing what had been arranged and asking questions such as, 'How much will it cost?' and, 'What will I have to do?' so that it could be clear evidence with me listening, Kiki started shouting, 'You can fuck off. I'm not having any of this.' I just had to make my arrest and hope we had enough evidence. In fact The Professor pleaded guilty and received six years' imprisonment, and the other two involved got three years apiece.

One occasion when my disguise proved rather too successful was when I was an undercover man buying a lorry load of whisky from some thieves. The plan was that when we were all together in the warehouse I would give a signal to other officers and then be allowed to make a dash for freedom when the raid began. To make it look absolutely genuine, one officer was detailed to chase me but, unfortunately, in the squad was also a new detective who did not recognise me and had not been briefed. He took off with the 'plant' chaser and soon outstripped him. When he was gaining on me I thought it was time to surrender and ran into the garden of a nearby house so I would not be seen giving myself up. I tried to signal to the officer that I was one of his own but it was no use. He fancied himself as a rugby player, tackled me just above the knees and I landed in a stagnant ornamental fishpond. I was not best pleased, although I soon realised it was no fault of the young officer. I was even less pleased when the officer who was to have 'chased' me arrived in time to pull me out and, seeing me, burst into laughter saying, 'If that's what you get for going undercover, leave me out.'

On 8 August 1963 the biggest theft the world had then known went off. The night train from Glasgow to London was stopped at the remote Brigedo Bridge, Cheddington, in Buckinghamshire. A gang of armed thieves coshed the driver, smashed their way into the high-value-package coach and stole 120 mailbags whose contents were estimated to be worth over £2.5 million. Even now the Great Train Robbery has a certain romanticism about it which has not attached to the later and bigger raids such as the Security Express and Brinks Mat robberies. There had been thefts from trains before in recent years, particularly on the London to Brighton line, but these had been relatively small affairs.

First reports of the Cheddington theft were vague but, as the day wore on, it became clear that this was a major robbery. Buckinghamshire was one of the smallest of the county forces and the Chief Constable, Brigadier Cheney, quickly realised he did not have the manpower at his disposal to deal with such a major incident. He used the facility that was available to all provincial constabularies. He called in Scotland Yard.

Officers from Scotland Yard had been made available from 1907 when the then Home Secretary, Herbert Gladstone, wrote to the Commissioner saying he felt that it was desirable that the services of a small number of detectives should be available for enquiries in difficult and important criminal cases committed outside the Metropolitan Police District.[3]

It then fell to the officers of Central Office, New Scotland Yard, to take on this responsibility. As the majority of cases they investigated were murders, they soon became known as the Murder Squad. It consists of ten Chief Superintendents in charge of squads of men who are committed to investigating a variety of criminal cases. These range from extradition and fugitive offender cases, banknote forgery and coinage offences, bribery and corruption, international lotteries and crimes relating to government departments. There is no question then that these experienced investigators are simply sitting around waiting for a telephone call from a provincial or overseas force. They are well occupied with their daily responsibilities. What there is in force is a rota system with three on stand-by awaiting call-out. Being one of the three was known as 'being in the frame' and as a call was taken, then the next one moved up a place. Number One had a suitcase ready, packed with a current passport in case of an overseas job, and the famous 'murder box'. It meant that officer had to be available twenty-four hours a

---

[3] One of the first, if unsuccessful, investigations was undertaken by Inspector Dew who later arrested Crippen. He was sent to Salisbury to find the killer of a crippled boy, Teddy Haskell. Unfortunately by the time he had arrived all the blood had been cleaned away under the supervision of the local police. Flora Haskell, the boy's mother, was arrested, and was defended by the young Rayner Goddard who later became the Lord Chief Justice. She was acquitted after a re-trial.

day and ready at very short notice to go anywhere in the world.

The current Number One was Gerald McArthur who had only recently been appointed to the squad and who, although he had considerable experience in all manner of investigations, including murder, whilst serving in various divisions of the Met, had never been appointed to assist a provincial force whilst on the Murder Squad. He chose as his assistant an old colleague of mine from Paddington, Jack Pritchard. Their role was an advisory and directory one, as was that of any member of the Murder Squad when he was called out. Although this was standard procedure, it did not satisfy the press or the public. Why, it was asked, were only two men detached from the Met to solve the world's greatest robbery? In turn it was decided to supplement McArthur and Pritchard with a larger team. I was a part of it.

Aylesbury, where the inquiry was based, throbbed with activity, speculation, rumour and excitement. The world's press swarmed everywhere like mayflies on a warm summer's afternoon. It was impossible to walk two yards or go for a sandwich and a half pint of beer without being accosted by a reporter or photographer. Of course this was completely understandable. This was WORLD NEWS. Every snippet of conversation or chance remark could be turned into the latest headline, and anyone leaving the headquarters was the object of a battery of flashbulbs, on the off chance he might be someone interesting.

Indeed this was the first time I had seen at close quarters the in-fighting and back-biting which went on in the higher echelons of the police. Each officer wanted some of the glory from this, the world's greatest robbery. Each wanted to be seen as the instigator of this or that line of enquiry, preferably when it had turned out to be a successful one. More senior detectives visited Aylesbury than any scene of crime before and probably since. They all gave notice of their arrival to the reporters and made sure their best side was showing when the cameras clicked. Every senior officer was out to make a name with *his* arrests and have *his* photograph in the papers. All gave short crisp quotes suggesting that they were really overlording the operations, and then shortly afterwards they were driven back to London.

Through all this Gerald McArthur maintained an air of unruffled equanimity. He knew who was really in charge. Unfortunately the record has never given him any of the credit for the magnificent job he did. Few members of the general public realise that he was the man at the helm.

I was put to work with an Inspector Richard Chitty, who later became a Deputy Assistant Commissioner, to organise the control room and introduce the Yard's 'system'. Dick Chitty was a master of this. Within a couple of days the production line system was fully in operation and I was looking for a chance to get out into the field as quickly as possible.

The Great Train Robbery was a job which had been hawked like a film script around the underworld for some time. The blueprint had been carefully worked out and had been offered to a number of suitable clients. It had been on offer so long that when it happened a number of people were not surprised. It was well known at the Yard that an Irishman was responsible for planning robberies and then selling them on to the perpetrators. The first of these was at Ericson's Telephones in Beeston in Nottingham. This was the first big hijack after the war. He went on to plan many others and detectives would say, 'That's got Mickey's stamp on it,' because the planning was meticulous.

Whilst I was at Paddington there was one job he gave me. We never met but he either knew or had heard of me and we had a series of telephone conversations. I was never quite sure why he blew the whistle but I suspect he had not been paid for the plan for this particular job.

It was a nice job really. Each week money was collected from an office block in Eastbourne Terrace by a GPO van. Mickey told me there would be a Ford Zephyr motor car and four people in it and another bloke at the bus stop and so on. When the people came out with the loot, etc., the men in the

Zephyr would attack them and the man at the bus stop would be a back-up helper.

It was a perfectly simple operation to mount, and when the raid was scheduled to go off there I was standing in my shirt sleeves on the steps of the office block having an argument with my 'girlfriend', a woman detective, Betty Reid. Two of my men were the 'office workers' there to hand the money over to the GPO men. Sure enough, as the exchange was made, the Ford car appeared with four men in it, drove up and then slowed down. After the exchange was made it roared away up the road.

We arrested the only one left, the man at the bus stop, who had a long steel bar up his sleeve and got five years for conspiracy to rob. When I got back to the nick, Mickey was on the phone in a rage. 'You've fucked it up completely.'

I said, 'What are you talking about? We had everything laid on. They just didn't stop.'

'No,' he said, 'Of course they didn't fucking stop. These two blokes of yours – the ones in the waistcoats who handed over the cash —'

'Yes,' I said, wondering how he knew they were 'my chaps'.

'They came out of the office – the real ones never, never do that.' It was an example of how meticulous his planning was. He had obviously detailed in his plan that the office workers handed over the cash and went straight back to their duties. The fact that they did not alerted the robbers and the job was off.

I am sure from all the information I had that he drew up the plan for the Great Train Robbery, but it was Bruce Reynolds who honed, polished and fine-tuned it. I don't think he devised it. It had been on the shelf and available for anyone who wanted to take it on, but he did a lot of research on it. He joined a fishing club, took photographs, went to Euston to see how the coupling on hydraulics worked.

I can remember standing on the embankment at Brigedo Bridge and realising what a perfect place it was for the unloading operation. Looking around, there was only one building in sight, a farmhouse, the telephone wires to which had been cut. Then, a short walk down the track, was a white flag resting on an overturned barrow. This was the signal for the driver to stop the train so that the high-value-package carriage was precisely above the embankment on the bridge. This had been separated from the rest of the train, leaving the sorters, who might otherwise have been a problem wondering what the delay might be, a mile down the track. The exercise had not only involved the uncoupling of the train but the disconnecting and reconnecting of the vacuum pipe controlling the braking system. I have always believed it to have been a perfectly planned and well-executed operation. The only flaw was the gratuitous violence meted out to Jack Mills, the train driver.

There have been a number of theories about a sinister and mysterious 'Mr Big', rather like Steve McQueen in the film *The Thomas Crown Affair*, who masterminded the affair but who was never caught. I discount this. There also was a story that one of the friends of the Krays, who actually came from South London, was involved, but whether he put up money I don't know. I believe that the mastermind as such was Reynolds, with the brilliant Gordon Goody as the quartermaster sergeant, the Number Two. An operation of this size needs financing and the money for it was provided by the 'City Gent' job at London Airport in 1962. This was a robbery alleged to have involved Gordon Goody, Bruce Reynolds, Charlie Wilson, Roy James and some others. Wilson and Goody were charged and acquitted whilst Mickey Ball, who pleaded guilty, received five years' imprisonment.[4]

Now the planning for the big one could go ahead. It was another example of fine planning that Leatherslade Farm had been selected as a temporary hideaway, and discipline over the job had been very strictly observed. I believe Gordon Goody was the man who kept the troops under control. Before the job

---

[4] Perhaps the best account is in Piers Paul Read's *The Train Robbers*, W.H. Allen, London (1978).

he could do this, not only because of his forceful personality but by constantly referring to the rewards on offer when the caper was finally pulled.

I believe it was when, back at the farm, the team tore open the mailbags and found they had netted £2.25 million that they realised they had hit a jackpot beyond their hopes. Discipline went to the wall after that and, from being a well-drilled and regimented body, the robbers reverted to type and once more became individuals blinded by wealth, each one eager to go off and spend it for himself.

They were not helped by the fact that McArthur put out an announcement that he believed the robbers were still within a 30-mile radius of Brigedo Bridge. (Leatherslade Farm was about 27 miles away.) Then when the friend of a neighbouring farmer circled the area in a plane they really thought the game was up and the exodus from the farm was rapid and frenzied. All these things led to a break-up of the tight control which had been exercised by the leaders. The belief spread that it was only a matter of time before the farm was raided, and as a result the team began to split up, taking with them suitcases filled with money.

There has also been a theory[5] that there was a Judas, someone who was meant to go to Leatherslade Farm and set fire to it, destroying all trace of its previous inhabitants, but who failed to carry out his task. One story was that a client of Brian Field, the solicitor's clerk involved, had been paid to burn it. I don't believe that. I was at the farm almost immediately it was found and whilst there were two vehicles there from which petrol could have been siphoned, there were no inflammable materials round about to which anyone could have easily put a match.

---

[5] Advanced first by Peta Fordham, journalist wife of Wilfrid Fordham, in *The Robbers' Tale*, Hodder & Stoughton (1965). Fordham defended Mary Mansell and John Daly, both of whom were acquitted. It was advanced also by Ernie Millen in *Specialist in Crime*, George G. Harrap & Co (1972).

It was fascinating to watch the Yard's painstaking fingerprint expert Maurice Ray at work. There had been about 15 men holed up there, eating, sleeping, playing games, going to the lavatory, and yet they had left really no fingerprints. Had it been their intention to have the place burned down, then there would have been no need to worry about prints. Consequently one would expect to have found them on door panels, light switches, bathroom fittings, the walls, everywhere.

It was clear that Maurice Ray and his team had scoured every inch of the place, seeking any traces left by the inhabitants. Every room was daubed with fingerprint powder, but nothing of consequence was found. It was only by dusting the most unlikely places that evidence did in fact surface: a sauce bottle, a faint palm print on the tailboard of a lorry, a saucer put out by Reynolds for the cat, and a Monopoly set, probably left behind in the mad scramble to get away. In Goody's case there was only the faintest trace of yellow paint on a shoe to connect him to the farmhouse. There just weren't the million fingerprints lying about as one would expect if a team of 15 or so men had been there for a week.

It is my theory that the fingerprints they left were so inadvertent and unusual that they were terrible mistakes rather than evidence of the belief that there was no worry because the place was going to be torched anyway. If that had been the case then whoever had failed to burn the place down would have met with a very nasty accident. I've never supported that view at all.

Early on at Aylesbury it became quite clear that a London team had executed the job. The job had been on offer for some time and informants had done part of their work. Despite the precautions taken by Reynolds and Goody, the Yard knew some major villains were about to pull something big. But it was only after the robbery that they knew what.

A list was quickly put together of those thought to have been involved. After all, there was only a handful of people in the country who were capable of such a job. It was then the real work of finding the evidence began.

Maurice Ray and Ian Holden, the forensic scientist, provided the foundation upon which the detectives could build, but tracing the suspects, their questioning, and the breaking of their alibis was left to the Flying Squad under the direction of their newly appointed chief Tommy Butler. It was on this job that he really came into his own. This was what he really loved – chasing top-class villains. It became a personal vendetta. He undertook a totally ruthless and dedicated operation which would finally result in the whole team being netted.

And so a second base – 'the London End' was established for the inquiry in Scotland Yard, in the Flying Squad office. Butler, first in in the morning and last out at night, now changed his tactics. He still played his cards very close to his chest. His team was given the minimum of information needed for a surveillance operation or to make a quick arrest.

A good example of this was the way he sent his 'twin', Detective Chief Inspector Peter Vibart, the man with whom he was meant to have the greatest rapport, and me to Leicester after Gordon Goody had been arrested.

Goody's had been one of the earliest names in the frame as an organiser and prime mover. Police in London had visited his mother's address and some of his known hideouts, but with no positive result. On 23 August we had the news that he had been detained in Leicester. Butler sent Vibart and me to Leicester with no instructions about what we were to do. Now usually a superior officer would have told us either to question him in detail there and then, or perhaps ask about an alibi, or just to bring the suspect back to the office and talk about nothing but horse-racing on the way down. Not so with Tommy. We had no instructions whatsoever. I suppose it was that we were so in awe of him that we didn't ask before we left Aylesbury. Along the M1 Vibart said to me, 'Nipper, stop at the next service station and give him a ring to see what we are to do.'

But at first many of the suspects were brought in, questioned and then released. These included Hussey, Wisbey, Goody, Brian Field and Lennie Field. This gave the impression he was only on a 'fishing expedition' and that he had no real evidence to back him up; otherwise he would have charged them. This was a most unusual practice for Tommy. Normally, and it was well known amongst the villains, once he had his hooks into someone it was seldom they left the police station except to go to court. As a result some of his junior officers began to be worried that he was going soft. Nothing of the kind: he was merely playing a game of patience. By seeing them and having a quiet, apparently friendly chat, he had persuaded them that, so far as they were concerned, it was a routine inquiry. He had opposed the publication of photographs of some of the leading suspects and had been overruled by Ernie Millen, the Commander of the CID. Butler had rightly feared that men of this calibre would simply go underground or flee the country. The others were lulled into a false sense of security. When it came to some arrests it was only a question of asking them to report to the Yard which they did quite happily. This time they did not leave. Tommy was a canny operator.

He went to the farm for the first time on 17 August and I took him on a conducted tour. As he walked through the rooms looking at the debris he smiled his wry smile. 'Pity. With a bit of luck they could have all been nicked here, Nipper. But never mind, we'll get the bastards.'

He was right, of course, Within a matter of weeks nine of the fifteen finally charged had been arrested, and another five had been posted as wanted.

There had been a breakthrough the previous day. A Dorking man, John Ahearn, was giving a lift on the pillion of his motorcycle to Mrs Nina Hargreaves when the small-engined machine began to overheat. They pulled off the road into a sheltered area of woodland where only a few yards from the road, sitting on a tree stump rather like an altar, was a beautiful embossed suitcase. They opened the bag and were astonished to find it was crammed with used banknotes. They knew at once they had stumbled on part of the Train Robbery haul and contacted the police. A dog unit arrived with other officers and began to search the ground. A little further into the wood they discovered another bag. The total count was £100,900.

I was sent with a Detective Superintendent Malcolm Fewtrell from the Buckinghamshire Constabulary to recover the loot. He was a charming man and, looking back, although we travelled together around the countryside following leads, it seems we mostly went about collecting recovered money.

Fewtrell was an independent man and so managed to avoid the in-fighting and controversy amongst other senior officers in the inquiry. When we arrived at the wood I was amazed to see how obvious the case must have been. It would have been visible even from the road. It was almost as if it had been put there to be discovered. Right opposite from where the suitcase was found there was a field of fern in which it was almost impossible to see anything. With a bit more planning the suitcase could have remained undetected for years.

Anyone less honest than Mr Ahearn and Mrs Hargreaves might have been tempted to keep the swag, but at that time anyone seen with a suitcase was fair game for a stop by an officer. The country was in the grip of GTR mania. Anyone stopped with more than an ordinary roll of banknotes would certainly be invited to 'assist the police with their enquiries'. Hundreds of calls were received from up and down the country giving information about this or that person acting 'suspiciously' by spending money freely. Any spare moment of Joe Public's was spent in debating what he would do with his share, how he would hide it or disguise it, get it out of the country and where he would go to live happily ever after. And we, the investigating officers, were not above joining in the speculation.

One beneficiary of the find was the press. The next weekend what seemed like half southern England came out to play 'Find the Train Robbery Money' for which, of course, there was a substantial reward. The photographers had a great time shooting pictures for the Monday morning editions.

At the bottom of the Dorking suitcase a German hotel receipt was found in the name of Herr and Frau Field. This was Brian Field, the solicitor's clerk, and the £100,900 was obviously his share of the proceeds. Brian Field, a very good-looking smooth-talking man, had been managing clerk to a solicitor, James Wheater, who had offices in the West End. He had been fairly easy to link to the job because Wheater's firm had been instructed in the purchase of Leatherslade Farm. Field had defended a great number of villains over the years, including Goody in the Airport robbery. Once the hotel bill had been found, Jack Pritchard had been keen to arrest Field but orders 'from above' countermanded him. Nevertheless, Jack was convinced we should find something worthwhile at Field's home near Pangbourne, where he lived with his good-looking German wife Karen. After a great deal of lobbying Pritchard was allowed to apply for a search warrant and execute it; so one morning around 5 a.m. we arrived to awake the occupants. Brian Field came to the door and, although his expression of amazement did him credit, I have no doubt he was expecting a dawn call.

'Hello, Nipper,' he said. 'What on earth are you doing here?' As if he didn't know! Jack told him and then, whilst we ransacked the house, Karen, bravely playing the part of the hostess, made us coffee. But it was clear from Field's behaviour there was going to be nothing on the premises that day. We left with Field smiling and waving from the doorstep, his arm around his attractive wife as if he didn't have a care in the world.

Field was a real smoothie and a man of great charm. I had known him when he was defending, and in his professional life he was always extremely straight with me. If he was going to do something he would tell me in advance and not spring it on me in the witness box. For his part in the Train Robbery he was eventually charged with conspiracy to rob, and convicted. He was sentenced to 25 years' imprisonment but, on appeal, his conviction for conspiracy was quashed and he got five years as a receiver. I saw him again when in 1966, after his release from prison, he came into West End Central about Jack Buggy's murder. Later he changed his name and remarried, putting his past behind him. When he was killed in a road accident his new family was completely shattered to learn his real identity.

The following day I was back at Aylesbury where I had the responsibility of organising a team to clean up the farm before it was handed back to its owners. This meant removing all traces of the fingerprint powder from doors, walls, mirrors and so on, and moving out the incredible quantity of stores that the robbers had brought to the farm. There were dozens of eggs, packets of tea, rolls and rolls of lavatory paper, tea urns, cooking utensils, beer, and, of course, beds and mattresses, which were to have been their lifeline if they had kept to their original intention and stayed at the farm until the initial hue and cry had died down instead of panicking and fleeing in all directions.

There had already been an earlier breakthrough in the enquiry. On 11 August Roger Cordery, a man brought in as the electrician to work the signals on the track, and his friend William Boal were arrested in Bournemouth where they had had the misfortune to attempt to rent lodgings from the widow of a police officer. They had bought a vehicle and a substantial sum was found in it. The money was lodged in the Chief Constable's safe and the gloom which had descended over the investigating team lifted a bit.

But it was after the finding of the suitcase that things started to happen. A caravan owned by James White, one of the robbers, was discovered at Box Hill, Surrey, and on 20 August I went there with Malcolm Fewtrell where we were met by a Chief Superintendent 'Chalkie' White from the Regional Crime Squad. At the site we were snapped by an enterprising photographer. It made a lovely picture. There are the three of us standing with expressions of annoyance on our faces. The reason was that none of us had a key to the van. We had forgotten to pick it up from the local nick. When it was brought in we found it contained £30,000. At least we went back to Aylesbury with another suitcase full of money.

As the money was being recovered, it was stored in the safe in the police station at Aylesbury. I remarked to Malcolm Fewtrell, 'Do you know how much we've got in, sir? There's around half a million in there and only two police officers in the station all night.'

'My God,' he said, 'I've never realised that before.' He then sellotaped the whole of the safe door and proudly said, 'That should hold it until morning. We'll have to do something else then.' He then drafted in another two officers to reinforce the complement on duty and the next morning the money was moved to one of the major banks.

There is a sequel to the story of Jimmy White's caravan. Reporters and photographers sent to cover this particular 'crime of the century' were often short of news. They were camped out at The Bull in Aylesbury where they had the best rooms and first choice of seats in the bar. McArthur and the rest of the police were in the King's Head. In a case like this good relations with the press are essential. Consequently Gerry McArthur held a press conference every day to which he invited all the national press – there were no favourites – and they kept the public interest in the enquiries going. Quite apart from being short of news, they were often short of pictures. At that stage there was little at which they could point their cameras, and so the discovery of the caravan and its removal to Aylesbury was a godsend. Could they take pictures of Jack Pritchard, me and some other officers examining it? Of course they could. So there appeared a photograph of us standing around with screwdrivers looking as though we were about to take the van to pieces. Of course we did not do so – we had had our suitcase of money out of it and the van was just left standing in the police garage at Aylesbury for a considerable time. Later, when White was arrested, long after the main trial, he made a statement to the investigating officers and added, 'But you never found the money in the van though did you?' He then told them that behind some of the panels of the walls of the caravan was around £9,000, part of the proceeds. Sure enough, there it was. So much for the diligent search and stripping of the caravan by the police! The explanation was really quite simple. He was a carpenter and had removed the panels lining the van, putting the money behind them. At the time he thought it had been 'weeded' by the officers who had first searched the vehicle.

From then on, arrest followed arrest. Goody, Hussey, Wisbey, one after another Butler had them. He never let up, even after the main body of the team had been charged and convicted. His campaign to trace Charlie Wilson after his escape from Winson Green Prison in Birmingham, his persistent dogging of Buster Edwards until the man lost his nerve and surrendered, and his patient tracking of the mastermind Bruce Reynolds have all been well documented. The accounts bear testimony to Butler's determination. This obsession which persisted until the day of his retirement – something I believe he had postponed to complete his enquiries – has ensured his place in the annals of criminal investigation. I wonder whether the exertion and stress brought about his early death shortly after that retirement.

The long sentences passed at the trial have been the subject of much discussion. I believe they set the standard. This gang, who pulled off the biggest caper in criminal history, must have known that if they were caught the punishment would be of a similar standard – top weight. It had to deter others from robbing the Queen's Mail and discourage the use of violence. That used against poor Jack Mills was quite gratuitous. He was completely outnumbered and could easily have been overpowered without the blow to the head which may have contributed to his death seven years later. This put the attack in an even more reprehensible light and no amount of gloss can overcome it. These men were professional criminals of the highest quality who set out on an enterprise they were convinced would be successful. Even so, had they known before they started out that they would be nicked, I still think they would have done it – just to say they pulled the biggest caper of all.

Prison did not do many of them any good by way of reformation. Boal died whilst serving his sentence and others were re-convicted for serious crimes. Charlie Wilson was shot dead in Marbella in 1989. Biggs, one of the most insignificant of all involved, has become a national hero, following his escape from prison and the press hand-outs he gives from his bolt-hole in Brazil.

The police investigation of the Train Robbery was an outstanding success, so far as arrests and convictions are concerned. The failure was in recovering only a fraction of the money stolen. Of the total of £2.6 million taken from the train, only some £400,000 was recovered. There have been a number of suggestions, apart from the Mastermind theory, as to where the money went. First, there are always other expenses. If someone put some more money up for finance they would be in for a share; if someone provided a lorry or a car or a safe house, then so would they. Apart from that, I have no doubts. Escapes from prison are expensive and so is living in the underworld when your face is on a wanted poster. The members of the gang were blackmailed and ripped off for hundreds of thousands of pounds by their friends in the criminal fraternity.[6] Buster Edwards, Roy James, Jim Hussey, Jimmy White, Biggs and Gordon Goody all suffered in this way. Honour amongst thieves – forget it. It is pure bullshit.

Once the arrests had been made, the investigation wound slowly down and I returned to London. It had been good experience on a number of levels. First it introduced me to the bickering at high level which I would meet again later in my career, but more importantly it was an introduction to the investigation of a major crime which served me in good stead. When the time came to leave, I was sorry to go. It had been a pleasure to work under Gerry McArthur and Malcolm Fewtrell. Brigadier Cheney never pretended to be a policeman. He was a fine administrator and organiser. He had professionals to do the coppering job. He called me into his office where I found Gerry, Malcolm and Jack already there, gave us a glass of sherry, made a short speech of thanks and presented Force ties to us all.

---

[6] See Piers Paul Read's *The Train Robbers*.

Gerry McArthur went on to become the head of the CID for Hertfordshire and was later appointed the Assistant Chief Constable and Co-ordinator of the No. 5 Regional Crime Squad. During his time there, victims of the Richardsons' 'Torture Trials', recognising him as a man of integrity, went to him and, much to the chagrin of some of the elders at the Yard, he began the investigations which led to the conviction of the brothers and their henchmen. I met him on the steps of West End Central Police Station, just after he had detained a number of members of the gang. 'I'll tell you what, Nipper,' he said, 'the Train Robbery was nothing compared with this lot.'

Brigadier Cheney retired and his Force was swallowed up in an amalgamation, re-emerging as part of the Thames Valley Police. Malcolm Fewtrell retired and lives on the South Coast. Jack Pritchard, who died recently, left the force after 30 years – during which time he rose to a uniformed Chief Superintendent – and became a black cab driver.

I always regarded the tie given to me at the end of the inquiry as my lucky one and wore it when I attended promotion selection boards. Over the years it has justified my faith in it because I passed them all. The next to come was my selection to Detective Inspector. I then learned that I was to leave the frying pan of Paddington for the fire of the East End.

CHAPTER SIX

BY THE SUMMER OF 1964 there were a growing number of rumours that the Kray twins were operating a protection racket directed primarily against bookmakers, publicans, and club-owners in the East End. Protection could take one of two forms and sometimes both. Either there was the straight fee or percentage of takings paid weekly, or there was 'nipping', when the collectors would simply help themselves to bottles of scotch or wine. There could also be a direct demand for a loan of one or two hundred pounds 'to help the twins out for a day or two' or in some cases for a larger sum 'to conclude a business deal'. In this case a set of gold cuff links inscribed 'RK' would be left as security for the loan. A day or two later the return of the links would be requested as 'Ronnie has got to go to a posh dinner up West'. The money was never repaid. Whichever method was used, the victim soon got the message and his name went onto the permanent nipping list.

There had been no direct complaint that anyone was being approached to pay protection money because the victims did not feel it worth their while to risk a complaint, but their activities were so blatant that reporters had started to write a great deal in the national press regarding the Krays' activities. It came to a head when the *Daily Mirror* carried an editorial on 13 July commenting that:

This gang is so rich, powerful and ruthless that the police are unable to crack down on it. Victims are too terrified to go to the police.

Witnesses are too scared to tell their story in court. The police, who know what is happening but cannot pin any evidence on the villains, are powerless.

The next day the then Commissioner, Sir Joseph Simpson, had made a statement to the press that he had asked senior officers for 'some enlightenment' on reports that enquiries were being made into allegations of a relationship between a homosexual peer and East End gangsters.

On 16 July the *Mirror* ran a front page story: 'The picture we dare not print'. This was initially thought to be a picture of a peer in a homosexual position, but it turned out to be of Lord Boothby, a former Conservative MP and television celebrity, seated innocently enough on a sofa between the Kray brothers. He had been approached after Ernest Shinwell, the fraudsman son of the late Manny Shinwell, doyen of the Labour Party, had devised a scam involving setting up a company and building houses in Uganda. This was to be a very smart con and Shinwell approached a friend of his, Leslie Payne, who was effectively the accountant for the twins. In turn Payne approached Boothby to join the board of the company, but sensibly he was not interested. Nevertheless he had agreed to have his photograph taken with them.

Boothby not only retained Arnold Goodman, then Harold Wilson's solicitor and himself an *éminence grise* in the Labour Party, to issue a writ for libel but, in a letter to *The Times*, refuted all the stories going round about his association with the Krays and denied that he was being blackmailed. 'I am not a homosexual,' he wrote.

I have not been to a Mayfair party of any kind for more than 20 years. I have met the man alleged to be 'King of the Underworld' only three times, on business matters; and then by appointment in my flat, at his request, and in the company of other people.

Later he was to receive agreed damages of £40,000 from the International Publishing Corporations.

The Labour MP for Brixton, Marcus Lipton, put down a question in the House of Commons asking the Home Secretary what reports he had received about extortion from club-owners and what action he was taking.

The action that was taken was that I was detailed to set up a specially formed squad working from City Road. I hadn't been long as the DI down at Commercial Street when, a fortnight after the *Mirror* editorial, the Area Chief Superintendent – the equivalent now of Commander – Fred Gerrard decided to pre-empt directions from the Yard. On 27 July he came to see me at Commercial Street Police Station.

'I've got a special job I want you to do for me . . .' He waited for my reaction and so I said:

'Good, what do you want me to do?'

'I want you to get a little team together and have a go at the Krays.'

'Right,' I said.

He looked at me quizzically. 'Is this going to be a problem for you?'

I realised at once what he meant and replied angrily: 'No, of course not. I don't know them.'

'Good,' said Gerrard, 'Come to my office tomorrow morning and we'll work out the details.'

The twin brothers, Ronnie and Reggie Kray, born on 24 October 1933, with Reggie a few minutes the elder, had grown up with their seven-years-older brother Charlie, in the East End of London. Before the war they had moved to 178 Vallance Road, where they lived with their mother, to whom they were devoted. Her father had been a well-known professional boxer, 'Cannonball' Lee, and for a little while it seemed that they and Charlie would make a career in the ring. Reggie certainly had talent and won all his fights. Ronnie had an indifferent record, whilst Charlie, at one time a fancied welterweight contender, finally retired after a bad beating at the Albert Hall from the then undefeated Lew Lazar. He hadn't fought for nearly a year. That night, 11 December 1951, all three had fought on the bill. Reggie won on points, Ronnie was disqualified.

Their boxing careers, which had begun in their teens, were probably the highlights of their non-criminal career. They spent much of their National Service, in 1952 still compulsory, in the Glasshouse, facing a string of disciplinary charges for assault and desertion. On their release they took over the Regal Billiard Hall in Eric Street, Mile End. The owners had been having considerable trouble with fights, breakages and even threats to burn down the premises. Now the twins offered to mind it for £5 and the violence stopped. Soon they became the legal tenants. It was a pattern to be repeated throughout their careers.[1] They were on their way to a life of protection and violence.

Over the previous years the Krays had been taken on by the police but not concentrated on. Before Gerrard formed my squad the CID had never taken their actions personally and I think they should have done. If ever there was a shooting and the overwhelming level of opinion amongst detectives was that this was down to the Krays, the attitude had been that you went along to see them first and they said, 'No we've got an alibi'. Then you would go out and look for the evidence. It should have been the other way round. This is what always appalled me even before I started the first enquiry. You'd talk to the CID officers and they'd say, 'Oh this is down to the Krays,' and you'd say, 'Well what are you doing about it?' And the answer was they were doing nothing about it. They never sort of took up the cudgels. They never got keen enough or personally involved enough to want to have a go. That was the sort of thing that always surprised me.

Even forgetting the Krays for a moment, if for example there were lorry loads missing, experienced officers would say 'That's down to Tom so-and-so,' and when you asked, 'Why not do something about it?' the reply would be, 'It's no use, he's too big' or, 'Nobody would give evidence against him.' It

---

[1] There are many accounts of the Krays' early career. One of the best is John Pearson's *The Profession of Violence*, Grafton (1984).

was a poor attitude overall and one which was unfortunately commonplace. Shortly after I had arrived in the East End I was having a drink in a local pub with a Detective Sergeant who had a reputation for being a very active man with a string of arrests to his credit. Across the bar was a big, well-dressed man who was entertaining a crowd of his friends.

'Who's he?' I asked.

'That's old so-and-so,' said the Sergeant, 'He's well at it. Jump-ups, lorry loads, blaggings, the lot. He's a right tasty merchant.'

My next question floored him. 'Why don't you do something about him, then?'

He spluttered, searching for a satisfactory reply, but could not come out with one. Like many others he had adopted an attitude that had become an almost acceptable form of behaviour. In turn the Divisional officer used his heavy case-load of break-ins as an excuse. He also considered that, as some of these people were such big operators, the Flying Squad should be taking them on. Of course they weren't, and in turn they would have said, if asked, that the guys were operating over such a large area that it was the Regional Crime Squad that should be dealing with them. In this way the local officer could salve his conscience. This was one of the reasons why the Krays were able to remain at liberty for so long and to foster the belief that the police were impotent in dealing with them.

If you are persistent enough you'll usually find someone who will give evidence, even if he doesn't particularly want to. But nobody did that with the Krays. Probably the normal Divisional detectives didn't have time to do that. Say there was a robbery and someone said 'that's down to the Krays', the detectives couldn't devote more than a week or ten days to getting the witnesses, and if they said they didn't want to know, no pressure could be put on them. The detectives have limited time. Although the Krays were known and accepted as the bigger-time villains, it still didn't justify ignoring all the other cases they had.

I don't believe they'd corrupted police officers on a scale that was sufficient to give them a licence. True, in 1966 Ronnie did make a complaint that a Detective Sergeant had taken £50 from him to allow him to have free run of the Baker's Arms in Northiam Street, but I think this may have been something of a pre-emptive strike. When the man was suspended and prosecuted, Ronnie failed to appear to give evidence at the committal proceedings and a warrant was issued for his, Ronnie's, arrest. After two trials at the Old Bailey the jury still could not agree on their verdict and the Crown offered no more evidence against the officer.

The only time I had anything approaching evidence that they had corrupted an officer was at the murder trials in 1969. We intended to call a senior officer to make some formal proof, and whilst I was waiting outside No. 2 Court a private detective, George Devlin, who had been employed by the Krays, sidled up to me to ask if the prosecution was calling this officer. When I told him they were, he said, 'Don't, they've got him on tape accepting £200.' I went straight in to tell David Hopkin, the Director of Public Prosecution's representative on the trial, and the man was not called. Of course, there was not sufficient evidence to mount even disciplinary proceedings against the man.

The police were the natural enemies of the Krays, but what the twins had done was to create a situation where people believed they were very deeply involved with the police and that they were paying huge sums of money for protection and information. If the twins were not able to buy off a bloke whom they had attacked with a grand and the words 'that'll keep you quiet', they had a second ploy. They would say to the victim that if he decided to go and tell the police about the incident he should not forget he was wasting his time because any statement he made they would have within twenty-four hours. A lot of people told me that. 'I'm not making a statement – the Krays'll have it within a day.' This belief was something the Krays generated intentionally to negate any statements being made by their victims. They could and did produce dummy statements. All they needed to do was produce one printed with the caution 'Metropolitan Police, Statement of Witness' and wave it at the victim who never got the chance to examine it closely. In this way people became convinced they'd got the police in their pockets.

It was just a part of their campaign but, so I thought, it was a hurdle that was surmountable, although it didn't excuse the fact that for years they operated with no real attack on them by anyone with a certain amount of dedication. When my little team, less than ten strong, was formed, this was the first time someone had said, 'Let's find out what they're really up to,' and been able to keep at it for a period of time.

The immediate thing for me to do was to go and see what they actually looked like, and the first time I saw any of the Krays was in the Grave Maurice, a seedy pub in the Whitechapel Road, one of their favourite haunts. I learned that Ronnie was to have a 'meet' with Michael Barrett, then a TV interviewer. All I was told was that the 'meet' would take place sometime in the early evening, not before 6 p.m. I went on my own, dressed in tatty old gear with a cloth cap and carrying the *Evening News*, then a broadsheet, opened at the racing page. I got a drink and a sandwich and sat back to wait. From where I sat I had a good view of both the door and the snugs for seated customers. At that time they were still empty.

They came within half an hour, in a large American car. First a man named 'Duke' Osborne got out, his hand in his jacket pocket so it seemed he was carrying a gun. He looked up and down the road, came into the pub and gave the place a swift East to West – I was the only one who was there and he ignored me – checked out the lavatories, went back out onto the pavement, and gave a nod in the direction of the car. Through the open door I watched as Ronnie Kray unfolded himself from the back seat, straightened up, and hurried across the pavement, flanked by minders.

For a moment I could not believe what I saw. His hair was smartly cut and gleaming and his gold-rimmed spectacles firmly in place. He was wearing a light camel coat which almost reached his ankles, the belt tied in a casual knot at the waist.

For all the world he looked like something out of the Capone era. Once inside the Maurice, the minders selected two booths and Ronnie sat in one whilst the minders collected two gins and a whisky from the bar. Ronnie remained in solitary splendour with his men in the next booth until Barrett arrived. He was wearing a neckbrace at the time and the minders did everything but frisk him. He was escorted by them to Ronnie's table before they went back to collect his drink. At the end of the interview Osborne and the others went out, 'swept' the street, and then Ronnie hurried to the car. I have no reason to think that this was anything other than for show. It was not a period in the life of the twins when they were facing a war with anyone.

In a way it was a joke but, at the same time, it was a bit unnerving. I'd heard all these stories about the Krays, and here was Ronnie behaving exactly as their reputation suggested they would do. If it had been mocked up for a TV serial you'd have said, 'Come on, this is a bit over the top.'

However, the joke of 'Duke' Osborne and his finger in the pocket was on me. A few weeks later a small boy was brought into the police station at Bethnal Green after he had been found in possession of quite a nice wireless, obviously well beyond his price range. Although it was quite clearly stolen he stoically refused to say how he had come by it and so his father was called to the station. He was a typical East Ender with no time to waste. He heard the facts and then asked the boy where he had got the radio. The boy still wouldn't say so he slapped him across the face saying, 'Nah, you tell 'em or you'll get one on the other bleedin' side.' The reaction of the boy was swift: he began to cry and soon told all. His father, now completely satisfied, left the room. 'Rotten bastard,' muttered the boy, and, when he was told by the officer he shouldn't speak like that about his father, blurted out, 'Well he can have a go at me over a poxy wireless but he don't say nothing about that lodger in our house and all the guns under his bed.'

The lodger was Colin 'Duke' Osborne, one of Ronnie's boyfriends, and it was only after our search of his room that I realised the finger in the pocket probably was a gun. Osborne, who came from a decent family in Westminster and was known as 'Duke' because of his upper-class manners, was the armourer for the Krays, whom he had met when they had settled some gambling debts of his. For possessing the firearms he received a seven years' sentence and died in prison.

At first my squad consisted of ten aides to CID, some of whom had never even heard of the Krays in passing, drawn from various districts. It was never going to be a covert operation. The men were drawn from almost every Division from what was then Three District. People would suddenly disappear from their regular duties and friends would ask 'Where are you going?' and 'What's it all about?' It was pointless to try and keep it under cover. There was also a Detective Constable whom I picked myself. Trevor Lloyd-Hughes was well known to me from my Paddington days and had always impressed me by his dedication and ability. He was of enormous help, and later when I formed another squad in 1969 I again co-opted Trevor. My faith in him was not misplaced. He rose to the rank of Commander and, sadly, he died as a serving officer, at the young age of 52.

Any thoughts I had that the investigation would be concentrated but short were soon dispelled. The journalists who had written the articles were interviewed but could do nothing more than repeat stories they had heard. I went to see my old friend Jack Spot, the 'ex-King of the Underworld', who had employed the Krays as minders for his bookmaking pitch at Epsom when he was at war with Billy Hill, but now he was down on his luck and knew nothing. In fact he was rather hoping to capitalise on the interest in the Krays with another story in the newspapers about old times.

There was a story that protection money was being paid by an Italian restaurant near the British Museum in Store Street, and that two of the Krays' henchmen collected the contribution weekly, but the owner denied the rumour and this line of enquiry was abandoned after observation failed to identify anyone remotely connected with the Krays, let alone the two named men, visiting the premises.

At the time there were stories circulating that the Krays had slashed the buttocks of people who refused to be intimidated and pay protection money. The story went that these people had been brought before a 'court' presided over by a twin or other senior member of 'the Firm'. A prosecutor outlined the facts and although the poor devil was allowed the benefit of 'counsel' he was inevitably found guilty and sentenced. It was said that Ronnie's favourite sentence was a buttock-slashing with a razor so that 'Every time he sits down, he'll remember us.'

Every hospital in the Greater London area was asked for its records but no one could be traced who had attended hospital after such a 'slashing'. What I did not know at the time was that the Krays had a tame doctor who treated such wounds.

One line of enquiry did seem about to produce something. Of course I got a lot of stories which various people leaked to me and which had to be investigated to see if there was any corroborative evidence. Most came to nothing, but one story had been circulating that the twins had used extreme violence to a man over a debt due to their swish West End gaming club Esmeralda's Barn. David Litvinoff was a well-known and quite well-to-do gambler who had run up a considerable debt, I believe around £800, to the club. He ran the debt as a kind of bank overdraft, paying off a bit when he won, running up the debt when he lost, but this did not suit the twins. This became a personal debt to them. The story as I heard it was that first of all Litvinoff was put under some pressure, and then when he was unable to pay he was called to the club. A sword was placed in his mouth and pushed, with the result that he received a terrible gash which split his cheeks.

I saw him by appointment in the Carlton Towers Bar in Chelsea. Looking closely at him it was possible to see faint scars across his cheek. He told me that he had gone immediately to Paris for plastic surgery. I thought that, at last, I had found a victim who would be co-operative. Wrong. Litvinoff said he had no intention of making any written statement or assisting in any prosecution, maintaining that although he had been attacked he could not identify his attackers. Perhaps he was consoled if he saw the film *The Krays*. In it, one of the most horrific moments is the sword attack upon him. Someone must have told the film-makers about it.

A third line of enquiry which came to nothing involved such well-known nightclubs as Danny la Rue's, Edmundo Ros's Coconut Grove, Al Burnett's Stork Club and a number of others. The owner of one was interviewed on a number of occasions and I thought that he was halfway there to a situation when he would say 'yes, I am being blackmailed', but when it came to a second visit he had his manager with him, and on the third occasion there was the unwelcome figure of a solicitor. As for the others, they all vehemently denied they were paying protection money. Al Burnett agreed the Krays were regular customers, saying, 'They're good customers. They always pay their bills and I've never had any trouble from them at all.' Like the other club-owners he denied paying any protection money to anyone. 'I'm too big for these people,' he added.

Years later, when the second Kray enquiry took place, I found the same wall of resistance and fear amongst seemingly respectable club-owners. I can quite understand it. These clubs were doing good business and the publicity from bringing a charge would have had the effect of closing the club down in a matter of minutes. So far as Esmeralda's Barn was concerned, whatever the pressure put upon the former directors and shareholders, on paper this had been done in a wholly legal manner. There was nothing for us there.

We then turned to concentrate on bookmakers, both in the East End and in Central London. At first, members of the squad did this in person but it was found to be too time consuming and I could not justify the manpower being used, so I devised a questionnaire and sent it out to local CID officers to canvass betting shops in their areas. This produced no more positive results than had any of the other enquiries, but reports were beginning to filter through that bookmakers were being 'persuaded' to hand over money under various pretexts. For example they would be asked to subscribe to a fund for the wife of a man recently sent to prison, or for the welfare of a local face who had fallen on hard times or who was ill in hospital. Other bookmakers were offered the services of men who would help in the collection of bad debts. Of course a retainer would have to be paid for this service. Most common, however, was that a retainer had to be paid to protect the bookmaker from 'gangs' who would smash his shop or interfere with his customers. Even so, the Krays could not be positively tied in to these operations, despite the fact that certain bookmakers were kept under observation, as were people who visited the Krays regularly.

Our operation was a very open one. We quite brazenly kept observation outside their house, as it was my intention to let them know we were going very heavy-footed into certain areas and eventually we obtained information that the main source of their income was from either setting up or financing Long Firm frauds.

Long Firms, or LFs as they are known, are a simple and relatively easy swindle to operate. A business, perhaps in ladies' dresses, is set up, goods are bought on credit and paid for properly, more goods are bought and also paid for. The operation is expanded to take in household goods, children's toys, sweets, anything, and then finally when a line of credit has been established a very substantial amount of goods are ordered, which are then sold off below cost, the premises closed and the suppliers and possibly the bank are out of their money. Of course, suppliers needed references before they would extend lines of credit, and so the LFs were set up in cells of five or six with each cell producing references and cross-references for the others. A properly run LF could, even in those days, produce a profit of between £100,000 and £150,000.

Until then Long Firms had been dealt with by the police in a pathetic way. First, the company had to go bust and there had to be some complaints from losing creditors; then it would be sent to the Board of Trade for an investigation. This took about 18 months and then, if they found grounds for concern, the papers went to the Fraud Squad for another year's investigation. By this time witnesses would have disappeared. One LF man used to take his wife around the world for a cruise at the end of each operation, confident that things would have blown over by the time he returned.

Operators knew that because of this protracted method of doing the investigation the chances of being nicked were remote, and of being convicted even more so. An LF operator would employ staff on a casual basis for a very short time, ensuring a very rapid turnover of personnel so that a commercial traveller could come in and find there had been a change of manager almost fortnightly. This was a positive way of dealing with it, so that when it came to an investigation no one could be identified as being 'the manager' of the firm throughout its life and someone who should have known what was going on. All these other people – if they were ever found – would be able to say, 'I don't know what was happening. I was only there two weeks.' Another trick was to employ a 'blower man' who ordered the goods over the telephone and so gave witnesses no opportunity of making an identification.

What I decided to do was to steam straight in so that when my people found what they knew to be an LF – and they were fairly easy to identify – we would go in and nick all the books, look at all the people who had given them references and go into them as well. It would be clear what they were up to and so then I would go for warrants and prosecute them for conspiracy.

My hope was that by going into the LFs we would find somebody who would involve the Krays. They were remote in the sense that they took no active part in the running of these companies but they scooped the pot at the end – or it was brought to them. We knew they visited some of them to see things were going all right. The people running the LFs may not have been members of the actual Kray firm, but they had been recruited because they looked the part or they had previous experience. There's a certain amount of ability required to run an LF – a certain amount of front – theatrical ability almost. So from time to time if one of these people stepped out of line it was necessary for one of the brothers to go along and have a word or simply go along. There was one instance where we knew Reggie had been along to the premises – he had been tailed – and so we pulled in the bloke who was running it. He was a real thug of a man, the sort who if he went into a pub and said 'All out' everyone would go without question. When I saw him at Commercial Street Police Station I asked him if he was running the firm. Then I said, 'The fact is the Krays are running the firm.'

He replied, 'The Krays?'

'Yes, Ronnie and Reggie. You know the Krays.'

'Krays, Krays, I've never heard of them.'

'You're a man who knows the East End of London. How can you not know the Krays? It's like not knowing the Queen.'

'Wait a moment, let me think.' He sat a while and then said, 'No, I've never ever heard of them.'

He was a hedger. It was always a question of 'a word, Mr Read', intimating that if such and such a thing happened he might do so and so. He was a man who almost came across, and if we'd got something more from him and something from another and another we'd have embroiled the Krays, but it never came to that in the end.

Another man went down for 18 months, and I had high hopes he would come across. I saw him just before he was sentenced at the Old Bailey and he asked me to go to see him in prison. It turned out he had managed to get himself into Grendon Underwood, a psychiatric prison regarded as an easy place to serve a sentence. When I booked in at the gate I asked the officer if my man was running the prison yet.

'Not yet,' he replied, 'but he's in charge of the stores.'

He was a man who took a pride in his work. When I saw him he told me he had shown the Krays how to set up a really good LF, but added, 'They weren't really interested. They were much too greedy, wanting money from Day One. They just didn't have the patience to run them properly.'

At the end of the day the investigation was quite successful in that we began prosecutions against six separate companies.

But, as the inquiry ran on, Fred Gerrard and I were under a great deal of pressure from the Yard to wind it up, and whilst Gerrard was away on leave I was called to the Yard by Ernie Millen, the Commander, and asked what was happening.

It is difficult to explain the jealousy and interaction between bosses in the CID. It is unbelievable. I was amazed at the way people acted and reacted against each other. Millen was antipathetic towards Gerrard, whom I believe he saw as a bright investigator who should have gone further than he did. He stood out amongst his contemporaries as an investigator, an administrator and a solid and honest police officer, by whom generally one would want to be led. Millen would never have called for me whilst Gerrard was there. Gerrard would have said, 'Don't ask the boy, ask me.' Nor would Millen have wanted to face Gerrard directly. If he felt strongly about something, Gerrard would have told him to get lost. So the fact that Millen called me when he heard that Gerrard was on leave is indicative of the method he employed. It was very much an attitude that it wasn't his game and therefore we weren't going to play it either.

I certainly did not want to impart information, but he was several ranks my superior and I had to say something even if it was not the full story. When I was asked how things were going I was reluctant to talk about it.

Millen could have justified his behaviour if he had said that the Commissioner wanted to know what was happening, but he never did. To me it appeared sinister to wait until Gerrard was on leave and then call and cross-examine me. Instead of trying to give encouragement to a junior officer by accepting we had arrested over 30 people, Millen was scathing, saying things like, 'You're never going to get anywhere with this. It's time you packed it in.' He belittled the whole investigation and suggested it was time it was wound up. Now had he been talking to Gerrard, the conversation would have gone differently. Gerrard was an enthusiast and a bullshitter who would have said, 'We'll nick them in a week,' which would have kept him quiet. I really wasn't in a position to say that. In turn I said we were arresting a lot of people and, although unfortunately they weren't saying anything, we were hopeful. The interview was something which coloured my view of Millen from then on. I'd never worked with him in the sense that he had never been my immediate senior officer. To me he was always a guv'nor. To pull rank like this was, I felt, both unnecessary and something which should have been beneath him.

When Gerrard returned I told him what had happened. In turn he was furious and went straight to see Millen, wanting to know why questions were being asked behind his back. Even now I am not quite sure what it was about. There could have been a half-sinister reason why Millen wanted to know what was happening, but there could also have been a very good reason: so he could have said to the next man up the line, the Assistant Commissioner, 'It's coming on good and we're going to get some results,' or to say for his own protection, 'Well, it looks as though it's going to fold.' He could have got this information from Gerrard, and that is what he should have done. Talking to me was the wrong way to go about it, but my gut feeling is that Gerrard would have bullshitted him, telling him things were going along very well and that it was all a matter of time.

It had run about six months, which is a long time for such an enquiry. A murder investigation runs for about three months, and then you think of saying it's about time to pack it in. It was a concentration of manpower which couldn't be afforded. The work should really have been done by the Fraud Squad. My argument was that the people involved were minions, and if I could have got one on the table and screwed him enough he might have blurted out a name or have said, 'They're involved in this way.' The enquiry justified its existence because we did a lot of work and committed around 70 people for trial on Long Firm and conspiracy charges. But, when it came to it, we had not done much more than chip away at the edges of the Kray empire and cause a good deal of inconvenience to them. Yet the object of the exercise had been to nick the twins, and truthfully we were no nearer at the end than the day when we started it. There was a wall of silence which I had found impossible to climb. The LF side fell away just as the protection side had done.

Then there was an extraordinary turn-up for the book: something which seemed at the time an amazing piece of luck. In early January 1965 I received a telephone call from John Donald, a DI at Marylebone Lane, with information about a West End club-owner, Hew McCowan, who was the son of Sir Cargill McCowan and was a wealthy man in his own right. He lived just off Oxford Street, and Donald had known him for some time. McCowan used to frequent a little club, the Music Box, in Panton Street near Piccadilly Circus, where he would pick up boys and take them back to his flat. His apartment was amazing. It was a most elaborate place with a bank of slot machines which worked on half-crowns. When you went in he would give you a fiver's worth to play these machines. In the film *Topkapi*, there was a toy parrot which recorded a woman's laughter to fool the police whilst the museum was being robbed. McCowan had bought it and had this in his flat as well. The boys he took back would nick things left, right and centre. In turn McCowan would report the thefts, Donald would arrest the boys and then McCowan would refuse to go to court to give evidence. Now McCowan had told Donald he was being pressurised by the Krays to pay protection money for the Hideaway Club in Gerrard Street.

I went straight over to Marylebone Lane to take a statement, and a curious one it was. The Hideaway had previously been named the Bon Soir and had been owned by a Gilbert France, proprietor of the Wardour Street restaurant Chez Victor, in partnership with Frankie Fraser, of the Richardson gang, and Albert Dimes who had fought Jack Spot in Soho some years previously. A young man, Sidney Thomas Vaughan, had been the manager, but was then in dispute with France, and because of this and financial difficulties the Bon Soir was closed in the early autumn of 1965. France had met McCowan at Vaughan's 21st birthday party, and in October an agreement was signed giving Vaughan *carte blanche* to run the premises.

In turn he had to pay France's company, Gerrard Enterprises, £150 a week. McCowan employed Vaughan as his agent and manager and spent some £4,000 in redecorating the premises and opened for business on 16 December.

According to McCowan, profits from the club were expected to be £1,100 a week from takings of about £2,500. He had already met the Krays through a Johnny Francis and their accountant Leslie Payne, when they called at his flat to try to interest him in an investment in a housing project in Eastern Nigeria. McCowan had said he was not particularly interested, even though profits of £2.25 million were being suggested for an investment of £0.75 million. He had, however, mentioned that he was thinking of opening a West End club. Francis arranged for McCowan to meet the brothers in the Grave Maurice where he alleged that Reggie had maintained it was essential that two of his men be installed in the club before its opening to provide against trouble. A figure of 25 per cent of the takings was suggested. At a subsequent meeting McCowan said he was told the percentage was to be 20 per cent after the first month, then 30 per cent and finally a half share. At a third meeting the percentage, so McCowan alleged, was to be 50 per cent from the start. Tempers, so he said, became frayed and finally it was agreed that the profits should be divided more or less on a scale rising to 50 per cent after the first quarter. Vaughan wanted to make sure that he had sorted out the prior agreement he had with France and insisted that a contract be drawn up by a solicitor in Shaftesbury Avenue.

A table for ten was reserved for the Krays on the opening night. They never arrived, and when McCowan complained about this to Francis he was told that the brothers had thought they would have an interest in the place and not just be guests.

In the early hours of 19 December Teddy Smith, a writer who had had plays broadcast by the BBC and was a friend of the Krays, arrived at the club, very drunk, and caused some trouble and around £20 worth of damage to furniture in the reception room before being thrown out by waiters. When McCowan next saw the Krays, it was pointed out that this sort of thing would not have happened had one of their men been on the door. This time it was agreed that 20 per cent of the takings would be paid to the brothers. McCowan asked for a written agreement, and was told he would get one when they all next met. Then he telephoned Donald.

I also took a statement from Sidney Vaughan who, at that stage, seemed to be more help than McCowan himself. McCowan would, I thought, over-egg the pudding a bit. He would tend to elaborate too much. Although an active homosexual, and therefore subject to attack from defence counsel, he did not dress flamboyantly, nor had he exaggerated effeminate gestures. He seemed to feel very strongly about the matter, and I was sure however that this time he would see it through to the end.

Sidney Vaughan, who was then 21, seemed to have a quick brain and undoubtedly had a more retentive memory than McCowan. I thought that he would make a truthful and convincing witness. It would have been helpful to have had a copy of the agreement, but even without it I decided that I had sufficient evidence to make arrests.

At that time the Krays were living in the Glenrae Hotel in the Seven Sisters Road in North London. It had been a pleasant hotel for commercial travellers with a little drinking club in the basement, but gradually it had been taken over by the twins and their entourage. A Phoebe Woods had bought it in 1959 and had spent a considerable sum doing it up. For years it was a popular and well-run club with no trouble, until September 1964 when her son James was attacked by three men. Whilst he telephoned the police, the men threw bottles and beer crates through the windows. As a result Mrs Woods shut down the club. Three weeks later three men came into the hotel waving knives and advising her husband that he had better reopen the club. Mr and Mrs Woods reported the matter to Highbury Vale, their local police station. Two weeks later another man attacked Mr Woods whilst he was in the basement kitchen.

Within a matter of weeks Billy Exley, a long-standing friend of the Krays, had become the club's barman. His relief was

Sammy Lederman, also a close friend of the twins, whilst the doorman was Bobby Ramsey who had been charged, along with the Krays, with Grievous Bodily Harm some years earlier. The brothers moved in to Rooms 1 and 2.

It was in the hotel that evening that Fred Gerrard and I made the arrests. Billy Exley was behind the bar dispensing good cheer, and the room was full with other members of the team. The arrests went perfectly quietly. Reggie asked if he could say goodnight to his girlfriend, something we did not allow, and called out to Charles, his brother, to get them a brief. Ronnie, who was found to have a sheath knife in his hip pocket, appeared too overwhelmed to reply. One of the minders was arrested at the same time and so was Billy Exley. The twins were taken to Highbury Vale Police Station where they were charged.

Ronald replied grudgingly, 'It's taken you long enough. This has all been in the *Mirror*.' He asked me who had nicked them and when I told him it was Superintendent Gerrard he asked again, 'Yes, but I mean who's it down to? Somebody must have put the finger on us. We haven't been out blacking people, you know.'

Reggie added, 'What's this man got the needle to us for? This is definitely not our game.'

Teddy Smith was also arrested. He admitted he had 'done up a club', but said it was a drunken brawl and he had got the worst of it. Of Johnny Francis there was no sign. He had left England and had gone, we learned later, to Torremolinos from where he was planning to go to Mexico.

Once the Krays were arrested Phoebe Woods became hysterical, screaming with relief, and literally threw herself at my feet saying how glad she was that things were over, how all her customers had been driven out of the club and how there were bills for the rooms and drink amounting to over £100 outstanding. 'Take them away and never let me see them again. You've saved my life. Please take them away,' she cried.

She was so upset that I decided not take a statement from her there and then. Instead I arranged that she should call at the police station next day. What a mistake that was! The next morning she was at Old Street Magistrates' Court, dressed to the nines and looking a completely different woman. She wore a fur piece and high heels. Her hair was smartly done and she was smiling and confident. She offered to stand bail, insisting that the management of the club by the Krays was an arrangement with which she and her husband were perfectly satisfied. The difference between this assured, well-turned-out woman and the pathetic wretch who had been grovelling at my feet the evening before was remarkable. I just couldn't believe the transformation.

The 'brief' retained by the brothers was a man called Emmanuel Fryde, known in the trade as Manny. He may, or may not, have qualified as a solicitor in South Africa, it was never clear; but now he was working as a managing clerk for the firm Sampson & Co., who had offices near the Old Bailey. He instructed Victor Durand QC, then as now one of the top half-dozen barristers who specialised in criminal cases, and a young man, Ivan Lawrence, who was beginning to make his way and reputation as a defender and who later became QC and a Member of Parliament. Lawrence claimed at the bail hearing that, whilst there might have been a proposal that McCowan should pay up to 50 per cent of the takings of his club in return for an investment by the brothers, there was no pressure of any kind to make him do this and no evidence that he was frightened by the Krays. 'Only suggestions and discussions had taken place,' he said.

But 'Mick' McElligott, the stipendiary (or qualified and paid) magistrate would have none of it. 'A rose by any other name smells as sweet,' he commented. When Durand offered two sureties totalling £4,000, McElligott replied: 'I am satisfied so far as I can be at this stage that there are other persons at large who would be in a better position to interfere with witnesses or impede investigations were you at large.'

He remanded them in custody for a week and there followed, over the next few months, a series of bail applications, all of which were refused, ending with an application to the House of

Lords.[2] The Krays first went to a High Court judge by way of appeal against the decision by McElligott and were refused. They then tried to find another more sympathetic High Court judge and were thwarted. Eventually the House of Lords ruled that once a High Court judge had refused bail a defendant could not 'shop around' to find another who might be more likely to grant him bail, nor could he go to the Divisional Court to get that judge's decision overturned. So, in a way, the Krays gained more status when their names appeared in the legal reference books as *R*. v. *Kray, Kray and Smith*.

Meanwhile Lord Boothby tried to do his part for the brothers, asking in the House of Lords whether it was the intention of the Government to imprison the Krays indefinitely without trial.

But there were other problems in the investigation. It had long been my hope and, indeed, expectation that once the Krays were locked up some of the many victims of their violence would come forward to give evidence. I was confident that, in this way, the whole enquiry would snowball and we would really build up a substantial series of charges against the Krays and members of the Firm.

It was a fatal mistake. I could not have been more wrong. No one came forward at all. At the time I felt angry at this lack of response by the community, and I did what I could to counteract it by revisiting possible witnesses. At least I could now explain that the Krays were inside with no prospect of release until their trial. They could therefore speak with more confidence, I urged to no avail. People were still convinced that the Krays would walk out, as they had done on previous occasions, and so they were not about to commit themselves to supporting a prosecution as insubstantial as this one. It was also pointed out that other members of the Firm were still about, and so what difference did it make that the twins were temporarily under lock and key?

[2] Kray and Smith (1965) Ch 736.

Of course they were right. With hindsight I can understand their attitude, however frustrated I was at the time. The Krays were almost at the height of their power. They exercised control over an indeterminate number of villains collectively known as 'the Firm', and the fear of this name coupled with their own was quite sufficient to keep witnesses away from me. Nevertheless, the knowledge didn't lessen my disappointment and I began to wonder what was really necessary to nail the Krays for even *some* of their crimes. Then, tragically, such case as there was against them began to fall apart.

The man I considered to be the main witness, Sidney Vaughan, was beginning to act very strangely. I had men watching the Krays' house in Vallance Road when suddenly on 20 January, three days before the committal proceedings were due to start, I received a message 'Sidney Vaughan's going down the Road.' He went to the Krays' house and almost immediately Tommy Brown, an enormous ex-professional boxer, and another man came out, got in a car, went up the road at top speed to come back a few minutes later with the local vicar, the Reverend Albert Foster, who was hurried into the house. Although I did not know this at the time, what happened next was that Vaughan made a little statement to the vicar saying he wanted to change his testimony because he realised he wasn't telling the truth and that McCowan was paying him £40 a week to commit perjury.

Obviously I had to find out what was going on, and I had Vaughan brought to my office and asked him to explain his unusual conduct. He now told me his statement wasn't true and this whole thing had been cooked up by McCowan. I could not believe what was happening to me. I was already aware that because of his sexual predilections McCowan was a questionable witness. Now Vaughan, whom I had always regarded as the stronger of the two men, was reneging on *his* version of the events. My substantial case was crumbling before my eyes.

I was then left with the prospect of, at the very best, a reluctant witness at the committal proceedings. In fact, from the prosecution's point of view, Vaughan was worse than reluctant: he was positively hostile and was treated as such when he gave evidence at Old Street. He was shown the statement he made to us but insisted that no demands had been made directly by the Krays and that all negotiations had been dealt with by Francis. Both the brothers and Edward Smith were committed for trial at the Old Bailey, but it was an unsatisfactory state of affairs.

Three days before the trial began I had received information that Roy East, the crime reporter of the *People*, had tape-recorded certain conversations between McCowan and a man known as Johnnie. Listening to these tapes, it was clear that Johnnie was offering money if McCowan would not give evidence at the trial. A further meeting had been arranged between McCowan and Johnnie, and I immediately told David Hopkin[3] at the Director of Public Prosecutions' office, suggesting that the police attend this meeting, but he advised against it.

There had been other developments. In the early hours of 1 March, a Peter Byrne had telephoned the information room at Scotland Yard to say he had been assaulted by four men at his home in Lisle Street just off Leicester Square. He said he had been gagged and tied up before one of the men had produced a pair of tailor's scissors and threatened to cut his face. One of the other men had stopped him saying, 'No, McCowan only wants him frightened.' Byrne would not make a written statement. During the day Fryde came to the Old Bailey where the Director of Public Prosecutions (DPP) had an office and asked that no officer involved in the Kray enquiry interview Byrne. I therefore arranged for a Detective Inspector from West End Central to take a statement from Byrne. He went to Savile Row with Sid Ray, the Sergeant from Albany Street who had given evidence in the Wakeham 'razor blade' case and was

[3] Now Chief Metropolitan Magistrate and Chairman of the British Boxing Board of Control.

now another managing clerk with Sampsons. Ray produced a statement which, he said, had already been taken by a private investigator. He refused to hand over a copy and advised Byrne not to make a statement unless he, Ray, was immediately given a copy. The gist of his story was that he knew something about McCowan and that he was also a friend of Vaughan's. McCowan had learned that Vaughan had been to his, Byrne's, flat and wanted to know what had been said. When Byrne had refused to tell him he had been threatened and this attack was the outcome. Another appointment was made for the next day so that Byrne could look through photograph albums to try to identify his attackers, but he never kept it.

The trial began at the Old Bailey on 8 March 1965, very much earlier than would be the case nowadays when a delay of up to a year could be expected. Ronald Kray was now defended by Petre Crowder MP QC and Ivan Lawrence, Reginald by Paul Wrightson and Montague Sherbourne, and Smith by Kenneth Richardson and C. R. Cole. The prosecution was led by John Mathew, Senior Treasury Counsel.

On the second day, whilst McCowan was still giving evidence, Manny Fryde tried to abort the trial. After the luncheon adjournment he appeared in court with the story that he had a witness who would say that he had overheard a juryman discussing the case with a police officer. The witness was a man who had been questioned during the investigation into the sale of the shares in Esmeralda's Barn, and Fryde identified the juryman in question who was asked to stand down. The juryman objected at the time, and later when I interviewed him he vehemently denied that he had been speaking with anyone. One solution to the problem, and the one at which I believe Fryde was aiming, was to get a new jury. He clearly did not like the look of the one we had, thinking it looked too intelligent. However, after counsel had discussed the matter with the judge, it was agreed the case should proceed with eleven jurors.

McCowan behaved splendidly in the witness box, sticking rigidly to the story he had first given to me, and successfully withstanding a probing examination by the three barristers for the Krays and Smith. He readily admitted his sexual preferences, which in those days were looked on in a much less tolerant light than today. Frankly I admired the way he conducted himself throughout the investigation and the trial. I had offered him protection, something he had rejected out of hand as he similarly dismissed the suggestion that he leave London and stay with friends in the country. Instead he continued to frequent his West End haunts and stayed at his flat where everyone knew he could be found. I was forced to accept that his courage at this time was commendable, even though I thought it bordered on the reckless.

Vaughan, on the other hand, did not 'come up to proof'. He insisted the sole reason he made his original statement was because of pressure from McCowan who threatened to withdraw his financial support. Another application was made to treat him as hostile, and after argument it was agreed that the deposition at the committal proceedings should be shown to him, but not his original statement. None of the defendants gave evidence, but Byrne repeated the story of his attack, and the Rev. Albert Foster told the court of Vaughan's 'confession' to him at Vallance Road. I didn't hold out much hope for a conviction when the jury retired. The Recorder, Judge Carl Aarvold, had told them, 'If you think that because of Vaughan's evidence you cannot rely on McCowan, then that is the end of the case.'

Nevertheless the jury was out for three and a half hours before they returned at 5.45 p.m. on 18 March for the foreman to say rather apologetically that they could not reach a verdict, which in those days had to be unanimous. They were sent out again but came back within half an hour to say they still could not agree. A re-trial was ordered to begin on 29 March. In the mean time the Krays and Smith were in custody.

By then John Mathew had decided that Vaughan would not be called. It was apparent that his word could not be accepted on so many different points that he could not be put to the jury as a witness of truth. The decision was bitterly opposed by defending counsel who wanted him at least produced so that they could cross-examine him, something Mathew declined to do. The judge indicated that Vaughan might be called by the Court and therefore open to cross-examination by everybody, but after McCowan's evidence Petre Crowder said that none of the defence counsel wished this to happen. By this time a private detective, George Devlin, had been hired to investigate McCowan's background, and there is no doubt that the defence was able to make great play of the fact that he had been involved in a number of trials where he had alleged blackmail in three other cases. He had also spent some time in a psychiatric hospital.

This time, with the evidence for the prosecution relying solely on McCowan, the jury retired for only ten minutes before returning a verdict. The judge, Mr Justice Lyall, warned them that if they regarded McCowan as an unreliable witness they could not be sure of the guilt of the accused and so must acquit. It was a foregone conclusion. All the defendants were discharged but applications for their costs in the second trial were refused.

For me this was a disaster. I felt it would have been better not to have charged them rather than to have them acquitted after two trials. It was not so much a personal thing, more that I was concerned that their reputation was further enhanced by the failure of the prosecution. Their followers might now believe they really could walk on water. I also felt angry that as the officer in charge of the investigation I had been unable to make the case more reliable or support it in some way with further charges. From a personal point of view it was a blot on my record and certainly no boost to my career. All I could hope was that my superiors would appreciate that I had taken the initiative, had a pop at the Krays and showed that they were vulnerable. As I commiserated with my squad, I was at least able to remind them of the arrests and convictions over the Long Firm frauds which had gone some way to cutting off the Krays' income.

That afternoon they bought the Hideaway Club, renaming it the El Morocco, and later held an acquittal party co-hosted by a South London villain, Freddie Foreman, who was later to stand trial with the twins over the disappearance of Frank Mitchell from Dartmoor Prison. I decided we should have one last look at the Firm gathered together in celebration, and update our already extensive intelligence records, so with Trevor Lloyd-Hughes and two others I went to Gerrard Street to check out the identity of everyone who went into the club. We also wanted to give them a bit of aggravation to show them that even if they had been acquitted they still weren't forgotten. I was in a telephone box opposite the club, noting names, when George Devlin, the private detective who was employed by the Krays, pulled open the booth door and said, 'Hello, Nipper, what are you doing?'

I said I was just ringing home to say I would be late. It was a feeble excuse which he was far too intelligent to accept.

He said, 'That's bullshit. I know what you're doing. If you want to see who's here why don't you come inside? It's no problem.'

It was a case of either accepting or backing off. I told Lloyd-Hughes what I was going to do. He offered to come with me but I thought this might cause too much reaction from the Krays and in I went. Inside the foyer I was greeted by Gilbert France who told me to come through. Well, of course, it did cause great consternation. I was wearing a heavy overcoat which I kept on and I felt as if all eyes were on me. I knew most of the people there and nodded to a few. Ronnie stayed apart but was visibly absolutely furious. Reggie, who had a more leisurely approach, didn't seem to mind very much. The atmosphere soon became electric, and I thought it time to go after clocking as many people as I could. I can't say I was sorry to be back out on the street again.

In his book *The Profession of Violence*, John Pearson makes much of the story as a high for a chapter ending, and unfortunately it has been repeated in many other books and articles. He says that I was photographed having a drink and that Ronnie Kray was able to boast 'with one glass of champagne he had chased his most dangerous enemy in the police out of the West End for good'.[4] He then makes the astonishing claim that I thought it a good idea to enter the club and meet the twins face to face as 'It was the first time they had met'. He overlooks that he had already described my observations in the Grave Maurice and that I had arrested them and of course been in their company in both Bow Street Magistrates' Court and two trials at the Old Bailey. He concludes the chapter by saying that there was a Yard inquiry and I was cleared of any improper contact with the Krays, was promoted and sent to help Superintendent Butler on the Great Train Robbery which had in fact taken place two years earlier! I was not promoted for nearly another year.

In fact what was published was a picture in the *Daily Express*, and I was delighted to see that the man who was said to be me was the actor Edmund Purdom. I was flattered. Since when did I ever look like Edmund Purdom? In its story the *Daily Express* said one of the guests was 'Nipper' Read. That morning I went to see Fred Gerrard and told him what had happened and that I had had my two Sergeants with me checking names, which were later supplied to the intelligence department. Later I was telephoned by Ernie Millen who said, 'Be at the Albert at one o'clock.' I went to the pub near Ludgate Circus and there he introduced me to Percy Hoskins, the crime reporter from the *Express* whom I'd never met before. He was profuse in his apologies about the report, saying it was most unfortunate and that certain steps would be taken within the company. He hoped that I wouldn't be taking any action against the newspaper. At the time it seemed so inconsequential that I had no intention of doing so. Had I realised what capital Pearson and others were going to make

[4] *The Profession of Violence*, p. 172.

I might have adopted a very different attitude. As recently as last year I was approached by a producer from Channel 9 of Australian television to do a short interview. He asked me if I had any old photographs I could bring along. 'What kind?' I asked. 'The one of you drinking with the Krays would be nice,' he replied.

'If you can find that one I'll pay *you* a million dollars for it,' I said.

There was never any police investigation or disciplinary proceedings. It has annoyed me because, if there had been a photograph, in the subsequent trial that's the first thing the defence would have produced. Quite reasonably they'd have wanted to discredit me in any way they could and if there had been a photograph of me drinking with the twins in a nightclub it would have been a case of 'How do you explain that, officer?'

The Krays returned to the East End in triumph. Although people didn't actually line Vallance Road to welcome them, it almost seemed like it. 'Krays Back Home' boomed the headlines, showing the three brothers in the now-famous picture of the cross-hand shake. They had scored again over the police, and their supporters were jubilant.

We continued enquiries into the tapes obtained by Roy East of the *People*, but it was decided there was insufficient evidence to mount a prosecution which would have any reasonable chance of success. As for the Krays, soon they announced they were going to forsake the West End and 'lead a quiet life'. Reggie said that he would soon marry his girlfriend Frances Shea. Both the twins threatened to sue the police for wrongful arrest and malicious prosecution but they never did.

Fred Gerrard told me he thought I deserved a rest and said he had put my name forward for a new six months' middle management course known as the Intermediate Command Course at Bramshill. 'Of course,' he said, 'you've got to pass the selection board first.' Wearing my Buckinghamshire tie I did so, along with 23 other officers from Forces all over the country. After my return from the course I heard that my promotion had been confirmed and I waited in Old Street Station in some anticipation to learn to where I would be sent. It was another six months before I moved – hardly being chased out of the East End.

CHAPTER SEVEN

ON 9 MARCH 1966 I was promoted Detective Chief Inspector and was transferred to West End Central, certainly in the eyes of the public the most prestigious of all areas. It covers a wide area from Marylebone down to St James's and, of course, Soho and Bow Street. This enormously busy area was covered by two stations known as CD1 and CD2, housed in one building in Savile Row. The other station on the Division, Bow Street, covered Covent Garden, Drury Lane and the Strand. There had been a station at Vine Street but this had been bombed in the war and had, effectively, never been reopened.

This was my first jaunt 'up West' and although I was thankful to be leaving the East End, quite frankly I didn't fancy it. Your promotion starts the day you move and although in theory it was always possible to refuse to be transferred, in practice that would have been the end of your career. In next to no time I would have found myself filing traffic reports in Whetstone. The West End didn't have the same workhorse relationship that other nicks did. It was more confined and never seemed to have the same broad scope of crime to investigate that you would get at Paddington or down the East End. You wouldn't get a decent housebreaking – the odd shopbreaking, perhaps; but on the whole it never appealed to me because there wasn't the same diversity. The West End had a more transient community: there were tourists who were ripped off or robbed, but you knew it would never come to anything because the next week they would have gone back to America and that would be the end of the witness.

The man I replaced was Wally Virgo who later became a Commander and who featured in the 'Trial of the Detectives', held a hundred years after the one in 1877.[1] Curiously enough, I later followed him onto the Murder Squad when I left the West End.

In 1966 Soho had an even uglier face than it has today. Dirty bookshops were everywhere and 'near beer' joints, 'clip' joints and cinemas showing pornographic films attracted the oddest types and tourists who wanted to see the naughty bits of London. In turn, they became the victims of the unscrupulous operators of these establishments who picked them clean.

Prostitution and clubs were controlled by a small number of men who had taken over the territory after the breaking-up of the Messina operation and the retirement of Billy Hill and Jack Spot. Over the years there had been a constant struggle to determine power and control and as a result there were spontaneous bursts of violence as one or other faction tried to establish and redefine territories.

At the time the smoothest operator of them all was Bernie Silver, who had seen the disasters that happened when rival operators fell out, and had the sense to realise that a *rapprochement* was necessary between at least some of the operators. He therefore formed a liaison with a Maltese, 'Big'

---

[1] Virgo was convicted in 1977 of conspiracy and sentenced to 12 years' imprisonment. His conviction was later quashed by the Court of Appeal on 15 March 1978 on the grounds that the trial judge had failed to give the jury an adequate direction on the definition of corroboration. Virgo died some years later. His solicitor, Victor Lissack, who was later to defend Donaghue in the second Kray trial, always maintained his belief in Virgo's innocence.

The original 'Trial of the Detectives' occurred in 1877 when a third of the detective branch of Scotland Yard stood trial, charged with conspiracy. The allegations were that they had taken bribes and had warned suspects of raids. Sentences of two years' imprisonment were imposed. This trial and its aftermath led to the founding of the CID.

Frank Mifsud, and had cunningly tried to avert all-out war by involving all interested parties in a kind of co-operative, running clubs and near beer and clip joints.

It had been worked out so there would be no rivalry and inter-club warfare between them. Say A and B owned the Star Club, B and C owned the Spangled Club, C and D the Banner Club and D and A the America Club. If, therefore, premises owned by Silver or Mifsud were attacked, the other operators would suffer by it. There was therefore no incentive for anyone to cause trouble in another club. It worked after its fashion, but there was always an undercurrent of feeling and a belief that violence was never far away.[2]

Near beer joints, of which there was one or more in every street, yard and alley in Soho, worked very simply. Young, attractive and scantily dressed girls stood outside the premises, which were often on the first floor or in the basement of buildings. Subtly, and sometimes not so subtly, they would lure customers inside with the veiled promise of sexual intercourse. Once inside, the men were like moths round a flame, unable to resist the flattery and spiel of these 'come-on' girls. They would pay exorbitant prices for non-alcoholic drinks such as shandy and blackcurrant juice for themselves. Each drink came with a cocktail stick and the girl was paid by the number of these sticks she collected during her stint. Their function was only to rip-off the customer for as much as he would pay without complaining. There was certainly no requirement by the management that the girls had to have sex with the clients, although many did as a side operation. If so, they took the man to a local address or hotel.

Two years earlier the Refreshment Houses Act 1964, which

---

[2] In November 1967 two Maltese men, Anthony Cauchi and Tony Galea, were convicted of conspiracy to commit damage to property by fire and explosives. Cauchi was also found guilty of placing an explosive substance in the Keyhole Club. The property under attack had been owned by Silver, Mifsud and their friends. Silver later received six years for offences relating to prostitutes.

required clubs serving any form of refreshment, including soft drinks and sandwiches, to have a licence, had given the right to the police of entry into premises. And enter in they did, causing a certain amount of trouble to the 'clubs'. Clubs were closed down on a regular basis by magistrates sitting at Marlborough Street and Bow Street, with the result that many proprietors did not bother to renew their licences. So the premises reverted to being clip joints where a version of the corner game was played out. There was now no pretence that drinks would be supplied or that the girl was a hostess. Money was obtained on the implicit understanding that sexual intercourse would follow. Of course, now, most of the girls never had any intention of having sex and so for the same to succeed a delaying tactic had to be introduced.

Mostly the girl would persuade the punter that the address was some form of club and that her employer forbade her to leave before a certain time. She would then ask the man to wait around the corner to meet her as soon as she was free. Often the man would wait two or three hours 'around the corner' before he realised he had been done up like a kipper. Under the clock at Victoria Station was a well-worn favourite, Marble Arch, by Big Ben, Charing Cross, outside the Ritz or the Regent Palace Hotel and Leicester Square were frequently named by the punters who had spent many wasted hours waiting there. The one I liked best, even though I found it hardest to believe, was Morden, a station at the very end of the Northern Line. I asked the Dutch seaman why the hell he had gone that far to wait for a girl. He replied, in attractive broken English, that he had paid her £100, adding, 'Well, this is where she tells me she is living.'

Of course these men contributed to the loss of their money, and even when they reported the matter to the police they were often unwilling to go through with the charges because of fear of exposure to their wives, family, friends and employers. Often they were men from the provinces or sailors who would go home or sail before any proceedings could be processed through the courts. It was better to write off their loss and put it down to experience.

As a result of what they considered amounted to immunity to prosecution, the girls became more and more brazen, and so occasionally the clients took reprisals of their own. The most tragic example of this was when, on 25 April 1966, three young men out to celebrate a birthday were tricked at a club in Lisle Street and thrown out by bouncers. They found some rubbish in the street, doused it with petrol and threw it into the passageway of the clip joint at No. 23. Far from its being the minor annoyance the boys anticipated, the rubbish set fire to other material and soon the whole premises were ablaze. Sadly, a perfectly innocent man had decided to try to find a lavatory on the premises and, unable to get out in time, burned to death.

All we had to go on was the first name of one of the boys and the fact that it was his 21st birthday. We announced that we would check the names of everyone born that day 21 years earlier – something which seemed to be an impossible task. It would not have been impossible, but it certainly would have been boring. But, when it came to it, there was no need. A photograph was published of officers starting to make the list at Somerset House and the boys, thoroughly shocked by what had happened, went into Tottenham Police Station with a solicitor to confess to what they had done. They were later convicted of manslaughter and received sentences of three and four years' imprisonment.

Of course there were many other incidents when punters, frustrated by waiting at one or other of the rendezvous, returned to the club and demanded their money back. The normal course of events was that they would then meet one of the club's bouncers and would sustain a black eye or broken jaw for their pains. Once again the fear of disclosure of the illicit sex behind the assault hampered many a prosecution.

Another common scam at the time was the 'blue film' racket. This was another popular version of the 'corner game'. The scenario was usually that of a smooth-talking spiv standing outside an open doorway and inviting tourists to see a blue film. As a come-on, he might have postcards showing explicit sex scenes 'from the film'. After taking the punters' money he would direct them up to the second floor and then simply move on to another suitable doorway. There were variations, of course. Sometimes the spiv would actually go to the second floor with the punters and ask them to wait whilst he went into the projection room to check the film. Off he would go down the back stairs. If their luck was in, they saw a film made in Scandinavia showing a woman undressing or nudists playing volleyball.

With the World Cup coming up in July, I was afraid that both thefts from visitors and more examples of violence would occur over the summer months. Tens of thousands were coming to London and many who would drift into Soho during the evenings would become the victims of the villains who were waiting to fleece them.

There was not only the problem of the clubs and our own thieves but also the con men who would come from Australia, the fraudsmen and tricksters from Mexico and Venezuela, the dipsters from Italy, second-storey hotel thieves from the States, drug-pushers from Holland and the heavies, GBH merchants from Germany. All these and others travel the world and congregate for any international sporting occasion or world or trade fair of sufficient size that runs for long enough. The World Cup was certainly both of those and the thought of the havoc those kinds of villain could create, coupled with our local talent, was very depressing.

So I formed a squad of officers from 'C' Division (West End Central). It was only a small one, 11 officers and myself, with a very positive mission: harass and shut down the clubs, and then maintain a blanket policing operation on the West End. This I believed would keep down the foreign villains to a minimum.

The first job was to visit the clubs and take down the names of the girls present. They were also given the 'warning formula'. In other words they were told in no uncertain terms that their freedom to fleece the suckers was over. It was also explained to the proprietors, or their front men, that they were committing offences of theft or of obtaining money by false pretences and they had better change their lifestyle. It was all to no avail. The pickings were far too easy and the clubs continued to flourish – for a time.

It was now time to show them exactly what we meant, and soon the girls found that the 'punters' were in fact plain clothes officers. In June seven girls were arrested for obtaining money by false pretences or straightforward theft. In the week leading up to the World Cup a further 21 arrests were made by the squad, mainly for theft. From time to time I would lead part of the squad to raid the premises and again all present were logged and cautioned. It was interesting to see the girls' reactions – this kind of police activity was new, but still they didn't get the message.

Then one girl decided to go for trial at the Inner London Sessions instead of having her case dealt with by magistrates, which was the more usual way of doing things. In those days a case could be heard at Sessions within three weeks or so, and she received a sentence of nine months' imprisonment. Word soon got around the others and by the start of the Cup only four of the clip joints remained open.

The resources of officers at West End Central were always stretched, and my squad was a further drain on manpower, so it was decided to call in officers from other Metropolitan police districts. The West End was divided into nine crime patrols with three Sergeants and two detectives posted to each. All had personal radios and I patrolled the division in a radio-equipped car. It was later acknowledged to be a good example of how effective saturation policing could be. By the end of the operation on 31 July only one clip joint was still in business and that only on a haphazard basis. During the period, reported crimes dropped by nearly a half, whilst clip-joint complaints had gone down from 205 in the first week to 12 in the last!

The bosses, of the police, if not the clubs, were well pleased. My report went to the Home Office and commendations were given. It was announced that the squad should be kept on although, as with everything, it was gradually allowed to run down because of lack of resources. Even so, the crime rate in the West End was stable for some months to come.

If Silver and Mifsud thought they had a tight hold on Soho and were immune to outside attack, they had a shock when the next February two Maltese, Anthony Cauchi and Tony Galea, were accused of plotting to cause damage by fire and explosives, and Cauchi of placing explosives at the Keyhole Club in Old Compton Street. All the premises involved belonged to the Silver–Mifsud connection in which the two men had no share. After a re-trial at the Old Bailey and an ugly scene when the police had to be called to deal with two dozen Maltese who had suddenly arrived in the lobby to hear the jury's verdict, they were convicted and sentenced to lengthy terms of imprisonment. Once more a fragile peace was restored.

Sid Kiki, in whose betting shop I had posed as a clerk, was a regular informant, providing good information. He wouldn't ever give his name over the phone, believing that it could lead to all sorts of complications. One evening in May 1967 he telephoned me. 'Listen,' he said, 'You've got another Ginger Marks[3] on the manor. Come and see me in the morning and I'll give you the full SP.' He still had a beautifully furnished flat in Hyde Park Mansions where Jack Spot had once lived; tea and toast were on the table and Kiki, hands stuck through his braces, began by asking if I knew of a man called Jack Buggy. I said I had never heard of him and so he asked if I knew of the Mount Street Bridge Club. Yes, I knew of that place. At one time it had been quite a fashionable card club but as the years had passed it had become little more than an illegal gaming club run by a man, Franny Daniels, and his nephew Charles 'Waggy' Whitnall.

'Well,' said Kiki, 'this fella Buggy was knocked off in there a few nights ago and his body has been done away with. Apparently he was making a right nuisance of himself. Albert was called in at the end.' Albert was Italian Albert,

[3] Ginger Marks had disappeared in January 1965 following a shooting incident in Cheshire Street, Bethnal Green. His body was never found and no charges were ever brought.

Big Alby or plain Mr Dimes, the friend of Billy Hill who ten years earlier had battled with Spot in Soho and was still a power in the West End. If Albert was involved this was serious.

'Take it from me, Nipper,' said Kiki, 'Buggsy's a goner. You'll find out he's left the face of the earth.'

That was all he had for me, but his information was always good and it was enough for me to pull Buggy's file from CRO.[4] American-born John 'Scotch Jack' Buggy had come to England with the American forces and had been a Glasgow hard man. In 1961 he had been sentenced to nine years' imprisonment following the shooting of another man outside the Pigalle Nightclub in Swallow Street. The man, Robert Reeder, had apparently complained about the noise Buggy had been making. During the time he had been in prison, Buggy had served part of his sentence and become friendly with at least one of the Great Train Robbers, Roy James.

I looked at the file on the club which was also known as Lederers, and then I went to see my Superintendent, Arthur Butler, who on his retirement became Security Consultant for Security Express. He suggested we walk round to the club to see what was going on. We arrived about 3 p.m. and there were a couple playing kaluki, some people watching television and not much else going on. We both noted that there was a nice new carpet on the club's floor and no signs of nerves from anyone. The club was hardly a hive of activity. Back at the office we both agreed that, although there was nothing to show for it, we had a gut feeling something was wrong. Arthur sent me to make some enquiries and I went to Buggy's address in Kilburn. I also found that his girlfriend, Ann Phillips, had received a telephone call from him on 12 May, telling her to meet him at her mother's stall in Kingston Market. He had not shown up, and two days later she had told the police in Sutton he had gone missing.

---

[4] Criminal Records Office at New Scotland Yard.

Now all sorts of rumours started to fly around the West End. The night before Buggy disappeared a gelignite bomb had gone off in the hallway of the club in Mount Street. He was known to have been involved in protection rackets in the past. Could the bomb and his disappearance have been connected to them? Ann Phillips told the *Evening Standard* that he had given up that part of his life but could she really know that? Then there was a suggestion that he owed £20,000 to a big-time syndicate. Another version was that it was a Mafia-backed killing, and yet another that Buggy had been protecting a man who had turned against him.

There was also the story, and this seemed to be the most credible one – it was certainly the one which lasted the longest – that he had gone in search of money belonging to Roy James and said to be held, but unaccounted for, by a man who frequented the club. It was said that the man had been given the money to mind but, when the Train Robbers' appeals were dismissed, he went on a spending spree and blew all the money he had been asked to mind.[5] Buggy's mission was to try to recover at least part of it. As to Buggy's death, the firm rumour was that he had been shot in the club at around 3 p.m. and his body wrapped in a carpet and taken away. There was a secondary story that he had eventually been killed in a garage in Kingston-upon-Thames.

The next stage was the finding of his red MGB sports car in Maida Avenue by the Grand Union Canal. In it was a key to a safe deposit box which he always carried. It was now obvious to us that he was dead and a murder investigation was started. Police frogmen started to search the muddy waters of the canal and we, with the help of forensic experts, began an inch-by-inch search of the club's Regency-striped walls and its

---

[5] In his book, *The Train Robbers*, Piers Paul Read endeavours to account for the total monies stolen in the raid, apportioning shares to each man. He lists £76,000 as having been stolen by the man deputed to guard Roy James's share.

spanking new carpet, which we ripped out. Of Buggy there was still no sign.

There was little room at West End Central Police Station, which housed much of 'C' Division, and so I decided to reopen Vine Street, just off Piccadilly, which had been more or less closed since the war. A small unit from the Firearms Section had occupied part of the premises as a temporary measure and now they were moving out it seemed the right place to which to move the murder investigation.

With the exception of the Kray case I can't recall dealing with people who were so blatantly lying as they were in the Buggy investigation. What was both surprising and annoying was that many of them were really ordinary men and women, not the type of villains from whom one would expect a wall of silence. Some of them may have been on the fringes of low-life, but they were not what could be called real criminals. They may have been involved in illegal gaming but that was no big deal. What had they to hide? Had they actually witnessed the murder and thought that perhaps made them accessories? It was difficult to decide, but I know we questioned them for hours and, after they had been released, pulled them in again when some small new piece of evidence turned up, but we still got nowhere. There were no variations. No one would crack.

There was no doubt in our minds that Buggy was dead. But where had he been killed and by whom? Two men who we thought could assist and so wished to interview were out of the country. Most unusually a photograph of Buggy was sent to the newspapers together with a description of his clothes, including a black polo-neck sweater. But nothing came of this either.

And so with nothing to go on, the enquiry began to peter out. Arthur Butler decided I could leave the squad under the direction of one of the DIs and return to normal duties. I had the opportunity to go to the Derby meeting at Epsom as head of the CID there. I thought a few days at the races would do me good. I had been working hard, getting nowhere and banging my head against the brick wall of silence. So I reported to Chief

Superintendent Frankie Davies, known as Jeepers, with the rest of the team, as his Number Two, looking forward to some sunshine and nothing too demanding for the rest of the week. I had my men lined up in the police room behind the stands and was parading them in front of Jeepers when an officer came in, took him on one side and spoke quickly in his ear. In turn Jeepers called me to the back of the room.

'Leave that to me, Nipper. It's back to the West End. Buggy's body's just surfaced in the sea. Hard luck, mate. Let's hope you've at least a winner there.' And so, instead of staying at the meeting and eventually seeing the Australian jockey George Moore ride Royal Palace to victory, I left the track and battled my way against the crowds to get back to the station and on to Savile Row.

Arthur Butler was waiting to tell me the story before going down to Seaford where two off-duty police officers out fishing had seen something floating. They had cast for it, hooked it and reeled in Buggy's body. He had been wearing his black polo-neck sweater and his arms had been bound with baling wire. He had also been gagged. In his back pocket was his driving licence and some correspondence. An examination by the pathologist Francis Camps showed he had been shot twice. In theory this could have become a Sussex case, since the body was found there, but I suspect the local Detective Superintendent Bill Rostron was delighted when Arthur Butler came down to Seaford that night to say he would take the investigation back to London.

So we began again, and made not much more progress than we had in the previous weeks. One of the men whom we wished to interview, Waggy Whitnall, was in Vienna where, after negotiations, he agreed to be interviewed in the presence of a London solicitor, Andrew Keenan. Nothing came of that interview and he remained in Austria.

But when it came to it, no one was arrested and charged that year, or for the next six either. Then in the middle of the enquiry I was promoted to Detective Superintendent and was taken off the case and sent to the Murder Squad itself.

There was, however, an interesting sequel to the story. On his deathbed in 1973 Albert Dimes is said to have ordered that the police be told the truth about Buggy's death. In any event enquiries were renewed and then Donald Wardle, a member of a team of Australian shoplifters who, at the time, was serving nine years for blackmail, made a statement. As a result, Whitnall's uncle Francis Daniels, then aged 63, and Abraham Lewis, who was two years older and had been working at the club at the time of Buggy's death, were charged with his murder. Wardle maintained that he had been in the gaming room of the club on the afternoon of Buggy's death when he had heard three shots. Daniels, he said, had come out and told him and other players to go home.

By the time the men came to trial I was the National Co-ordinator of the Regional Crime Squad and was called as a witness to give evidence of the long interviews I had had with both Daniels and Lewis during the original enquiry.

In November 1974 both men were acquitted, and so the death of Scotch Jack Buggy still remains a mystery. Like all unsolved crimes it has been taken out and dusted down over the years and even more reasons have been put forward for the slaying.

Personally, I still think it was something to do with the Train Robbery money. Shortly before I left 'C' Division I was surprised when I heard a Mr Field had called at Savile Row asking to see me. I was even more surprised to discover it was the former solicitor's managing clerk, Brian Field. He told me he knew Buggy because he had served part of his sentence in the same prison, and that there was no doubt in his mind that Buggy had heard the story of the handing over of the money from the robbery for safekeeping. According to Field it was common gossip in the prison, and I believe that Buggy thought he could score by setting himself up as the official collector.

CHAPTER EIGHT

I WAS PROMOTED TO Superintendent in 1967, during the Buggy inquiry. At that stage in your career you normally go to see the Assistant Commissioner to receive both congratulations and details of your posting, which usually meant serving on a Division for four years and then, if you had a run of luck in solving serious crimes and murders, it was off to the Murder Squad. This was the *crème de la crème*: it was what being a detective was all about and everyone who was, or wanted to be, a detective had the Squad in his sights. This was Scotland Yard and these were the people who had given Scotland Yard its international reputation, making them the envy of law enforcement agencies all over the world. I had been involved in a number of murders including the on-going Buggy inquiry, I had done myself some good with the success of the World Cup Squad and I had achieved a bit of favourable notice in the right quarters. For the moment I assumed that I would be sent to one of the busier Divisions, D, N or E. I wasn't really concerned. At the age of 42 I'd made it to the top of the ladder.

I reported to the Yard and, instead of seeing the Assistant Commissioner, I was marched in to see the Commander, Ernie Millen,[1] one rung down the ladder, whom I had met some

[1] Millen had been involved in a number of famous cases and according to his biography, *Specialist in Crime*, had provided the breakthrough in the Great Train Robbery investigation.

two years earlier during the Kray investigation and who was the head of the CID. He was known as 'Hooter' but I never discovered whether it was because of his nose, which was prominent, or because he had a voice like a foghorn. He was a big, heavy man with an abrupt manner who had a strong Flying Squad background and, like all who had served in it, thought it was the answer to all ills. He knew that I had been approached on a number of occasions to join that squad but had refused, and he could not understand this obstinacy. I had never been one of his 'boys', and indeed he had been scathing in his remarks over the first Kray investigation. I had only met him on rare occasions since then and I certainly had not gone out of my way to put myself in his sights. Not only was I not one of his 'boys', I was not one of his favourite men at all. However, when I heard what he had to say I realised that my appointment had been nothing to do with him at all.

'Well,' he barked in his usual brusque manner. 'Do you know where you're going?'

'No, sir. I've no idea.' This was true. Usually there is some leakage about where a new Super will be posted, but the wall of silence about my future was on the same level as that erected by the witnesses in the Buggy case. Try as I might, I had not been able to find out where I was going.

'C1,' he barked, and then, seeing my look of disbelief and pleasure, quickly added, 'but if you think you're being sent out to the provinces to murder inquiries you've got another bloody think coming. You're going to do a special that is, at the moment, top secret. The ACC is away at the moment but he'll want to see you as soon as he comes back. Meantime I expect you've got plenty to clear up on 'C', so you'd better get back there until you're notified he's back.' I felt like jumping up and down but instead, with a respectful 'Thank you, sir', I turned and made my way to the door. My hand was on the knob when I heard him say, 'By the way.' I turned but he did not even look up as he mumbled, 'Congratulations.'

I was on air. I didn't give a damn what the enquiry was. I had done a triple first: the first postwar Superintendent to be posted to the Murder Squad; the first ever to be sent on promotion from Chief Inspector, and the first to go without serving a period of grace on a Division. This was something of which I had never dreamed. The Murder Squad was top of the pile and I was delighted. Later, when I was in a trough of despair about the way things were going, I would regret that I hadn't been sent to some quiet Division where I could have soldiered on without too much aggravation. But for the moment . . . I was ten feet tall.

The call to attend on the Assistant Commissioner (Crime), Peter Brodie, came a few days later. Brodie, who had been Chief Constable of Stirling and later of Warwickshire before taking an appointment as one of Her Majesty's Inspectors of Constabulary, had graduated from Hendon College as a Detective Inspector under the Trenchard scheme. At the time of his appointment as ACC he believed that as Joe Simpson was a relatively young Commissioner this was as far as he was going to go. When Simpson died suddenly and John Waldron took over as a caretaker Commissioner, Brodie saw avenues opening that he had not previously considered, and thought he could make it to the top. What he had done, however, was to fail to take account of the interloper who had just joined the Force, Robert Mark, who had just been outvoted for the post of Chief Constable in the newly amalgamated force of Leicestershire, and had joined the Met. He was only the second provincial policeman to be appointed to the rank of Assistant Commissioner and, although it may not have been apparent then, he was to prove too formidable an opponent to Brodie. There was a preliminary skirmish, then a bit of close in-fighting, and Mark emerged the clear winner. But that was all in the future.

For the moment, when he saw me, Brodie was confident and assured. By that time the Richardson gang had been broken and Brodie was riding high. There was, however, a cloud partly obscuring the sun in which he was basking. He was not best pleased that the complainants in the Richardson case had initially gone to the Hertfordshire Constabulary and insisted upon seeing Gerry McArthur who had headed the enquiry into the Great Train Robbery and was now Assistant Chief Constable of that force and the Co-ordinator of the No.5 Regional Crime Squad.

The victims of the Richardsons considered, quite rightly, that McArthur was trustworthy and it was to him alone that they were prepared to tell their stories of beatings and torture at the hands of the gang. They were emphatic in their assertions that they could not trust any of the CID in South London where the Richardsons operated, and McArthur was obliged to take all their original statements.

Politics dictated that the enquiry couldn't be dealt with exclusively by McArthur, and eventually a team was formed consisting of a mixture of his squad and Met officers. They worked very well together and were enormously successful. The Richardson brothers and many of their associates were arrested and charged with very serious cases of assault. They were jailed for long periods and the credit for the enquiry was shared between the Met and McArthur's team. His personal contribution to the operation was recognised by the award of an MBE. Brodie's belief was that, if he could score again, his hopes of following Waldron into the big chair would be much improved. Unfortunately for him, the first of the scandals of the Met would break before the end of the decade, and with it would go his chance at the jackpot.

That said, I thought he was a nice if naive man, and one who was too much influenced by the people he consulted. He was often badly advised and was not nearly inquisitive enough about the information supplied to him. His great quality and his redeeming feature was his passionate devotion to the CID and his chaps, by whom he badly wanted to be seen as a 'good boss'. Sadly, he was let down, time and again, by the men he had trusted and selected for promotion on the advice of others. Many were to feature prominently as defendants in trials at the Old Bailey throughout the 1970s.

His wish for a well-publicised success was apparent when

he spoke to me. 'Mr Read, you're going to get the Krays.' As soon as he uttered the words my heart sank, and the pleasure of my promotion evaporated. I could hardly believe what I was hearing. Although I had taxed my brain trying to figure what the 'special' might be, I'd never even considered the Krays. Not them again, I thought. My God, I'd had enough of the difficulties and problems they had posed the last time around. I didn't need them again.

Now Brodie was in full flow but I hardly heard him. 'We've got rid of the Richardsons and it's time we cleaned up the rest of London. The Krays have been a thorn in our sides long enough. Now you can do it any way you like,' he continued, 'but I'm looking to you to get the right result.' When he saw the questioning look on my face he realised his remark had been ambiguous and added, 'I know you will wish to run this thing entirely properly and fairly – I don't even need to say that. It is important to nail these bastards.'

He had realised by my silence that I was not exactly overjoyed at the prospect on offer, nor was I affected by his apparent enthusiasm. 'Always remember we are here to help in any way we can.' I wondered at the time exactly who the 'we' were, and later I was to discover he should have added 'or hinder'.

Well, there it was. Now I knew my fate and it gave me no pleasure. I thought, why me? Why not give someone else a shot? Why do I have to do it after all this time? I had been puffed up like a meringue thinking no one else had ever made the grade like this and then to find out what it was really all about was a great deflater. It was like being hit with a wet dishcloth. Brodie was still murmuring platitudes about how I was obviously the best man for the job, and how he knew he could rely on my skill and judgement, but I was hardly listening and it didn't serve to allay my feelings. I was absolutely pissed off. Until, that is, he questioned whether I was concerned about taking on these 'enemies of society'.

I was immediately alert and replied that I was only concerned about the enemy within. There was no need to spell it out. Brodie understood what I meant. He nodded reassuringly.

'May I select my own team?' I asked. I was already thinking of some of those I would ask to join me.

'Certainly,' he said, 'if they are available, you shall have them.'

My next question was my most important, and I was hanging on the answer. 'Whom do I report to?'

'Mr du Rose,' replied Brodie.

'And where shall I be working from?'

'We thought here, but do you have any strong views on the matter?'

I did indeed have very strong views. The Yard was the last place from where I wanted to mount an investigation. 'I don't mind working anywhere *but* here.' If there was to be any secrecy in this operation it wouldn't keep if I was working from the Yard.

'Very well, you can arrange that with Mr du Rose,' said Brodie, and with offers of congratulations on my promotion he bade me good-day.

My next stop was to see John du Rose, a slow speaking, cheroot-smoking man with a firm jaw and direct manner. He was a Deputy Assistant Commissioner and I had never worked with him before. I knew him, of course. Who amongst the detective branch had not heard of the legendary 'Four Day Johnny', so called because of his knack of solving a murder case in that time? He was the man who had overlorded the Richardson inquiry, the London nudes murders,[2] had rid the

---

2 The nudes murders became known as the 'Jack the Stripper' murders because the victims – all prostitutes – were found naked in the West London area in 1954.

West End of the Messinas[3] and who enjoyed the highest success rate on the Murder Squad for solving provincial murders.

We shook hands, he told me to sit down and asked whether I wanted a cup of tea. This was the first of many long discussions I had with John du Rose. Not all the subsequent ones were as pleasant. Nevertheless, I found him to be a good 'guv'nor' and I was later to find his strength and determination an enormous help as the enquiry progressed.

He asked what I thought of the job and when I screwed up my face slightly and began, 'Well –' he interrupted, saying, 'Yes, I know it's a bit of a ball-breaker, but don't worry. I'm sure it will come good.'

We talked about headquarters, and it was arranged that I should move to Tintagel House, across the river, on the Albert Embankment. This meant I would be away from the mainstream of the Murder Squad but, for the moment, offices were found for me on the 17th floor at New Scotland Yard. We then turned to the method of picking a team. He agreed I should find my own squad, but it was he who provided its first two members, both Sergeants from the Murder Squad, Algie Hemingway and Alan Wright, who were to stay with me to the bitter end. The three of us comprised the whole investigatory team for the first three months of the six-month enquiry.

Du Rose told me that we couldn't expect to keep the lid on the enquiry for too long, so it would be let out that I was conducting a high-level disciplinary inquiry into a major corruption allegation. This, in fact, was not a bad cover story. Before the creation of A10 (the Discipline and Complaints department) the Murder Squad officers would often deal with major complaints of corruption, and so it was quite an acceptable cover.

Du Rose was concerned with providing me with all the resources I needed, but the one thing I was delighted about

---

[3] The Messinas were a family of Maltese who controlled vice in London for a period of over ten years.

was that he never asked me how I intended to conduct the inquiry. In fact all the way through there were only a couple of occasions when he tried to interfere and, when I voiced my disapproval, he backed off.

This is not to suggest any timidness on his part. Far from it. But John du Rose had been there. He knew what it was like to be at the sharp end and how unwelcome undue interference from senior officers can be in those circumstances. We had a great deal of respect for each other and our relationship worked well.

For example, du Rose held what were known as 'morning prayers', and part of the deal when I was allowed to go to Tintagel House was that I had to return daily to New Scotland Yard and attend them. This meant reporting to him on the previous day's progress even if, in fact, nothing of any real interest had been achieved. It was really pointless to say, 'Oh yes, Sergeant Hemingway is going through the books of a supermarket in Southsea.' It was even worse that we had to line up and wait for the senior reporting officer to finish before we went in, particularly as I was the most junior. It came to a head when, one day, I ran into Tommy Butler waiting to make his report. 'Wasting my time,' I said to him when he asked how things were. By the time he had finished with du Rose I was seething. Du Rose's habit was to stand with an elbow on a filing cabinet, smoking one of his cheroots. 'What have you to tell me?' he asked, puffing away.

In a fit of recklessness I told him I had been wasting my time which could have been more profitably employed and added, 'If you want reports, call into Tintagel House on your way home. You're welcome to know anything at all about the investigation, but there's only three of us and I can't waste half a morning sitting outside your room.' I expected a right rocket for being so presumptuous but he took it in good part and from then on he would call uninvited at Tintagel House, either on his way into Scotland Yard or on his way home, for a chat to see how things were progressing. Even that he did infrequently. He just left me to get on with the job.

But for the moment I went to my office, and I have to admit I was proud walking down the long corridor which housed the Murder Squad to see that already my name was painted on the door. I was by far the youngest member and that, and my size, made me truly the Nipper. For the next two years I was hardly ever there to occupy it.

The guv'nor of C1 in those days was my old guv'nor from the first Kray inquiry, Fred Gerrard. Although he greeted me with a certain amount of enthusiasm, I detected a note of envy in his voice. Of course he had been made aware of my appointment, and also the fact that I was to bypass him and report direct to du Rose. I knew also that he would have wanted to be more involved, bearing in mind the disappointment of 1965. He told me that day that when my turn came as the stand-by detective he would put my name in the frame, as even the famous corruption case was supposed to be secret. That was how some months later, just as the crucial stages of the Kray enquiry were being reached, I found myself investigating the two-year-old murder of a prostitute found strangled on the foreshore at Dunlaoghaire in Eire.

What had the Krays and their friends been up to in the two years since I had last met them? To a large extent they had passed completely out of my sight. I knew, of course, of the killing of George Cornell in the Blind Beggar public house in the Mile End Road.I knew also of the disappearance of Jack 'The Hat' McVitie and the stories about his death. They were also said to have been involved in the disappearance of Frank Mitchell, the so-called Mad Axeman, from a working party at Dartmoor Prison. I knew they were still the Kings of the East End and the Firm was predominant there. But now I would have to get up to date on their day-to-day activities.

The story of the Cornell killing was that he was a member of the Richardson gang who had not been at the fight at Mr Smith's Club that had resulted in their mass arrest. Cornell was a hard and fearless man, mentioned frequently during the Richardson 'Torture Trial' as one of the most violent men in the gang. He had nothing but contempt for Ronnie Kray, whom he called a 'pouf' in public at the Astor Club. Ronnie, seething about the insult, bided his time but let it be known that if Cornell 'came on the manor' he was to be informed. On the night of 9 March 1966 Cornell quite brazenly went deep into the heart of Kray territory to have a drink in the Blind Beggar. He sat on a stool at the end of the bar with some four other men. It was around 8.30 p.m., a normal night in a popular pub. Indeed, a local Detective Inspector had been there a few minutes earlier, having a quick drink and sandwich. The door opened and, so it was said, in walked Ronnie Kray and 'Ian' Barrie.

The story was that Cornell merely looked up and said, 'Look who's here!' Those were the last words he ever spoke. He was shot with a Luger pistol at point-blank range by Ronnie Kray. The joke in the pub over the years was that the best thing to drink in the Blind Beggar was a Luger and lime. When the police tried to investigate the shooting they met with a series of blank responses. No one had seen anything at all, but it was common knowledge in the East End that Ronnie Kray had killed Cornell. Indeed later, as I began to re-investigate this murder, one well-known East End villain told me, 'Everybody knows Ronnie done it. Christ, they did everything but take the front page of the fucking *Times* to advertise it.' I also knew that Tommy Butler had been sent by the Yard to investigate it and even he, one of the most persistent and dedicated detectives, drew a blank. He organised an identification parade but no one picked out Ronnie. He was forced to call it a day when he met the orchestrated conspiracy of silence.

Cornell's widow, Olive, had mounted a campaign against them. She castigated them loudly and publicly and courageously. She had been round to Fort Vallance (the Kray home in Vallance Road) and, screaming abuse, smashed all the windows in the place. For this she had been brought before a sympathetic magistrate who had fined her the derisory sum of £1. But as with so many matters involving the Krays, of hard evidence there was none.

It was also rumoured that the Firm had been involved in

the springing of Frank Mitchell from Dartmoor. Poor Frank was one of life's tragedies. Since his escape he had simply disappeared. An ox of a man, he had been serving a life sentence on the Moor for aggravated robbery. His criminal career had been in the top grade for convictions if not for achievement. Unfortunately for him, he was of limited mental ability. Born in the East End, he had attended special schools since the age of eight. So, unlike the real masters of crime, he was for ever being caught.

At the age of 17 he was sent to borstal, and three years later received a second borstal sentence. Within a month of his release he had been sentenced to three months' imprisonment for receiving a stolen revolver and ammunition. Six months later, in March 1953, he went down for 21 months, and on 2 December 1954 he received three years' imprisonment. He was a most recalcitrant prisoner and in the first two days of his sentence he attacked a prison officer and was flogged. In July 1955 he was certified mentally defective and sent to Rampton, a secure mental hospital. In January 1957 he escaped and, whilst on the run, hit the occupant of a house – into which he had broken – over the head with an iron bar. On his capture he was found to be in possession of an iron bar and hatchets. This time he received nine years. Three months later he was certified insane and was transferred to Broadmoor. He escaped in July of the next year and, armed with an axe, broke into a house and attacked the owner and his wife. On his arrest he said, 'I want to prove I am sane and know what I am doing.' This time he received ten years and life imprisonment, to run concurrently.

On his recapture he was found not to be certifiable and was sent to Hull Prison where, during the attempted mass escape in April 1962, when his cell was opened by another inmate, he inflicted gross personal violence on a prison officer. On 13 May 1962 he slashed another officer with a knife, and for this he was birched. On 6 September Mitchell was transferred to Dartmoor, at which time the Chief Director of Prisons wrote that he should be treated in an unexceptional kind of way and should be accorded only those privileges appropriate to the stage of his sentence. He emphasised that under no circumstances should Mitchell be employed outside the prison without reference to the Commissioners for Prison. Three-monthly reports on his behaviour were called for, as well as for an immediate report if there was any reason to think that there might be a further outbreak of violence or an escape attempt by him. He was categorised as a prison trouble-maker and a potential escaper.

Then, for the first time in years, Mitchell seemed to begin to settle down. He worked well and in July 1963 he was removed from the escape list. In May 1964 the Prison Labour Board, an internal tribunal, recommended he should be employed on a working party outside the prison. This was put to the Prison Board and it was agreed he could go on the quarry party, which was a small and well-supervised group.

In turn he seemed to respond well. He kept away from other prisoners and worked on watches and model cars in his cell. Inordinately proud of his physique, he still maintained a strict exercise routine. There were regular demonstrations of his muscular development and his strength, an illustration of the fact that he could still be a threat if he so chose. He was also allowed to keep and breed budgerigars in his cell and he watched over their progress with an unusual tenderness for a man of such size and potential for violence. Then more freedom came his way when he was allowed on other outside working parties. In September 1966 he was transferred to the Honour Party, a much more loosely supervised group. This was the Dartmoor equivalent of the Prior Release Scheme, where prisoners nearing the end of their sentences were allowed to be employed outside prison, returning to their cells at the end of the day. The idea was, as had been the case with Niven Craig, to rehabilitate these men for a return to normal society. It is a scheme I have long thought to be rubbish. The only society to which this kind of man wished to return is the criminal society where he could hope to pull a quick bank job and sit and enjoy the spoils for a month or two.

Of course, he abused this freedom no end. No single prison guard could possibly restrain a man like Mitchell. The warders were too frightened of him to say or do anything. As one said, 'I just could not afford to have Mitchell troublesome.' Instead of working on the Honour Party, Mitchell was free to do what he liked. And what he liked was to go off into local pubs drinking and having occasional sex with women, the money for both of which was provided by the Kray Firm who sent men down to see him on a regular basis. Mitchell and a special friend became regulars at the Elephant's Nest at Horndon. Once he and his friend called for a taxi to take them to Tavistock, where they bought a budgerigar before taxiing back so they could rejoin the Honour Party.

On 12 December 1966 he went with four other prisoners, under the supervision of one prison officer, in a minibus to repair fencing on a firing range at Bagga Tor on the moor. That day the weather was too bad for work and after lunch the whole party stayed in a hut playing cards. At 3.30 p.m. Mitchell asked if he could go and feed some ponies in a nearby field. Fifty minutes later, the prison officer took the other four men to the point where they would be picked up by the prison bus but there was no sign of Mitchell. At 4.40 p.m. the police at Okehampton were told of the escape, and routine police measures were initiated, but by then he was miles away heading back to London in a brown Rover hired by 'the Firm' for the occasion. At 10.24 a.m. on 13 December Mitchell's prison clothing was found in a lay-by on the A30 some 30 miles from Tavistock, and an inquiry was told 'it was then assumed that he had made good his escape'. This was an interesting assumption in view of what I learned later in my own enquiries.

The next thing that was heard of him was from the newspapers. The *Mirror* and *The Times* each published letters signed by Mitchell and bearing his thumbprint impression on the bottom. Each asked for a release date. The Home Secretary of the day indicated he would be willing to speak to Mitchell, but when this caused an outcry he amended his offer saying it could only happen after Mitchell's surrender. The Krays were known to have been friendly towards Mitchell, and it was rumoured that members of the Firm had helped in the escape. Then the stream of letters dried up and there was no further word from Mitchell. He had simply vanished, and although there were reports, rather like those in Lord Lucan's case, that he had been sighted in Scotland, Ireland, Germany and most other countries in the world, he was never officially seen again.

These, then, were two of the major elements of the inquiry I was to conduct, and soon after the investigations started I learned of a third.

Jack McVitie, called The Hat, or Jack the Hat, because he always wore a natty trilby to hide his baldness, had disappeared. There were the usual rumours that he had done a runner, that he had blown himself up with gelignite, that he was in the foundations of any number of supermarkets, blocks of flats or motorway flyovers. It was also suggested that he had been dropped from a plane into the Channel and, most common, that he had been fed to pigs.[4] The most persistent rumour in his case, however, was that he had been killed in a basement flat somewhere in North London, but there was not much more to go on than that. What was clear was that Jack was missing and it was something I would have to consider very shortly.

Apart from those highlights I knew only of the rumours of protection being paid by quite fashionable gaming and night clubs in the West End, but here again, no complaints were being made by the victims.

From the beginning I had two excellent Sergeants to help

---

[4] Donald Hume did in fact dispose of the torso of Stanley Setty in just that way, flying a plane over Essex marshes and dropping packages from it. In 1969 the Hossein brothers were convicted of the murder of Mrs McKay. Although there was no absolute proof, it is fairly certain that her body was fed to pigs at their farm.

me. Algie Hemingway, who later became a Commander, and Alan Wright, who was called to the Bar, were with me to the end. Each deservedly received three commendations from the Commissioner for their work on the Kray case.

The investigation began in September 1967 and the first thing that had to be done was to pull the old files from Criminal Intelligence (C11) on the Krays and read up what information the Yard had on them. C11 had been set up to analyse information which had been received from any quarter and to disseminate it to the right area. You get information from one man, think it will be of interest and value to another on a different Division, and send it off. In theory that sounds wonderful, but in practice it hardly worked at all. For a start, police officers then were extremely jealous of sharing information. I have seen examples where officers on the Flying Squad have openly said, 'I have this information about X, Y and Z. I can't use it but there's no way I'm going to give it to the Regional Crime Squad.' There was this terribly petty sort of behaviour, even at high rank. Fortunately, over the years, this seems now to have completely disappeared, as methods of gathering and collating evidence have improved.

When Algie Hemingway came back from the intelligence branch with all the stuff on the Krays I received my first shock. There was not one single item added to the wealth of stuff I had put in during my Commercial Street days. Of this there was an enormous amount: car numbers, relationships, associations, places frequented, the sort of thing they might or might not do; and there was a lot of firmed-up intelligence, real bundles of it. Normally you would get a file and there might be three snippets in it. But because we had kept very good records, we had put in a ton of stuff and I believed it was important we did so. Now I found, to my dismay, that there wasn't another single fact in there. Later, at the trial, this was to prove something of an embarrassment. During the early days of the trial, one witness gave evidence that after the Cornell killing he had met an officer, whom he named, behind the stands at the Hackney Greyhound Stadium and given him information. He was cross-examined to the effect that he was lying, and the officer had to be called to agree the meeting had taken place and the circumstances reported to Tommy Butler. Nevertheless there was nothing to show that any action had been taken following the receipt of the information, and the officer was obliged to agree this.

Tommy Butler had spent six months in the East End, cajoling, pleading and threatening, to try to get some witnesses to the Cornell shooting to speak out. He had even arrested the Krays and put them on an identification parade but to no avail. In fact the barmaid in the Blind Beggar had point-blank refused to attend the parade. Nevertheless, there was nothing even about this on the file. To all intents and purposes I was starting with an absolutely clean slate. With hindsight it was probably just as well.

I made the very positive decision not to investigate the murder of Cornell and the disappearances of Mitchell and McVitie. Of one thing I was certain and that was I would learn from the mistakes on the first enquiry. This time I would make sure the whole Firm was nicked in one fell swoop. That way potential witnesses could not be got at and stories changed to suit the evidence I had accumulated. It was also essential to delay the arrests until there was sufficient substantial evidence on a number of charges to make sure that they were not given bail. I knew from my past experience that it would be useless to expect the victims of the Krays or their protection rackets to give me any help, although I did travel to Scotland to see one ex-club-owner. As was the case with others in the 1965 investigation, he simply did not wish to know.

The problem was where to begin. The East End was still the same. I couldn't really expect any help from that quarter either. The Krays were still both idolised and feared. People either loved them or they were terrified of them. Either way, no one was going to talk about them. And so I decided to go back to basics. The sort of thing to form the basis of an investigation would be to try to talk to old members of the Firm who had drifted away and who might be both disgruntled with the way things had been run and also, if they were on the fringe, to be subject to a bit of pressure from me. It was said the Krays threatened that 'no one ever leaves the Firm', but the boast wasn't entirely true. For reasons of ill health, or other acceptable subterfuges, some had managed to get off the roller-coaster. They were still conscious of the power the Krays wielded, but they were, in effect, my only hope. So I made a list of all the people, some 32 in number, whom I had met during my previous enquiries and who, as former members of the Firm, were the best to see in the hope that they would crack. I hoped some of them might, by this time, have become so dissociated from or dissatisfied with the new-style Firm that they might be willing to do something for me.

I saw everyone personally and, of course, I got a lot of rejections. For instance Billy Exley was now well divorced from the team, at least as well as he could be. I went to see him in early December 1967, as one of the first people, in a little flat in Woodseer Street in the East End. Once a good middle-weight boxer, his fighting days were long gone. He had had a heart attack and, a sick man, did not wish to help in any way. He could have been a mine of information but he clammed up. He had been associated with them for too long and knew too much about them for me really to expect him to crack at the first meeting. He was in an awkward position.

I suggested to him that he might have placed himself in a dangerous position by leaving the Firm, and he might talk to me in case later he was swept up in a series of arrests. 'Don't worry about me,' he said, 'If they come looking for me I've a shotgun behind the door and that's what they'll get. Don't worry, it's licensed.'

Slowly I worked through the list. Some interviews were interesting; most were blanks. But despite this I found that the more rejections I got the more I warmed to the task. I was determined to break this wall of silence. Both Wright and Hemingway were totally supportive and enthusiastic. I don't remember that all three of us were ever despondent at the same time.

What I was keen to do was to get to somebody who would not immediately go back to the twins. I believed that someone like Donaghue might have done that and blown the whole thing at an early stage. I knew in all conscience it could not go on under cover for ever, but I did want it quiet for as long as possible. So on the list were people who, even if they did not want to make a statement, would at least keep their mouths shut. What I also wanted from them was another name to go to: someone who they believed was feeling a bit strongly about what was going on. I had obtained a fairly good response from Exley. He didn't resent my going to see him; he pleaded, at that stage and as I expected, that he didn't want to know, and he didn't give me any more names, but he left it in a situation whereby I could always come back to him if anything blew up. I did go back and see him two or three more times and we had quite a good relationship. It worked out well because eventually my visits bore fruit.

With all the people I had met on the original enquiry I had formed a relationship. Whatever they were nicked for, they were told that what I really wanted was not them but the people behind them. They knew that and they knew I neither fitted people up nor abused them. My general reputation with people like them was good. They knew I wouldn't put things on them, or do some of the things other officers would. So I could go to people like that and reckon not to have the door slammed in my face. This was how I started, and eventually I got to see Leslie Payne. I had run into him years earlier, down in Commercial Street, and the relationship had been good then. It was 'Mr Read – Mr Payne': there was no coming the heavy hand or 'If you don't do this, then I'll do that.' So when I met him for the second go-round in early December there was a basic understanding, a platform on which I could start to build.

Payne, the *consigliere* and a financial wizard, was the man who had made fortunes for the twins by setting up cells of Long Firm frauds. He was far more intelligent than most of those I saw, the sort of guy who might want to do a deal, but

I had to remember he was a most experienced, even brilliant, con-man. I knew he couldn't be bullshitted, but he might be tempted. When I saw him for the first time it was just a 'fishing expedition'. Algie Hemingway had arranged a meet at Lyons Corner House in the Strand and, for me, it was like a meeting of old friends.

Of course he wanted to know what was in it for him. What could I promise him? Think of the possible repercussions, Mr Read. With Payne it was like a game of chess. He moved a pawn, I moved a pawn. We were old adversaries and we both knew the rules. We sat drinking our coffee like two civilised people and learned a little more about each other. I promised I would deal with him honestly and fairly – but he already knew that or he would not have seen me in the first place – and I asked the same in return. The meeting ended with a promise to meet again, and I could see there was hope. When I gave Hemingway an account of the meeting he was elated. We were both convinced that, sooner rather than later, Payne would come across and, as it turned out, we were right.

The reason he gave for divorcing himself from the Krays was that he could no longer control their unnecessary violence. He liked to feel he was cultured. He enjoyed the good life that crime could provide. He liked dining well, drinking good wine and having stimulating conversation. On the face of it he was the managing director organising things, but they were going off having bursts of violence, eroding the discipline he was trying to build up. Simply to say, 'I represent the Krays' was all that was needed in the middle and late 1960s. They didn't need the violence by that time. The violence they had exercised in their early days had been necessary to establish themselves as bosses, the men running the underworld. Now they had done that and their reputation had spread, Payne knew all he had to do was to mention their name and he could get whatever he wanted. But when they then committed some further violent act he came to realise he was wasting his time. Although he tried to do something about it – talking them out of it, telling them that they could become gentlemen of leisure

– they would suddenly revert to totally gratuitous violence, something he did not regard as sport. He was also appalled by their stupidity. He preferred the company of people similar to himself. At least there was a challenge in having a conversation with another intelligent con-man. So he left the Firm.

When we next met a few days later I knew I had to force him to make a decision. There could be no bullying. Payne would have baulked at those tactics, but it needed a firm hand. I explained that I wanted a statement from him regarding his activities with the Krays. I warned him that in the statement he would have to admit to certain involvement but I promised that I would do what I could to make sure he was not prosecuted. Payne was nobody's fool. He knew the score on matters such as this, and realised that my best hope of getting near to the Krays was to get someone like himself to talk. For him a statement to me would get him off the hook of a prosecution and possibly a substantial sentence.

I suggested that, if he would feel more comfortable, he could have his solicitor present, and I guaranteed that no one else would see his statement. His immediate question was, 'Does that include the Yard?' and I assured him it did. I told him, as I was to tell all possible witnesses, that there was no need for him to sign the statement at this stage. I would only ask him to sign when I had built up a sufficiently strong case that he was not the only person who would be giving evidence.

Nevertheless he still needed a prod. Perhaps not a big one, but a prod nevertheless. He was, after all, about to make a tremendous career decision which would affect him and his family. I played my trump card – the one about his being liquidated.

'Have you heard you're on the list?' I asked.

He knew exactly what I meant. The list was Ronnie's notorious hit list of people he wanted to be rid of for one reason or another. For half a second he hesitated and, when he answered, it was not with his usual confidence. 'No, have you?'

I pressed home the advantage. 'As a matter of fact I've

heard it very strongly. I'm surprised you haven't heard a buzz.' Watching his face I knew I had him. For some reason Leslie Payne had allowed himself to be out-conned. It was many months later that I learned that he *knew* I was right.

Had the Krays left him alone, all would have been well. He was, on the face of it, too deeply implicated to go to the police and inform on them. Anyway, that was not his style. But this was something the Krays were not prepared to chance, and it was to prove their downfall. Once Billy Exley began to talk to me, so many pieces of the jigsaw fell into place and I learned that Jack 'The Hat' McVitie and Billy Exley were sent to shoot Payne. It was not a very good hit squad. Jack, now well into drugs, was the hit man; Billy, with heart trouble and losing his nerve, was the driver. On the way, according to Exley, Jack produced a gun 'as big as a bleeding cannon'. When they arrived at Payne's home McVitie knocked boldly on the door, which fortunately was opened by Mrs Payne. 'He's not in,' she said.

'That's all right,' said McVitie and off he and Exley went.

'Good job he wasn't,' said McVitie after they had left, 'I would have blown his fucking head off.'

It sounds comic and amateurish with no plotting-up, no ringing to see if he was likely to be home, or making a meet, but it was a near miss for Payne. Nevertheless, even then, I don't think he was absolutely terrified by the twins. He always believed he retained some control. The incident, in its turn, was something which led, in part, to McVitie's death. McVitie had been given £1,500 to perform the task and, instead of repaying the money, he kept it.

But Payne suspected what I said was true, and there was still a contract out for him, and perhaps my assertion removed any possible doubts from his mind. He knew now that the McVitie call was unlikely to have been a social one. This was what tipped the balance and made him the very first Supergrass.

To take Payne's statement, 146 pages long, I chose the library of a quiet police section house in Marylebone. He clearly could not be seen at Tintagel House, and since the

Three times winner

All time loser: Jack the Hat in happier circumstances

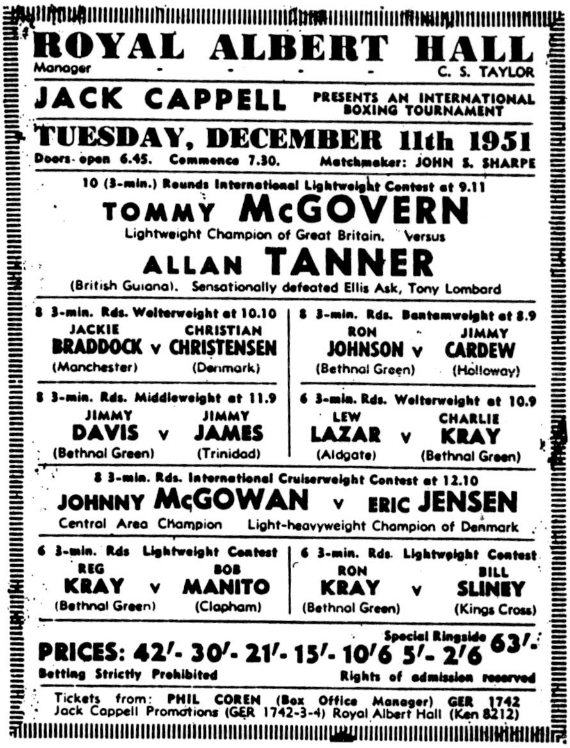

ROYAL ALBERT HALL
Manager - - - - C. S. TAYLOR

JACK CAPPELL PRESENTS AN INTERNATIONAL BOXING TOURNAMENT

TUESDAY, DECEMBER 11th 1951
Doors open 6.45. Commence 7.30. Matchmaker: JOHN S. SHARPE

10 (3-min.) Rounds International Lightweight Contest at 9.11
TOMMY McGOVERN
Lightweight Champion of Great Britain. Versus
ALLAN TANNER
(British Guiana). Sensationally defeated Ellis Ask, Tony Lombard

8 3-min. Rds. Welterweight at 10.10
JACKIE **BRADDOCK** v CHRISTIAN **CHRISTENSEN**
(Manchester) (Denmark)

8 3-min. Rds. Bantamweight at 8.9
RON **JOHNSON** v JIMMY **CARDEW**
(Bethnal Green) (Holloway)

8 3-min. Rds. Middleweight at 11.9
JIMMY **DAVIS** v JIMMY **JAMES**
(Bethnal Green) (Trinidad)

6 3-min. Rds. Welterweight at 10.9
LEW **LAZAR** v CHARLIE **KRAY**
(Aldgate) (Bethnal Green)

8 3-min. Rds. International Cruiserweight Contest at 12.10
JOHNNY **McGOWAN** v ERIC **JENSEN**
Central Area Champion Light-heavyweight Champion of Denmark

6 3-min. Rds Lightweight Contest
REG **KRAY** v BOB **MANITO**
(Bethnal Green) (Clapham)

6 3-min. Rds. Lightweight Contest
RON **KRAY** v BILL **SLINEY**
(Bethnal Green) (Kings Cross)

PRICES: 42/- 30/- 21/- 15/- 10/6 5/- 2/6 Special Ringside **63/-**
Betting Strictly Prohibited Rights of admission reserved

Tickets from: PHIL COREN (Box Office Manager) GER 1742
Jack Cappell Promotions (GER 1742-3-4) Royal Albert Hall (Ken 8212)

Two losers, one winner

Soho Rangers FC: left to right: includes Stanley Baker, George Wisbey, William Stayton, Tommy McCarthy (Bert's brother), Albert Dimes, Frankie Frazer. Front row: Bert McCarthy, boxing promoter, Eddie Richardson and others

Reggie outside Fort Vallance

Right to left: Reggie, Jack "Kid" Berg, Ted "Kid" Lewis, Charlie, Terry Spinks, and Ronnie – champions all

Right to left: Ron Coles, Gerry McArthur, Malcolm Fewtrell, self, Jack Pritchard and others at the end of the case (© Daily Mirror)

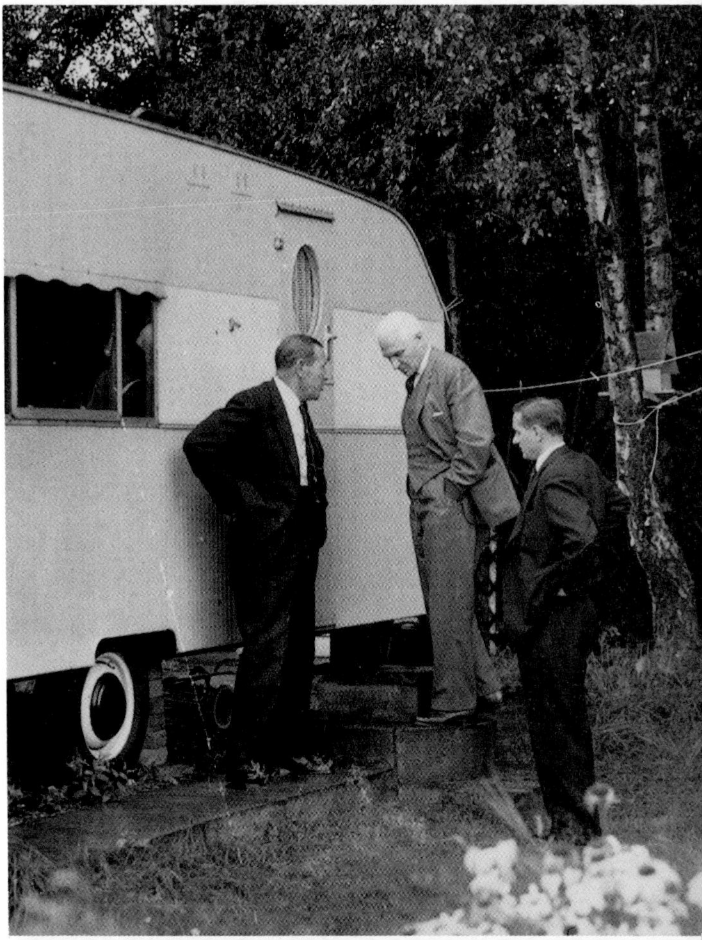

'Chalkie' White, Malcolm Fewtrell and self outside White's caravan at Box Hill. "Who's got the key?"

Reggie and Ronnie (© Daily Express)

Frank Cater and I coming out of Bow Street Magistrate's Court (© Evening Standard)

Four in hand: Self, Lloyd–Hughes, du Rose and Cater (© Daily Telegraph)

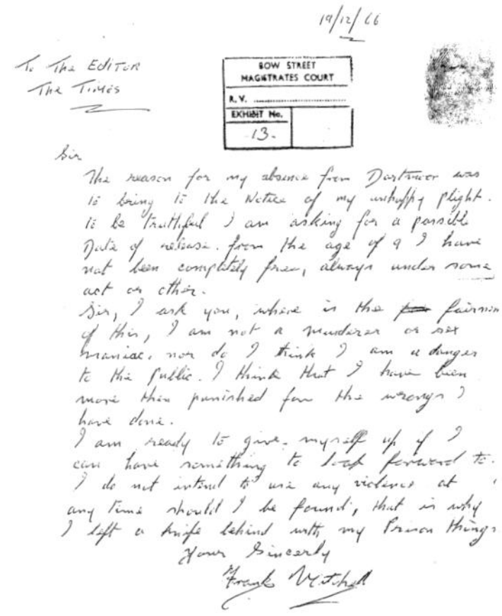

19/12/66

To The Editor
The Times

BOW STREET
MAGISTRATES COURT
R. V. ....
EXHIBIT No. 13.

Sir

The reason for my absence from Dartmoor was to bring to the Notice of my unhappy plight. To be truthful I am asking for a possible Date of release. from the age of 9 I have not been completely free, always under some act or other.

Sir, I ask you, where is the ~~fa~~ fairness of this, I am not a murderer or sex maniac, nor do I think I am a danger to the public. I think that I have been more than punished for the wrongs I have done.

I am ready to give myself up if I can have something to look forward to. I do not intend to use any violence at any time should I be found, that is why I left a knife behind with my Prison things

Yours Sincerely

Frank Mitchell

Frank Mitchell's letter to *The Times* with his fingerprint to prove authenticity

The bar at the Blind Beggar

The “murder” suitcase. Note the needle at bottom right (© Commissioner of Police of the Metropolis)

Liza the nightclub hostess

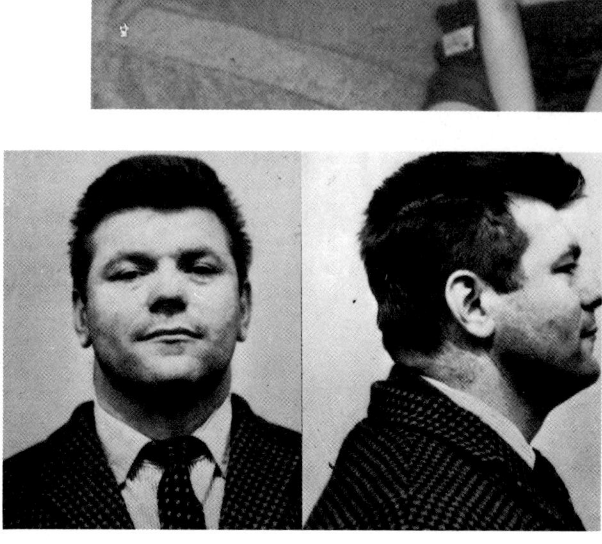

Frank Mitchell

Cartoon of the personalities in both Kray cases by Ivan Lawrence QC

Ronnie and Reggie with Judy Garland

"Latest society photograph of the Kray brothers."

Jak Cartoon
(© Evening Standard)

On appointment as National Coordinator of Regional Crime Squads for England and Wales (© Daily Mirror)

At Tintagel House, with view behind

Right to left: Self, daughter Maralyn, wife Pat and Maralyn's friend Alan

library was little used there was no possibility of a leak from that quarter. Besides, Payne looked more like a policeman than either Hemingway or I did. Payne, disdaining any offers of protection, came up from Tulse Hill every day, arriving at 9 a.m., and went home every night. It took three weeks, working six hours and more a day, to complete.

Payne was a fount of knowledge and, now that he had taken the decision to talk, information gushed out of him. He had a wonderful memory and, although he never produced any notes or other records, he was always so precise I often wondered whether he had prepared for this day by keeping some sort of diary to which he referred before our meetings.

The statement covered Long Firm frauds, stolen bonds, forged currency, the sale of drugs, blackmail and assaults as well as an enormous amount of general and background information about the day-to-day running of the Krays' enterprises. This was the first statement which gave me something really solid to work on. It was what I needed and it was the beginning of the destruction of the Kray empire. It is not possible to say whether without Payne a successful prosecution would have resulted, but certainly he was, at that stage, the principal informant and supplied most of the groundwork on which the investigation was based. He was the key which unlocked the door.

Whilst I was taking the statement it became quite clear that Payne's position was a difficult one. In disclosing some of the criminal activities of the Krays he was also involving himself and, strictly speaking, he should therefore be formally cautioned that he did not have to say anything else. This would also mean that, from then on, the statement would have to be in exactly his words without my asking questions on which he could give expansive answers. So on 11 January I broke off and went to see David Hopkin, the senior legal advisor, at the offices of the Director of Public Prosecutions in Queen Anne Gate. He and I had known each other since my early Paddington days and he had been involved with me in the abortive Hideaway Trial. With his background knowledge I knew he was the right man to turn to for advice this time. We discussed the situation at length and he took me to see Sir Norman Skelhorne, the then Director of Public Prosecutions. I argued that Payne should have immunity from prosecution for any offence with the exception of murder or other violence of any kind.

In any event he wasn't involved in any of the violence, and so that aspect did not trouble him, but the good thing, from my point of view, was that by the time he came to the end of his statement he was beginning to name names. Others had given bits of information which were useful, but there had been nothing concrete. There was still much work to be done. It was obvious that I could have preferred charges against the twins and others, but I was determined to benefit from my mistakes last time. No arrests would be made until I could ensure that a number of very serious charges could be preferred and also that other senior members of the gang would be arrested with the twins and not left outside where they could hamper my investigation.

One of the names Payne put up was that of Freddy Gore, who had been involved with him and the Krays in trying to establish the housing project in Eastern Nigeria. He had also been concerned in the smuggling of stolen bonds as well as in various Long Firm frauds and was potentially a most important witness. He and Payne went back a number of years and if Gore chose to co-operate he would almost certainly be able to corroborate much of what Payne was saying. Unfortunately there was a fly in the ointment. Years before even that, Payne and Freddy Gore had been involved in a Long Firm fraud when Payne had had John Mathew defending him. In this particular case Payne said to his co-defendants, 'My brief's done a deal and you can guarantee there'll be no bird involved if there's a plea.' In principle this was totally acceptable, but the result had been that Gore and another man pleaded guilty and Payne, who was third on the indictment, pleaded not guilty. The other two went down and Payne, who in his defence put all the blame on them, was acquitted. This did not really endear Payne to Gore, and there was a good deal of animosity between the two of them.

It was clear that the next person to be seen was Freddy Gore. As a rule he was an unco-operative man, and I certainly had no wish to disclose that Payne was assisting us. The problem was solved by Payne himself. He believed he could sweet-talk Gore into co-operating, and so we arranged a meeting in Lyons Corner House in the Strand, just by Trafalgar Square. Algie Hemingway brought Gore along to where Payne and I were sitting. As soon as they walked in, Payne, who had once been described by his counsel as having the ability to charm birds off trees, rose and with a cheery 'Hello, old chap' clasped Gore to his bosom.

Within ten minutes they were sitting quite happily eating buns and drinking tea together, and Freddy Gore said, 'I don't know how to deal with you; it's like a fucking mongoose and a snake.' It was true. Under the criminal code, what Payne had done to Gore and the other man was just about the worst possible thing you could do – off-loading it onto a mate, especially after he had set it up like that – but they'd worked together before that and had been friends. Now Payne was able to charm him round again in a matter of minutes. He was a man with an almost hypnotic charm when he put his mind to it. And so Gore made a statement about the Long Firms and other frauds which had been run, and in turn also provided names, so the investigation was blossoming.

The finer points in the statements of both Payne and Gore had to be corroborated in detail and this meant far more work than Hemingway, Wright and I could handle. I applied for an enlargement of the squad and so Frank Cater, a most experienced detective who had recently been on the Richardson inquiry, was seconded to me. Originally he came because of his expertise in fraud cases, but I soon realised his great potential and made him my Number Two. In his place on the fraud side I acquired Inspector Frank Holt, who took over the very difficult task of unravelling the puzzle of the Firm's international dealings in stolen bonds. WDS Sheila Acton and

WDC Pat Allen became the first women on the squad, and they were soon joined by six other detectives. Harry Mooney, an old associate of mine from Paddington days, now a Chief Inspector who was to become both a forager and the man who kept the lid on the East End after the Krays were nicked, came from the Yard, as did Superintendent Don Adams, a very experienced administrator.

It was Frank Holt who made progress in enquiries abroad. From the information I had from Payne and Gore it was apparent that the Firm had been dealing in stolen bonds, and it was on this I had decided to build the case. Basically the deal had worked like this. Bonds are sold in America and Canada in much the same way as insurance is sold here. They are sold by government agencies or by large public companies and have a maturity date for their redemption. In the meantime they are negotiable as money. Holders usually deposit them for safe keeping in banks or safety deposit boxes, but many keep them in their homes. Burglars who found them usually left them as being worthless or accepting that they would be unable to negotiate them. However, certain elements of the Mafia, realising that there was great potential in the bonds, let it be known they would be prepared to buy as many as were on offer. In the spring of 1965 more than $500,000 of these negotiable bonds were stolen from banks in Canada. They went straight into Mafia hands who, realising they were 'hot' and difficult to dispose of in the States, contacted the Firm for help in moving them.

Payne and Gore, together with another man, went to Montreal to pick up consignments of the bonds which were given forged registration certificates and then cashed in Belgium, France and Germany. It was, as the expression goes, a nice little earner.

Another witness, Lenny Hamilton, came through Payne because Leslie had been at Esmeralda's Barn when Hamilton had been branded for picking a fight with a friend of the Firm. That was another link in the chain. Hamilton was a very reluctant witness at first. He and I met on the Embankment and, after a period of skirmishing when I had to establish my credentials, he agreed to make a statement. It was the same with other witnesses: sometimes I would take Payne along with me to convince potential witnesses that I was on the up and up. Many of them knew Payne, and if he was with me it was easier for me to say, 'He tells me this and that. Now you have a word with him.' I would often leave them with Payne to have a private chat. The potential witnesses were obviously terrified that all this would get back to the Krays, and having Payne around was something of a comfort for them, to convince them this wasn't going to be the case.

The other thing was that I wrote into the statements a kind of proviso that the statement wouldn't be used without their consent or until such time as we had substantial evidence to arrest the Krays. What I wanted to be able to assure them was that they would not be the only witness out on a limb. Indeed sometimes I did not get the witnesses to sign the statements at the time they made them. I told them I wanted the story and that I wanted names so that I could go on to other people. I would be back later to have them signed if things worked out and a court case materialised.

Almost the same day that I obtained immunity for Payne, Sylvia McVitie, together with a woman friend, walked into New Scotland Yard to report the fact that her old man Jack the Hat had been missing since the end of October. She had been in the previous November to West Ham Police Station, but the inquiry had not really got off the ground, principally because she was not able to give any definite information as to where he might have been killed. It was clear my cover was breaking down, but at that stage I couldn't help the poor woman. I didn't know any more than she did.

I did on 8 March though. Ron Coles, who had been a Detective Inspector at Aylesbury when I was there on the Train job, was now a Superintendent on the Regional Crime Squad. He rang me to say he had an informant who wanted to see me urgently.

'Where and when?' I asked immediately.

'Tomorrow, twelve-fifteen in the Sir Christopher Wren pub in the City. It's a lady who says she knows you by sight.'

This was the first of three meetings I had with this very knowledgeable lady who effectively pinpointed the site of the McVitie murder. She told me that the killing had taken place at a party in a basement flat in Evering Road, North London. She wasn't sure of the number but said it was owned by a blonde woman with two small children. This was enough to go on and I called in Sheila Acton and Pat Allen and told them what I wanted.

'No problem,' said Pat Allen, 'we can go as market researchers. It's amazing what people will tell you if you give them a packet of Daz or a carton of washing-up liquid.' That's just what they did, and a couple of days later were back with the information that when they reached No. 97 they found a blonde woman, Carol Skinner, with two children in a basement flat. I had already given instructions that no approaches were to be made to her. For the present the Krays were still free and it would not be sensible to mount a full-scale investigation. I knew only too well how seemingly staunch witnesses would find an excuse to go back on their stories. Her name was noted and that part of the enquiry, apart from observation being kept on the woman, was put into cold storage to await the arrest of the Krays.

The inquiry was not helped by the fact that to keep some semblance of cover going I had to be in the Murder Squad 'frame' for requests from the provinces or other countries for aid, and so I was sent to assist in the enquiry into an allegation of murder by a young army officer of a prostitute on a Dublin beach in 1966. The evidence was that on the morning of 15 February the body of middle-aged Peggy Flynn had been found by a swimming pool at Sandycove Point. She had been strangled both manually and with nylon stockings. The previous night she had been out drinking in Lynch's bar which she left 'not drunk but drink having been taken' as the Irish quaintly put it. In fact she went to a hostel in Harcourt Street where she was allowed to stay for a couple of hours to sober up. She was later seen getting into a Triumph Herald in Merion Street.

The inquiry did not progress well and it was not until the autumn of 1967 that Fred Gerrard sent me, along with a member of the Garda, to see the young officer in the psychiatric unit of the military Royal Victoria Hospital, Netley. He made a statement to the effect that on the night of the murder he had had a few drinks with a friend and had later picked up Peggy Flynn. A row had broken out over money and he strangled her, first with his hands and then with a stocking. He had, he said, been driving his mother's Triumph motor car.

I went back to the hospital on 18 October and took another statement, this time in the presence of the man's solicitor, in which he retracted the first statement, saying he had been confused and now doubted the accuracy of it. This was based on the fact that his mother did not have a Triumph car at the time. He had clearly been on poor terms with his family, and medical evidence was called to show that under the influence of drink and drugs he could have reconstructed and confabulated the incident from things he had read in the newspapers. Guilt over his poor relations with his family had been transferred to the present case.

This inquiry was, as far as I was concerned, an interlude which was a complete waste of time during what was becoming an increasingly demanding investigation. On 5 December, keeping up my cover, I executed a warrant for his arrest, took him back to Dublin and forgot about the case. Then, inconveniently, in March I had to return to the Central Criminal Court there to give evidence in the week-long hearing. Following a four and a half hour retirement by the jury, the officer was acquitted. To my surprise I was asked to go down to the cells where the young officer shook me by the hand and thanked me most profusely for my honesty and the fair way in which I had given my evidence.

Back outside the court, after the case, in true Irish fashion, counsel in both prosecution and defence, the officer and his family, the Garda and I all went over to the nearest pub for a celebratory few glasses of stout. Drink was taken by many that night, but as I kept saying to them I couldn't see it happening in the Magpie and Stump opposite the Old Bailey.

On my return to England, I found that now the word was out that I was conducting a major inquiry. The Yard had, much to my annoyance, leaked details of the inquiry to the press. I was not pleased to read in the *Sunday Mirror* a report that 'Gangbusters Move in on the Top Mob', nor, in the same paper, that I was investigating the murders of Cornell, Mitchell and McVitie, or that one man at Maidstone Gaol was under special protection. This sort of thing did not help my team. It was quite apparent that any vestiges of cover I had left had been well and truly blown by our side. It was a typical indication of the attitude of the mandarins who sat on the Fifth Floor and who took great delight in revealing secrets after a Friday night drinking session to ingratiate themselves with the press and show off their extensive knowledge. Added to that there was, completely without my knowledge, a member of the Kray firm working as a double agent for John du Rose.

The inquiry itself was going well enough, but I still lacked that final breakthrough I needed to make arrests with sufficient evidence to secure convictions at the end of the trial. I couldn't afford another Hideaway Club case. The order was to stand back and see what happened, and something of a stalemate had now been reached. By now it was common knowledge in the underworld that my inquiry was progressing and the Krays were prepared to do something about it. I had a call from a detective 'Ginger' Hensley, who had more informants assisting him than anyone either before or since, to warn me. 'Listen, mister,' he said, 'it's very serious. I've been all the way to Brighton to see one of my best snouts and he says it's serious and to take care. That's all he had to tell me.' A contract had been put out on both my life and that of Leslie Payne. Before then I had continued to drive to and from Tintagel House using the same route daily, but now I started to look under my car before I started and when

I went home I made sure I varied my journey. By this time, however, I was spending many a night at Tintagel House on two easy chairs pushed together. In the morning I would go for an early Turkish bath at the baths in Jermyn Street.

Then in April I had the breakthrough which was to change the emphasis of the inquiry and to force my hand. During the course of the investigation I had established strong links with the Glasgow police. We had been working closely with them because teams up there had established connections with the Krays. Glasgow itself had been having trouble with protection rackets and there had been a fairly constant interchange of personnel between London and Glasgow gangs. If the heat was too much in Glasgow, men would come south, do a few small jobs, and stay awhile until the situation had cooled down.

On a number of occasions I flew up to Scotland to see Tom Goodall, then the Detective Chief Superintendent of the Glasgow City police, who knew more than anyone else about the 'Teds' in his area. We exchanged valuable items of information and the Glasgow officers were most helpful. Suddenly our relationship bore a spectacular fruit. One of the methods of gathering information is by phone-taps – not the kind used in American films where the detective goes into a basement, opens a circuit box and places a couple of crocodile clips across a line, but legitimate intercepts. These are sanctioned by the Home Secretary himself, and before he does so there must be proof that they are essential to a major investigation.

As a result of one wire-tap I learned that one of the Krays' closest associates, Alan Bruce Cooper, was sending a man, Paul Elvey, to Glasgow to pick up some dodgy gear. I passed the information to Tom Goodall who arranged for the necessary surveillance to be carried out on Elvey who, sure enough, never dreaming he was being watched, duly collected a suitcase. He was arrested as he boarded the plane for London. The case contained three dozen sticks of dynamite. Of course, in those days, security checks prior to boarding a plane were far less stringent. There was no X-ray scanner nor a body or luggage search. Elvey was just going to place his bag in the overhead locker.

Algie Hemingway and I flew at once to Glasgow where, in a schoolroom in nearby Paisley, I interviewed Elvey. At first he denied he knew what was in the case and it was only after hours of questioning that a story slowly emerged which, on the face of it, was so fantastic that, at first, I refused to believe it.

Elvey said that Cooper had told him it was the intention of the Krays to kill a man in the West End. The idea was to rig his car to blow up when the starter was turned. It was a long time before he told me the name of the intended victim – George Caruana, a Maltese club owner who had quarrelled with the mobster Bernie Silver. Caruana owned at least one club in Soho outside the Mifsud-Silver syndicate and, so the story went, the Krays had arranged to have Caruana killed. They had nothing personally against this man but there were benefits which would accrue to the Firm by his death. The twins would firmly establish themselves as Lords of the Manor and they would be able to exert pressure on Silver – whom I am sure did not want this extreme solution to his quarrel – and gain a share in one or more of his clubs.

At first I thought Elvey was totally mad. It was only when I obtained evidence to support the account that I realised he was telling the truth. His story was that not only was he to kill Caruana but, initially, he had been recruited to kill a man in the foyer of the Old Bailey by injecting him with cyanide by means of a suitcase with a concealed hypodermic syringe, which could be operated by pulling a ring near the handle. He said he had been supplied with both suitcase and syringe, and the cyanide to go with them. The man would initially feel only a sting, and there would be plenty of time for escape.[5]

When I asked the name of the potential victim, Elvey said he didn't know. He had been supplied with a photograph of the man, but after two abortive trips to the Old Bailey with the suitcase primed he had thrown the photograph away. I didn't realise it then, but the question of the photograph was to prove crucial. Had I done so, later in the enquiry I might have prevented an unfortunate setback to the case.

This was a plan devised by Cooper who had been instructed to set it up as a test of his loyalty. Elvey, a pale-faced youth who was a qualified electrical engineer, was really not the most likely person to have been involved in the plot. Later he, Elvey, had been given a crossbow which, according to him, was a most deadly and silent weapon capable of killing at 200 yards. It was an unheard-of weapon in the 1960s. He had practised with this until he was proficient, but no victim was suggested. When I asked him where the suitcase and crossbow were he replied quite blandly, 'In my garage.'

I telephoned Frank Cater in London who organised a search. It was true. There they were in the garage, barely concealed. I sent out an 'all points' for the arrest of Cooper as a matter of urgency.

Alan Bruce Cooper was not unnaturally known as 'ABC'. He was a shadowy figure, small, of slight build with thinning hair, a strong American accent and a stutter, particularly when excited. He was a clever manipulator with the ability to persuade others to do what he dared not. As a result he had been able to walk away whilst his associates were nicked.

Even his own family was not immune. His father-in-law, a

---

[5] Much mockery was made at the committal proceedings of this plan and the charges were dismissed; but it must be remembered that this was very similar to the way in which the Bulgarian defector Markov was killed with a poisoned umbrella tip.

previously respectable man, had been sent down for a long period over his, Cooper's, involvement in an LSD drug factory. Cooper had lived on the edge of the underworld for years keeping a toe, if not a foot, in the police camp. He had been pointed out to me at Bow Street Magistrates' Court where he had been watching his father-in-law's committal proceedings, but I had never previously spoken to him.

On my return from Scotland, Cooper was brought to me at Tintagel House and the interview did not begin well. He was stuttering in his fright and told me he knew nothing about either the dynamite or Elvey.

'Fine,' I said, 'Then I'm going to charge you with conspiracy to murder and that's all there is to it.'

He then protested and asked to see John du Rose. I told him I was running the show and asked him why. What he said came as a tremendous shock.

'If you contact John du Rose,' he said in his stuttering American drawl, 'he will tell you I am his informant.' He had, he said, been John du Rose's informant and spy for up to two years.

I simply didn't believe it and asked du Rose to come and see me. He did so almost immediately and I asked him if Cooper was telling the truth and that he, du Rose, was running him.

He accepted that they had been in contact for some time, but he was, he said, not really running him as an informant as such, and had really received no information worth passing on. 'If there had been, I'd have let you know, Nipper.' At the time I was furious and du Rose knew it. I got a bit emotional and queried whether I was trusted, but John was conciliatory and played the whole thing down. Eventually I calmed down, but so far as Cooper was concerned there was to be no messing about. I insisted on taking a statement under caution from him and said that, at this stage, there was no immunity from prosecution. Cooper had little choice at this stage. He knew from my attitude that he either made the statement or faced a charge of conspiracy to murder and he chose the easier option.

When I considered the matter and remembered that my target was really the Krays I realized that I needed Cooper to support the evidence of Elvey who, on his own, would have made little impact.

As Cooper spluttered through his statement he told me how he had the murder suitcase designed and gave more information about the identity of the proposed victim at the Old Bailey. This, he said, was to have been a 'contract' killing for the Krays but he was unable to name the potential victim. However, he did agree that the explosives collected by Elvey were intended to kill Caruana and this, he insisted, was at the behest of the Krays.

Of course he knew about the deals in the bonds and explained how these were to be negotiated. An influential member of the New York Mafia, Joey Kaufman, was due to arrive any day to discuss the disposal of the bearer bonds and counterfeit currency, he said. I asked him about the McVitie and Cornell murders and the disappearance of Frank Mitchell but he assured me he simply did not know anything about them. At this stage he was so terrified I believed he was telling the truth.

I had a problem. Cooper had been in daily contact with the Krays. If he did not appear or telephone them within a matter of twenty-four hours they would know something was wrong and suspect that he had turned against them. The word from the underworld was that when it came to nicking time they might either disappear abroad, or prepare to resist arrest. The last thing I wanted was a Chicago-style shoot-out, something I had to consider. Think what would have been said if it was learned that Ronnie had shouted, 'Top of the world, ma,' as he was hit by a few rounds from a police .32. More seriously, I did not wish to have anyone's life needlessly put at risk.

Nor could I turn Cooper loose. Either he too would go to America or he would give the twins an expurgated version of what had happened to him on his arrest, with a similar result. So for the moment I had him moved under police guard to a hotel in Surrey. Clearly, however, he had to be allowed to be 'back in touch' with the Krays on my terms. Then I remembered he had had a stomach ulcer, for which he drank gallons of milk, for some time, and I thought I could use this as the best cover I could devise. I spoke to a doctor friend and had Cooper admitted to a Harley Street clinic on the pretext that his ulcer had got worse and required immediate treatment.

Diet sheets and charts were arranged and, whilst the matron and my doctor friend knew the true position, the nurses believed that Cooper was a genuine patient. He had already told us of Kaufman's proposed visit and the high-powered conference which was to follow. I therefore made him telephone Ronnie to explain that he had been taken ill and was at the clinic. My idea was that he should persuade the twins to hold the proposed meeting in his hospital room. Frank Cater and I had his room rigged with microphones whilst we sat next door with the receivers and tape-recorders. It was a good plot, but it did not work. When all was ready Cooper began his party piece. He phoned Ronnie and told him what had happened. There was an abundance of sympathy, but Ronnie regretted that after a trip to the country for the weekend they were too tired to visit him. Instead they would send Tommy Cowley with some nice eggs.

Later the Krays were to say they knew the nursing home visit was a trap, but I don't accept this. They had no reason to think it. Frank and I packed up our things and were about to leave when we received a bonus. The door to Cooper's room burst open and someone said, 'Hi there, how ya doin'?' Joey Kaufman had arrived at the same time, and the recordings of their conversation were to prove invaluable evidence. Cooper asked him how the bonds would be delivered.

'Easy,' said Kaufman, 'I'll get them mailed to my hotel, the Mayfair.' It wasn't what I had hoped for, but it certainly was better than nothing.

By now I was convinced I had to act swiftly. The Krays were going to expect to see Cooper out and about, something I could not risk. It was prohibitively expensive keeping him in the nursing home and it was not safe to keep him there anyway. He was moved back to a safe house in Surrey. He exited from his luxury hospital, quickly followed by Messrs Read and Cater. Once back at Tintagel House, Frank and I went into a huddle. I was compelled to take action. There could be no more waiting. I called John du Rose and told him of my decision.

I called the pre-arrest briefing for the early hours of 7 May. I had previously discussed it with John du Rose when we had agreed on a strategy which was devised primarily to protect the witnesses in the case of a last-minute purge by the Firm. I needed more men and now I telephoned the Detective Inspectors in each of the ten branches of the Regional Crime Squads around London, asking them to arrange for their men to be available at short notice. The DIs, in their turn, were to telephone me at midnight. When they did I put them off until 3.30 a.m. I was simply not prepared to risk any sort of leak, and when they called back I told them to report with their squads at Tintagel House at 4.30 a.m. For once I followed Tommy Butler's line and did not say why they were wanted.[6] When they arrived the instructions were simple. At 6 a.m. sharp each team was to enter premises and arrest the occupants, tell them briefly the reason, and to make a thorough search. When they left, an officer was to remain on the premises to ensure there could be no communication with any members of the Firm who had temporarily avoided capture. All those arrested were to be brought to West End Central Police Station where I had arranged for a number of cells to be made available. Some of the squads were issued with firearms, and with photographs of all suspects; watches

---

6 This policy was also adopted by Commander Bert Wickstead in his swoops on the gangs in the 1970s. Once they had assembled he would lock up the members of the raiding party in a gymnasium so there was no chance of anyone slipping away to a telephone.

were synchronised and the teams were sent away to get into position. Cater and I had reserved the twins for ourselves. Naturally we had had them under surveillance for the past twenty-four hours.

The Krays had been in the Astor Club that night. They had taken Kaufman out on the town, starting with a party in the Old Horns public house before moving up West. They left in the early hours of the morning and went back to their mother's council flat on the ninth floor of Braithwaite House, Shoreditch. At five to six we took the lift to the ninth floor and crowded round the front door listening for any sign of movement. Suddenly we heard the lift start again and then with a great clank the doors opened and a milkman appeared carrying crates. This time I did not borrow his cap. Two of my men grabbed him and before he knew what was happening he was on his way to the ground floor again. Sometimes I wonder how many times he has earned a pint with that story.

At six o'clock precisely Algie Hemingway jemmied the front door. Two minders were asleep in the living room, and by the time I followed through both the twins had been handcuffed. Ronnie was found in bed with a young boy and Reggie with a girl. They too were arrested along with the minders.

When I told Ronnie he was being arrested he replied, 'Yes, all right, Mr Read, but I've got to have my pills, you know that.' He was referring to his supply of Stematol which kept him on an even mental keel. When Frank Cater told him he could not have them he pleaded with me and asked me to bring a letter from his psychiatrist which said he had to take two a day. Reggie was sanguine about the matter, saying he had had a late night.

Back at West End Central when I told them they would be charged with conspiracy to murder, Ronnie replied, 'All I can say is it's ridiculous. Murder, I don't know nothing about murder, do I? Did you remember my pills, Mr Read? I shall have to have them.'

Reggie said, 'Yes, Mr Read, we've met like this before. We've been expecting another frame-up for a long time. But this time we've got witnesses. There's plenty of people will want to help us.'

Kaufman was arrested in his rooms at the Mayfair Hotel, a stone's throw from the Astor nightclub. He vigorously protested his innocence but, following my instructions, the officers had asked the manager to inform them when a package came for him. Sure enough two days later it arrived and, when it was sent to the Yard and opened, it contained $190,000 of stolen bearer bonds, all daubed with Mr K's fingerprints.

At the other end of the sweep was poor old Billy Exley. When I later saw him I reminded him that when I had last seen him he had told me he would get a gun to defend himself against the Krays. Now a loaded shotgun had been found at his address. 'They don't bother me, Mr Read,' he said, 'Not on their own. They know I can take care of myself. But they've been threatening the old woman and the kid.'

CHAPTER NINE

IN NOVELS, ONCE THE suspects have been arrested, the detective takes his wife or girlfriend out for dinner. There is nothing like that in real life. Back at West End Central the cells were full to overcrowding with people waiting to be interviewed and charged. There wasn't time for a sandwich, let alone breakfast. Now the first person I wanted to see was 'Blonde Carol' Skinner whose flat I believed to have been the one in which Jack McVitie had been killed. I sent officers round to Evering Road and she was brought to see me and Frank Cater at West End Central. Whilst I expected a certain amount of initial resistance, I expected that we could eventually persuade her to tell us what had happened at her flat that night. To my amazement she denied all knowledge of the Krays and was emphatic that her flat had never been used for any unlawful purpose whatsoever. Frank and I spent some time with her explaining we had the Krays and the rest of the Firm under lock and key but she never even looked like cracking. After trying everything from threats to promises we were forced to let her go. It was the old, old story: the Krays were not yet locked up securely enough to enable people to talk about them. There was still the fear of what might happen if they walked free.

Once she was gone it was a question of getting down to the problem of interviewing the suspects I thought might be prepared to say something and give them the chance to help me and, of course, themselves. Whilst I could not make any promises, I told them the final arbiter in the matter, the

Director of Public Prosecutions, might view their position sympathetically. It was a waste of time of course. They all saw this as another ploy and one which, at this stage, they could contemptuously ignore. Then there was the sorting out of what charges were to be laid against each individual, most of whom were now calling out, literally, to be allowed to see a solicitor. The easy thing about that was they almost all, at that stage, wanted to see Ralph Haeems, an articled clerk of Sampson & Co., who had taken over the running of the Krays' docket from Manny Fryde who, although he still worked for the same firm, was now getting too old for the day-to-day hassles of criminal law.

Then came the task of physically typing the charge sheets – no word-processors then – which took 36 hours, and at times I thought we were never going to get to the end of it. Indeed it was just before 12.45 a.m. on 10 May before we started to have the prisoners charged by the Duty Inspector, and it was 2 a.m. before the last charges were put to the twins. The charges at that stage were two cases of conspiracy to murder, two of blackmail, six relating to stolen bonds, four of Long Firm frauds and one of Grievous Bodily Harm. When, some time later, Peter Brodie was shown the full list of prisoners, including the additional charges I had brought, he almost clapped his hands and jumped in glee. 'I'll have this blown up and I'll have it put in the Black Museum,' he said. But he never did. The only relics of the case in that museum at Scotland Yard are a large print of the David Bailey photograph of the three Kray brothers, and the Elvey suitcase.

By this time I had been continuously on the go since 7 May. Frank Cater and I had been watching over Cooper in the nursing home for two days, and when Kaufman had left I had decided to call the conference to decide on the plan of action. When it had been agreed that we would *go* I had drawn up the plans for the arrest and briefed the troops for the 6 a.m. raids. I was beginning to feel as though I would never get to bed – I had been sleeping on a makeshift sofa at Tintagel House for some weeks – but there was still a first appearance in court to be got through, let alone dealing with an excited press corps who were not only wanting details of what had happened but were speculating on future developments. The Krays were news.

Again, in those days, there was no Crown Prosecution Service in London to whom to pass the papers and who would take over the case. On the first appearance the officer in the case had to be there to fend for himself as he asked for an adjournment, outlined the facts of the case and indicated his objections to bail. He would then have to withstand a fair battering from counsel and solicitors for the defence. It would only be later that a file would be sent to the Metropolitan Police Solicitors' Department or, as in this case, the Director of Public Prosecutions himself.

I had arranged for considerable security precautions in the No. 1 Court at Bow Street where the 18 defendants appeared before Kenneth Barraclough,[1] then one of the resident stipendiary magistrates.

Neither the twins nor Charles Kray, who were represented once again by Ivan Lawrence, opposed a remand in custody, contenting themselves with letting it be known that they were 'innocent of all charges' and would, in due course, be able to prove their innocence, but Richard Du Cann appeared on behalf of Kaufman to ask for bail which, along with an application by Gordon Anderson, accused of conspiracy to defraud, was refused. It shows how money has changed in value. Kaufman was said to be a substantial businessman earning $20,000 a year. Nine of the defendants, including Billy Exley, were given bail to reappear on 31 May.

Although I told Mr Barraclough that I had no idea when I would be in a position to proceed, as a matter of urgency I was preparing a report for the Director of Public Prosecutions. Bail may have been more difficult to obtain in the 1960s than it is today, but the other side of the coin was that the seemingly endless series of remands which occur nowadays would not

---

[1] He later became Chief Magistrate.

be tolerated. Mr Barraclough said he expected committal proceedings to begin in not much more than a month. In some ways, the real work was just starting, with such a short time in which to compile the mass of evidence and for the papers to be sent to the DPP to prepare the committal papers.

The first consideration was the protection of witnesses. Several members of the Firm had, by being out of their ground at the time, avoided the sweep. It was possible they, and others, might be able to explain to potential witnesses the folly of going ahead and helping the wicked police by giving evidence and so, once again, sabotage the enquiry. To counter this I had already arranged for the massive deployment of police officers to provide a round-the-clock guard for the principal witnesses and to move them to safe houses in various places in the Home Counties. In the whole investigation it was this aspect which gave me the most headaches. It was to Harry Mooney and his team that I consigned the responsibility of rounding up the remaining members of the Firm and they soon began to get results.

The next step was to ensure that the defendants did not all go to the same prison, where they would be under the rule of the twins, where the defences of the lesser mortals might be tailored to suit those of their masters. In the event many of them were tailored, but it did make life more difficult for them at the time. Unfortunately as the men were only on remand, this proved difficult. They would need to attend court every week for the next month and then, in some cases, on a daily basis. My choice was limited to London prisons. The twins went to Brixton, and the others to Wandsworth, where I was greatly helped by the Chief of Security at the prison, the capable Jock Ions. We got on well from the moment we met and he promised to keep his ears open and let me know when any of the men there might wish to see me. It was he who sowed seeds of doubt and discontent into the minds of those involved on the fringe; and it was he who helped me when later I went to the prison and learned the true stories of what had happened over the past years.

The press was also very helpful. They were far different men – for there were few women – from some of those whom I met later in my service. They cultivated friendships but never abused them, and it was through these friendships they got their stories. People like Percy Hoskins, Tom Tullett, Ed Vale, Owen Summers, Norman Lucas and a half-dozen more were men I could trust and, more importantly, could be relied on to help in the direction of an enquiry.

Once things had settled down I had a word with Percy Hoskins, telling him that certain people were still at large and that I wanted to unsettle them. After the initial sweeps had been completed I had handpicked 35 officers whom I placed under the direction of Harry Mooney and I sent the remainder of the Crime Squads back to their various offices. I now told Hoskins that Mooney and his team were out scouring the East End to find those members of the Firm who had escaped the first trawl. The result of a headline in the *Daily Express*, 'Krays – New Moves Today', was that on 13 May Lennie 'Books' Dunn walked into West Ham Police Station.

He had been worried sick over his involvement in the escape of Frank Mitchell from Dartmoor and the Axeman's subsequent stay at Dunn's flat in the East End. Since the news of the arrests had broken, he had been waiting for the knock on the door which would signal his own arrest, or for the shotgun though the window which would put him out of his misery. When he saw the headline he became convinced that it referred specifically to him and it prompted him to surrender. This really was a breakthrough. Now we were able to get some real idea about what had happened to Mitchell after he had failed to meet the working party for the bus ride back to the prison. It turned out to be an extraordinary story.

I drove to West Ham Police Station at once but, even whilst I was on my way, he, Dunn, swallowed tablets in a gesture at suicide. He was convinced the Krays would get him and, because of the years of indoctrination at their hands, believed that even if the police could be trusted, which he doubted, they would not be able to protect him properly. In fact, as I heard much later, he had been considered a security risk by members of the Firm and there were plans afoot to throw him from the 14th floor of a block of flats where he then lived.

Dunn was a strange little man who ran a bookstall – selling, along with other magazines and books, mildly pornographic material – in the Whitechapel street market. He was by turns nervous, servile and timid and could then display a violent temper. He had known the Krays for years – who didn't in the East End? – and had gone out of his way to scrape an acquaintanceship with them. He was typical of those who hero-worshipped them. He frequented pubs where they drank and boasted of his acquaintance. The truth was they never noticed him, but to be in the same room was sufficient. Eventually he was identified as a camp follower and he let them know that he would do virtually anything for them. One thing he did, however, was to provide magazines and books which were sent to the 'aways' – people who were serving prison sentences.

However, his relationship with the Firm changed on 12 December 1966. At this time he was living alone in a ground floor council flat in Old Barking Road and a member of the Firm asked him for the keys to his flat, saying that he wanted a friend to stay there. 'When you get home tonight, a mate of ours will be in the flat,' he was told. Of course he willingly handed them over. At last he had been of some proper service. He couldn't wait to get home that night, but when he went back after closing up his bookstall he was both amazed and, in a way, horrified to find that the friend, sitting looking at his own picture on television, was Frank Mitchell. Now he, Lennie, had arrived. From being the mild man with the porno bookstall mockingly called 'Books' or 'Booksy', he had suddenly been propelled into the big time as a fully accepted member of the Firm. He was in a caper that was causing headlines every day. He, Lennie Dunn, had made it.

But when I saw him he was a pathetic figure, constantly grasping my hand and begging me to ensure his safety. His statement, however, was dynamite. Reports of Mitchell sightings had come in from all over the world. A senior Flying

Squad officer had been appointed to collate and assess these and he was convinced Mitchell was still alive and living abroad.

Now Dunn told me of the way in which Mitchell was guarded, how a girl, Liza, a big bosomy girl and an excellent cook, more or less kidnapped from Winston's nightclub, was provided for him. She and Frank had spent most of the time in the bedroom – well, they would, wouldn't they? – but there were other details. How there was a changeover in those guarding Mitchell, how he would exercise lifting himself on the doorframe and picking up his guards one in each hand. Dunn had been trusted to leave the flat to get the groceries, but had been ordered not to go to local shops where he was known in case his suddenly quadrupled orders aroused suspicion. As he proudly told me, 'I was the victualling officer.'

Lennie went on to say how he had watched Frank painstakingly copy out letters written for him which were sent on to various newspapers, asking for a date of release. He told of the row which had broken out when a message came that once things had been arranged, Frank was to give himself up. Frank had gone mad at this news, said Lennie, threatening that the Krays should tell him this themselves and that if they didn't come to see him he would go to Vallance Road and confront them. And finally he told how on 23 December Mitchell was taken from the flat by another member of the Firm, 'Big Albert' Donaghue, and he and Liza heard what he believed were four shots fired in the street.

At this point I was jolted out of the feeling of enthusiasm I had enjoyed as Dunn told his story. Frankly I found it unbelievable. I just could not accept that Mitchell could have been brought from Dartmoor, kept in a flat and then taken away and shot in the street outside that flat. Dunn was adamant, however, and he told his story with the kind of confidence one expects from a witness of truth. I hung on to Dunn, keeping him in custody for the moment. There were, after all, still a number of senior members of the Firm on the loose, and if he was telling the truth he was a vital witness.

Despite my misgivings about Dunn's story it was,

nevertheless, a tale which had to be followed up. Curiously it was not long before there was something to back up at least part of it. Others had seen the newspapers as well. I always felt that my relationship with Billy Exley would bear fruit. When he had been locked up at West End Central after his arrest I had made sure I spoke to him alone. He had been hesitant then, but I could see possibilities for the future. On 14 May I heard, with no great surprise, that Billy Exley wanted to see me, and so a meeting was arranged in the Lambeth Palace Road. Both he and his companion, a man known as Limehouse Willey, were in a highly nervous state.

'You know I've been off the Firm for some time and I've been a dot on the fucking card,' he began, 'expecting it at any moment.' He and his friend had just been a couple of mugs, he continued. 'With regards to Mitchell, I looked after him, know what I mean? I was taking care of him.' I cautioned him and warned him that anything he said would be taken down in writing and might be used in evidence against him. It did not bother him at all but he said he thought he ought to see a solicitor.

I didn't tell him that he had been named as a guard by Lennie Dunn and that if he had not telephoned me I would have been to see him. One of my problems was that I would have liked to tell witnesses like Billy the comforting news that others were corroborating their stories, but I could not. I had given a promise to each witness that I would not abuse his confidence by telling another that he had made a statement, and I stuck rigidly to this.

I saw him two days later at Tintagel House and asked if he wanted to make a statement under caution, something he readily agreed to. It was arranged that this would be done, not in the presence of his solicitor Tommy Edwards, a Welshman who had a large practice in the Mile End Road, but that it would not be signed before Edwards had had the chance to read it. Then next day in his solicitor's office Exley signed the statement. He was still terrified someone would find out what he had done. 'No one must know about it,' he said to Edwards, 'even in your office.' Edwards assured him that the only two people who would know about it were he and his secretary.

Exley's statement opened this up even more. Until then we had no idea how Mitchell had been brought to London. Exley was the man who had hired the car and he readily gave the name and address of the car-hire company. He also confirmed that a girl had been brought in to live with Mitchell for the few days he was at liberty. He knew her as Liza and recalled that she had been keen on serving Spanish food. She had arrived at the flat in the evening gown she wore in the nightclub, and he had taken her to her home to collect some more suitable clothes for her stay. He could not remember exactly where she lived but knew it was somewhere off the Bayswater Road. Later that month he made yet another statement clearing up some of the details.

This led to what was possibly the most brilliant piece of detective work in the case. Frank Cater set out, with this fairly flimsy evidence, to trace the girl Liza. And trace her he did. A week later he caught up with her. Frank took Exley for a drive around West London to see if he could recognise the address from which he had collected the clothes. This in itself is fairly standard police procedure. If, for example, a man admits to a number of burglaries but cannot remember exactly where they took place, the same practice is adopted. Exley was able to point out the house and so Cater returned on his own and spoke to the woman occupier. She had also been a hostess and recalled Liza, but nothing much else. Cater did not give up and returned to see if the woman remembered the name of Liza's doctor. It was not such a strange request. All sensible girls in the business have regular medical check-ups. She did not, but she recalled Liza had once been taken ill at the air terminal, which had then been in the Cromwell Road where now there is a giant supermarket. The girl also had a photograph of Liza.

Next Cater toured the hospitals in the area and again struck lucky. He found the doctor who had treated her and was provided with her real name and a family address in Leeds. Enquiries were made and her mother gave us her daughter's address in Battersea. But, she said, her daughter was just about to go on a world tour with her Australian boyfriend. Cater called at the Battersea address and found he was too late. He had missed the girl. She had left the week before. But when he questioned the other tenants they said they believed Liza and her boyfriend were still in the country. They had heard that the camper in which they were to travel had broken down. They gave Cater the name of the Paddington workshop to which it had been taken.

By the time Frank found the shop it was closed, but he did get – from the owner who lived in the flat above – the details of a car he had hired to them whilst their van was being repaired. He thought they were living in the Earls Court area, a home from home for young Australians, and Frank began a despairing sweep of the area. Earls Court was Little Australia, and his chances of finding the couple or the vehicle were almost nil. But he was always a lucky so-and-so. At about 2 a.m. he found the car parked outside a hotel. When he spoke to the hotel manager he knew his search had ended. He found Liza asleep in a bedroom on the second floor, woke her and told her she was being taken to New Scotland Yard to talk about Frank Mitchell.

He contacted me and then immediately set off for Tintagel House. As the car turned to cross Lambeth Bridge – nowhere near Westminster – Liza began to panic. She repeatedly asked where she was being taken and was told she was going to the Yard to see Superintendent Read. She was of course going to Tintagel House, but it was thought the word 'Yard' would calm her. Now she was crossing the river she became absolutely convinced the officers were part of the Firm and were out to kill her. As the car slowed for traffic lights she opened the car door and tried to run towards the bridge to throw herself into the Thames. Cater pulled her back into the car and tried to calm her. Suddenly she asked to see his hand. She ran her fingers over his palm and then quietened down. She had realised that he was a genuine police officer. When he asked her about it she replied, 'You don't have working men's hands.'

When I saw her she was still frightened but was much calmer. She was a handsome, well built rather than pretty girl with an exuberant personality. She could make you believe you were the only person in the room to whom she wanted to talk, and it was easy to see how she was a good hostess. What was more important from our point of view was that she also had an almost photographic memory. She could remember dates, times, places, what people said, what they were wearing, even what they ate. I was convinced from the start that I had here an outstanding witness. As I later discovered, she had an outstanding temper as well.

I began to go through her story of the bizarre circumstances of her involvement in the Mitchell mystery. She had been working as a hostess one night at Winston's when Reggie Kray and another man had virtually forced her into a waiting cab. She had been driven to East London and presented to 'Big Frank' as a gift. At first she had not been too keen on the arrangement but in her words, 'As time passed I was lost'. She described him as a 'ruthless demanding lover whose primitive passions electrified me'.

She confirmed Dunn and Exley's story, supplying more details of her own. As the story went on I waited, with bated breath, to hear what she had to say about the evening Mitchell disappeared. She confirmed she had heard shots and that some time afterwards Albert Donaghue had returned and made a telephone call saying, 'That dog is dead.'

'That was the moment,' she said, 'when I knew they'd killed Frank Mitchell.' Later that day she was ordered to attend a party the Krays were giving. There she was handed £100 and told she had earned the respect of everyone in the East End. She was also warned that she should keep her mouth shut about anything to do with Mitchell or, she said, she would be followed to the ends of the earth and would be dealt with.

When I saw her on 22 May I noted, 'Terrified of Krays – living under a cloud – saved her life – protection – appears very truthful – excellent memory'.

So far so good, but it was still the stories of Dunn, Exley and now Liza and no physical evidence. Donaghue had returned to the flat which he had wiped clean of fingerprints from doorknobs, lavatory handles, even light bulbs. A balaclava belonging to Mitchell had been taken away and burned. Everything relating to Mitchell's ten days there had been removed. Had she, I asked, any small keepsake from Frank? Fortunately she had kept a calendar taken from a magazine which Mitchell had given her. It was ringed with dates but we could not work out their significance, nor did she seem to know. She also produced a prison issue comb which she told us Mitchell had given her and which she had kept hidden from Donaghue. Thank God for her sentimental attachment.

I had the comb and calendar sent down to the prison but without much hope that they could be linked to Mitchell. Back came the totally unexpected reply from a prisoner that the calendar had belonged to him. The ringed dates were the ones when his budgies had hatched their eggs. The prisoner had given the calendar to Mitchell just two days before the Axeman had escaped.

This was a help but it was still not enough. Now I sent officers to Dartmoor Prison to go through the visitors' book there and to make enquiries at locals pubs and garages. As a result a young woman was traced who had been to visit Mitchell along with Firm members when they had told him of the plans for his escape. She had been to the Moor in May and June of 1965 with two brothers, who later gave evidence in the trial, when they had timed the route and later gave Frank the final details for his escape.

I now had enough evidence to prefer charges against three men for harbouring Mitchell. Later I was to charge the twins and Charles Kray with the same offence.

There was still, however, one major problem and that was the fact that there was no body. It was a similar problem in the case of McVitie. At one time it had been thought in English law that with no body there could be no proof of murder. The jurist Hale in the eighteenth century had laid down the proposition 'Never to convict any person of murder or manslaughter without the body being found', but that theory had been gradually whittled away in a series of cases.

In a South African case in 1879 the Chief Justice Sir H. De Villiers had commented:

> I never understood the law as to the *corpus delicti* to go as far as to hold that where witnesses swear they saw the person shot by means of a gun, and where they saw the deceased actually dying, a jury may be called upon to say there is no proof of death whatsoever.

Then in 1884 two seamen, Dudley and Stephens, had been shipwrecked along with a cabin boy whom they killed and ate while drifting on the seas, waiting for their rescue. It had been accepted in such a case that there need be no body. It was a similar situation in the 1948 case of James Camb, when a ship's steward was convicted of the murder of an actress Gay Gibson. Her body had been pushed through a porthole and had never been found.

But that still left cases where there was no body and where the allegation was that the murder had taken place on the land. In 1955 in the case of Onufrejczyk, a Polish farmer accused of killing his partner, the body was never found, but it was held that 'before a defendant could be convicted the fact of death should be proved by such circumstantial evidence as render the commission of the crime certain and leave no ground for reasonable doubt.'[2]

However, I now felt there was sufficient evidence to make charges in respect of Mitchell's murder, and three weeks after the Krays had been arrested they were charged with their first murder. In all, ten people were charged with Frank Mitchell's escape, harbouring and disappearance.

---

2 Archbold, *Pleading, Evidence and Practice in Criminal Cases*, ed. Stephen Mitchell QC MA and P.J. Richardson LLM LLB. 43rd edition (1988), Sweet & Maxwell, London.

I was well pleased with the progress that was made in that direction, but my actions did not suit prosecuting counsel. By this time of course the Director of Public Prosecutions, in the shape of David Hopkin, had been involved, and he had briefed leading counsel Kenneth Jones, with John Leonard as his junior. Both were to go on to become High Court judges. We were having regular conferences at chambers in the Temple, and once when we met, both of them complained strongly about my charging people with murder without my first consulting them. I told them that I believed, and I still do, that the officer in charge of a case should demonstrate that he is the one who is in charge. I take the view that the lawyers are responsible for the proper presentation of a case before a court and are in no way in charge of, or responsible for, an investigation into current matters. I know that this view was not liked by the lawyers, and with the coming of the Crown Prosecution Service there is now a different relationship between the investigating officer and the prosecutor. Nevertheless, I still firmly believe that a police officer is a police officer and a lawyer is a lawyer and that, whilst co-operation between them is essential, the two have very different functions in the criminal justice process.

Meanwhile I was still trying to find more evidence regarding the conspiracy to kill a man at the Old Bailey using the trick suitcase. An ex-speedway rider, 'Split' Waterman, a friend of Cooper's who was then serving a prison sentence for gold smuggling, was brought to me at Tintagel House. He agreed he had made the suitcase, of which he was rather proud, calling it 'a beautiful piece of craftsmanship' – but was unable to say anything else. It *was* a beautiful piece of craftsmanship. It was designed to allow a syringe to be hidden in the fabric with the needle protruding through the outer hide of the case. By pulling a small ring near the handle the contents of the syringe could be discharged. Waterman realised, of course, it was to be used to kill someone but he had neither the name of the proposed victim nor who was to use it. Indeed he made the point to me that one of his conditions when he made the case was that he was not to be told such details. It was not much in the way of evidence but, at least, it confirmed the story in my own mind.

When the Home Office pathologist, the late Professor Francis Camps, examined the case he described it as the most deadly murder weapon he had ever seen. He said that, had it been used properly, the victim would have been dead within eight seconds. He also added that the effect of the proposed poison would be to simulate a heart attack, and that no one would be able to identify this as murder, with the sole exception of himself, he told me modestly.

We were struggling with this one, and it was only much later that I heard the full story which went back to 1965. Apparently a friend of the Firm had been shot by a man who had discovered his victim had been having an affair with his wife. The victim had sought revenge and a plan had been hatched to kill this attacker. Watch had been kept but, unfortunately, the retribution was handed out to the wrong man. The proposed victim was walking along Cheshire Street together with a man called Ginger Marks, when a car drew up beside them and someone called out. Marks must have thought he heard his nickname 'Ginge' and stepped forward only to be shot and killed. The body was bundled into the car and driven off. The other man had, by now, run around the corner and climbed under a lorry parked there, clinging to the transmission link. When the mistake was discovered the 'contract' was renewed and the intention was to use the suitcase to kill the man. According to Elvey he had been given a photograph of the proposed victim, but he had destroyed it. It was only later when the man was named that a thought struck me.

When we had arrested the twins at Braithwaite House, the premises had been searched. Amongst the material taken away were two photographs taken in a club. The face of one man had been cut out. Although it was now really only of personal interest, I arranged with the photographer to produce his original and there in a group of three was the intended victim. It was his face which had been cut out and handed to Elvey.

There was also the continuing problem of the disappearance of McVitie. I had first interviewed Carol Skinner on 8 May when she had denied all knowledge of McVitie's death. She was seen again five days later by Harry Mooney when she made a statement confirming she knew nothing. This time I organised a search of her address but this revealed nothing that would positively identify the flat as the place where McVitie had died, and so once again the matter had to rest for the moment.

By the end of May, and with the remand hearing when those on bail would once again stand in the dock getting nearer, I began to hear whispers that one of the defendants in custody wanted to see me. In a serious case there is always likely to be one defendant who is on the fringe of things who wishes to try and improve his position, either by giving a bit of information on the side or by coming out and turning Queen's Evidence. As I have said, I put the matter to all the defendants when I had first seen them at the time of their arrests. I had been blanked out by them, and whilst I hoped someone would ask to see me – and indeed Willey and Exley had – I certainly would have given long odds against Charlie Mitchell sending out signals for help. I was also to learn from him just how much I was thought to be worth.

I had always regarded Mitchell, who had been accused of involvement in a number of the Long Firm frauds, as a real hard nose. He had maintained a cool detachment when he had been arrested, declining to answer questions without a solicitor, and although I had told him that if ever he wished to see me I would be available, he was one of the last people from whom I expected to hear.

The call asking me to go to see him came from his wife, and I went to see him in the afternoon of 5 June. He was quite straightforward about things, telling me he realised what the likely outcome of things would be and that he wanted to make a statement. I warned him it would have to be under caution. He said that he understood, and I went back to see him the next evening just before 6.30 and again on the following Sunday morning. What he told me was shattering. There had been a contract out on both me and Leslie Payne with a price of £50,000 for the pair of us. He, Mitchell, a wealthy man, had been the one who had been instructed to find the money and, so he said, a man had been hired in New York to come over and do the job.

Things fell into place because during a strip search of the cell of one of the defendants a series of messages had been found on toilet paper instructing someone called 'Junior' to 'do the business'. As a result I went to see an old friend, Alden McCray, head of the FBI in Europe and, as a matter of urgency, he had enquiries made back in the States. Incredible though it may seem, there really was such a man. He went under the name of Junior, and was stopped on information when he landed at Shannon Airport on his way to London. He was picked up at the gate, spoken to firmly and put on the next flight back home. I felt happier then.

So far as I was concerned, the turning of Mitchell was an incredible step forward in the investigation. The more I heard from him the more I was convinced he should be a prosecution witness, something with which David Hopkin, Kenneth Jones and John Leonard agreed. The effect it had on the Krays when his duplicity was revealed in court, from our point of view, could not have been better. As a matter of fact it was fantastic.

The No. 1 Court at Bow Street is a fine old panelled room which has seen some famous defendants pass through it. One of the first of these in the 1750s was the Italian adventurer Casanova, who was ordered to provide sureties for his good behaviour by the blind magistrate Sir John Fielding, brother of Henry who wrote *Tom Jones*. Other visitors have included such different figures as Crippen, together with his mistress Ethel Le Neve, Lord Haw Haw, and more recently Ernest Saunders and the other defendants charged in the Guinness case. The dock facing the magistrate, however, is small, holding four comfortably and five at a pinch. There was no possible way it could hold all the defendants in the Kray case at the same time and so we had had built a 'super dock'. On 25 June, the day of Mitchell's defection, they were all sitting there in their usual studiously unconcerned way when Kenneth Jones asked that Mitchell be allowed to stand down.

'He [Mitchell] has made a complete statement and it has been decided he should be used as a prosecution witness,' he told the Court.

Mitchell walked from the back row as though he was going to collect a prize at a Sunday School. Even then the twins could not believe what was going on. It was only later they realised the full implication of the betrayal and, by then, it was too late for them to show their displeasure in a tangible way.

Once Mitchell had come forward the message started to filter through to the lesser fry that there might be something to be gained from co-operation. It was not a message which Jock Ions discouraged. The next person who asked to see me was really rather a nice guy: Michael Kenrick, a fraudsman, who was one of the few members of the Firm for whom I had any sympathy.

I saw him late the next evening in Wormwood Scrubs where he was serving a five-year sentence. Kenrick was desperately afraid for his wife and child and concerned what might happen if the Krays knew I had been to see him. He was convinced that Alan Cooper had informed against him but I assured him his arrest was as the result of long observations by DI Holt and other members of my squad. Kenrick was presently charged with handling the forged bonds but could not face what he thought was bound to be a consecutive sentence. Unfortunately there was little that Kenrick could tell me. He was merely a pawn in the game but I promised to go back to see him. I wish I could have foreseen the consequences of that visit.

Now, parallel with the prisoners' fear, a further worry grew in my mind. I was fearful that news – which travels like lightning on a prison grapevine – would carry back to the twins. It was absolutely necessary that the meetings with the defendants took place away from the main wings of the prisons and out of normal hours. Algie Hemingway, my Sergeant, was keen on amateur dramatics and it was he who first 'became' a parson. He obtained the black stock and white collar and really looked the part much better than I did. He had something of a spiritual face and, as a practising Christian, could also bolster the disguise with the right word, quotation or gesture. We had kept observation together at London Airport on the gold and counterfeit smuggling offshoot of the main enquiry. He would be there as a cleric whilst I had a peaked cap to add to my grey suit. Who notices a chauffeur?

By the time the defendants were on remand in custody I had become the parson giving spiritual comfort in the prison chapel, helped by Jock Ions. I was able to carry a tape-recorder in a cardboard box which from a distance looked just like a Bible. I was also leaking little snippets of information which I knew would be passed about the prison to suggest that I was seeing far more people than, in fact, I was. The intention of this ploy was both to take the heat off those whom I was seeing and, at the same time, to cause more worry and discomfort to the others.

By the middle of June the defendants were beginning to break rank and at least a mild panic had set in. The next person to ask to see me was Cornelius Whitehead, later charged with being an accessory after the fact to McVitie's murder, the murder of Frank Mitchell, being an accessory after the fact to his murder, harbouring him after his escape, and a number of other matters. I saw him alone in the chapel at Wandsworth Prison on 22 June. In fact it turned out to be a feeling-out operation on both sides. I always believed him to be a fence-sitter and so it turned out. He was keen to tell me that those charged with the murder of Frank Mitchell had something which would 'definitely get them out'. He would not tell me what it was, preferring to say he would have to use it himself if the charges were not dropped against him. I told him that now matters were in the hands of the lawyers for the Crown and that to a great extent things were out of my hands.

The next day it was back to Wandsworth Prison in the evening to visit Tommy Cowley who also wanted to see me. He had been charged with two cases of conspiracy to murder and with harbouring Frank Mitchell. This was another probing exercise. He denied all knowledge of the charges, saying the witnesses were telling lies abut him. Now he was 'on the list'. Had he seen me with the authority and approval of the Krays? If not he was a marked man.

Four days after that I had a message from Jock Ions that John 'Scotch Jack' Dickson had asked for me. I saw him that evening in the chapel, in a meeting which lasted some twenty-five minutes and ended with him saying, 'For Christ's sake don't let anybody know you've seen me. I'd be dead. You know that, being here.' What he did not know was that he had become only one of a number who had the same fears.

These meetings were not all that productive. True, I was getting confirmation that the ranks were splitting, and confirmation also that McVitie really was dead, but it wasn't getting me that much further in the enquiries. I was also hampered by Harry, a small-time thief who told me he was able to pinpoint the spot where Mitchell's body was buried. In any investigation there are always a number of people who will offer help which turns out to be totally useless. They do it for a number of reasons. Sometimes they genuinely think they have evidence to offer, but more often it is because they think they can obtain some benefit in the way of reward money or help in their quest for remission or parole. Sometimes they do it just to make themselves feel important. The difficulty from an investigating officer's point of view is that until their evidence is proved to be absolutely worthless they cannot be disregarded. One of these was a small-time thief, really not much more than a gas-meter bandit, whom I first saw in Brixton Prison on 28 June.

On the face of it he was able to give some quite positive evidence and could place the spot where Mitchell had been buried. I made totally unsuccessful enquiries, and the next day when I saw him again I spoke to him sharply, telling him I was not satisfied he was speaking the truth.

'Mr Read, I wouldn't have called you here if I wasn't. I thought I'd convinced you yesterday,' was the plaintive reply.

I warned him of the consequences of perjury if he gave evidence which he knew was false, and with wasting police time, but he was quite adamant that he knew where Mitchell had been buried and so I obtained his release from prison for the afternoon. He led us a merry dance down to a farm near Tilbury. I had arranged that the Home Office would provide a team with an imagiser and there were hefty lads from the Crime Squad digging up what seemed to be acres of farmland. Within minutes what had been reasonable-looking pasture land looked like a First World War battlefield. It was all to no avail, and when I delivered the man back to Brixton I threatened him with all sorts of recriminations but he stuck to his story, saying that if he failed to find the place it was because it had been dark when he first went there. All he really wanted was an afternoon out in the country. When it came to it there was no point in wasting any more time on him.

And suddenly, after wasting valuable time with Harry, there was a major breakthrough. John Alexander Barrie, known as Ian, was arrested by Harry Mooney on Saturday 29 June as, broke, lonely, and rudderless without the Firm to guide him, he wandered back into the East End for a drink. The next day the barmaid at the Blind Beggar at the time of Cornell's shooting was brought to see me. She said she thought she could identify the second man.

'I think I could if I see him in person,' she said. 'To be honest I'm still terrified, but I'm going to see it through. I've made up my mind,' she told me. 'I'm not so sure of the second man as I am of Ronnie. It's his face. I only have to look at it to be scared, but I'm not so bad with the second man.' I asked her if she had seen that man either before or after the shooting and she said she had not.

All this was the result of the patience of Harry Mooney. I had told him to keep in touch with the barmaid, and he had done so faithfully, trying to calm her down and make sure she understood that she really had nothing to fear now the Firm had been arrested. Her children were mad keen on aeroplanes, and together with WDC Pat Allen, he would collect them all, most Sunday mornings, and take them to London Airport. Once there sometimes he went off with the kids to the observation gallery whilst Pat Allen stayed and chatted about things. Sometimes it was the other way about. Finally he had succeeded in gaining her complete confidence.

I saw Barrie in the cells at Bow Street magistrates' court about two hours after seeing the barmaid. I told him he was going to be charged with Cornell's murder, and that I had reason to believe the gun used was still in his constructive possession – in other words he knew where it was.

'I don't know where the gun is – that's the truth,' was his reply. He went on to deny any knowledge of the shooting but admitted he had been with Ronnie Kray that night.

So far as I was concerned this was sufficient. I did not want to hold an identification parade, causing my witness what would undoubtedly be considerable strain. If she picked him out it was no more than she was expected to do. If she failed to pick him out, whilst it would not be surprising after all the passage of time, it would be something seized upon by the defence.

I therefore charged Barrie and he appeared at court the following day. It was then David Hopkin intervened. He and counsel in the case considered it essential that an identification parade be held and despite my protestations they were adamant.

One of the problems was that Barrie had a distinctive scar down his face. The aim of an identification parade is to produce 'foils' who are of the same physical appearance. We could not find another eight scarred men, and so each member of the parade had a piece of sticking-plaster on his face. Imagine my delight when on 3 July the barmaid attended an identification parade at West End Central Police Station, calmly walked down the line and unhesitatingly picked out Barrie. Tommy Butler would have been pleased that after all the months of frustration he had endured things were now resolved and two men had been charged. Things were really starting to move.

Another part of the investigation began when, two days later, I received a letter from Chrissie Mills, the widow of Freddie, the former world light-heavyweight champion who had been found shot dead in his car in an alleyway outside a nightclub he owned at the top end of the Charing Cross Road in 1965. He had been shot through the right eye with a gun owned by, and borrowed from, a woman friend from the days when he had worked in a boxing booth on fairgrounds. Chrissie Mills was unwilling to accept the coroner's verdict that he had committed suicide, was convinced he had been murdered and asked me to look into his death. She also believed the Krays, who were regular visitors to his club, had been involved. This was just one of a number of alternatives to the official verdict which were flying around. In general, most people who knew Freddie could not believe that he would have killed himself.

The most usual version of the rumours had been that a gang operating a protection racket had been rebuffed when they had approached Freddie. Some time later one of the other small-club owners in the West End had been warned to keep up his payments – or else. He had been told that something would soon happen in the West End which would underline the warning. The something was Freddie's death.

For me and many in my generation Freddie had been a hero. Originally a fairground-booth fighter, he had been a boxer, not often showing a great deal of skill – you could see his punches starting somewhere near ground level – but with the heart of a lion. In a career lasting 14 years he had just short of 100 contests and innumerable battles in fairground booths. He had two contests for the world title with Gus Lesnevitch at the old Harringay Arena which are still regarded as amongst the best bouts ever. He took a terrible beating in the first contest in May 1946 when he was stopped in the 10th round but, in the second, two years later, he changed his tactics and, showing more style than usual, won on points. He told Frank Butler, the boxing writer who later became a member of the British Boxing Board of Control that, after his mauling by Lesnevitch, he had started to suffer from terrible headaches. I was one of thousands who saw Freddie give another gutsy performance defending his world light-heavyweight title against Joey Maxim at the Earl's Court Stadium on 24 January 1950. But he wasn't the Freddie of old and it was no real surprise when he was knocked out in the 10th round.

That was the last bout of his career. Very sensibly, he retired and became a celebrity, appearing in pantomime, on television on the famous 'Six-Five Special' programme with Pete Murray and Josephine Douglas, as well as being in constant demand to make public appearances opening fêtes and shops. Freddie was notorious for forgetting his lines, but his enthusiasm, personality and good looks carried him through. He was the Frank Bruno of his time.

Really, nothing would have given me more pleasure than being able to show that Freddie had not committed suicide. In those days there was much more of a stigma attached to the act than there is today. Moreover, if I could link the Krays to it my investigation would have a major boost. It would have been beautiful to have tagged this murder to them.

In his book[3] Bill Bavin suggests that I called to see Mrs Mills on 24 July 1968, disturbing her and her daughters as they were setting off to the cemetery on the anniversary of Freddie's death. This prompted him to speculate why in the middle of an investigation as important as the Kray enquiry I should make a casual visit to Tulse Hill on the off-chance of seeing Mrs Mills. In fact this part of the investigation took its place in the order of things and I did not go to see Chrissie until 5 August to keep an appointment I had made by telephone several days earlier. She was pleased to see me and her attitude was, 'Good, now something will happen.' She was utterly convinced Freddie did not commit suicide, but as for hard facts she could add little to what was common knowledge.

In essence the murder theory ran as follows. The Krays had been known to take over clubs. The Krays frequented

---

[3] Bavin, B. *The Strange Death of Freddie Mills* (1975).

Mills's club. There was money missing from Freddie's estate – something like £12,000, which was big money in the 1950s. There had been an unsuccessful arson attack on the club. There was the story that some weeks before Freddie's death small club owners who were a bit lax in paying were told something big was going to happen and this would be an example to them. Freddie had obtained a gun to protect himself and he had left the club saying he was going to an appointment. Usually Chrissie went with him to the club, but on that night she had been delayed and he had gone on alone. Therefore, so the theory ran, it all fell into place and Freddie had been killed to get hold of his club.

Chrissie Mills formally confirmed matters which were more or less common knowledge. Freddie had been an equal partner with Andy Ho in the club. The Krays, whom Freddie knew through Jack Solomons – the major boxing promoter of the 1940s and early 50s – were regular visitors to his club. It was no secret. There were dozens of photographs to prove this.

Chrissie also told me that her husband often used to go and sleep in his car in the alleyway. Andy Ho did not confirm this when I saw him.

But no one I asked could come up with anything. There was nothing from the West End, not a whisper. Faces I questioned would say, 'Oh Guv, you know better than that.' One heavy involved in such rackets to whom I spoke replied, 'We don't make examples of other people. If somebody don't pay we break *his* legs not somebody else's.' I talked to those members of the Firm who had collected money; the response was always the same. 'Freddie – no way,' they said. 'When the twins went to Freddie's place they paid. They'd never nip him. They were boxers too. He was their hero. You can bet every time they went there they paid. No danger.' I also spoke to those members of the Firm who were collectors in the West End. They confirmed Freddie's club had never been on the list.

I tried the other criminal elements in the West End who would certainly have known if Freddie had been in the grip of protection racketeers – in truth there weren't many – and again the answer was the same. Freddie was clear – there was no pressure from anyone.

One reply to that is 'well they would say that, wouldn't they?' But remember the atmosphere at the time. I was dealing with the dismemberment of the most organised gang ever established in this country. A number of lesser lights were going to be put out at the same time and 'bottles' were going.

In the end I could find no evidence to support the theory that the Krays or indeed anyone else had been involved in Freddie's death. The club was not doing well. Trade had fallen off disastrously and it wasn't worth taking over – even for free. Despite what Chrissie loyally said, Freddie had been a terrible businessman. He should never, in this world, have had a nightclub. When it was Freddie Mills's Chinese Restaurant it was fine. This was a new fad and Freddie with his bubbling personality made the customers welcome. But Freddie Mills's Nite Spot. . .! I suppose it was an effort to cash in on the girls and drinks racket, but it was not Freddie's scene. He was far too straight for that sort of business.

There were other problems, including the fact that he was a gambler. Chrissie said a regular but good one, but even the best have losing streaks. Somewhere along the line he had also had a girlfriend. Chrissie knew her name but we never saw her. She had covered her tracks and although, if I had mounted a major campaign, there is little doubt we would have been able to identify her, I did not think it worth while.

As with so many other sporting celebrities, his star was fading. Others younger were coming to take his place on the programmes. A great friend Michael Holliday who had appeared with him on the 'Six-Five Special' show had killed himself and he, Freddie, had been turned down as a member of a panel set up to discuss the Clay–Liston fight on television.

There were other, more disturbing problems connected with the club. Shortly before his death, the *Sunday People* ran an exposé claiming that some of the women who frequented the club were in fact prostitutes posing as hostesses. There was also a story that a round of drinks and a plate of sandwiches had cost £19 – a fortune at the time. There was no suggestion that either Freddie or Andy Ho had been involved, and clearly the villain was one of the waiters, but it did nothing for his image. Freddie was so upset he issued a writ for libel, but this was dropped when the newspaper produced proof of the allegations. He had also had a bad dose of flu – almost pneumonia – and had asked whether he could have a 'few quiet words' with his doctor. Andy Ho thought he was depressed.

What is certain is that he went to an old fairground acquaintance, May Ronaldson, who ran a shooting stall at Battersea Pleasure Gardens, a hangover from the Festival of Britain. He told her he was opening a fête in Esher the next week and was going dressed as a cowboy. When he asked to borrow a rifle, she readily lent him one, and he soon returned it. In the meantime he and Andy Ho had been summoned for supplying drink to customers who were not taking a proper meal, and for having an illegal fruit machine on the premises. The magistrates had fined them each £50. It cannot have helped Freddie's self-esteem.

A week or so later Freddie went back to May Ronaldson to borrow the rifle again. This time on the mantlepiece there were some of those rifle range bullets that have a soft head so they do not ricochet. May Ronaldson left him alone for a few moments to go and make a cup of tea and, I believe, it was then he took the bullet. Indeed sometime later she noticed three of the bullets were missing. It was with this rifle that he was killed. I am convinced that on the previous visit he had not seen any bullets. Now he had.

There are still many unanswered questions about Freddie's death. If, as he suggested to Chrissie, he was going to keep an appointment, why not at the club rather than in his car outside? It has been suggested that this was because the location was one favoured by villains – somewhere in the dark, away from the public's view. Well, that's not my experience. Villains are as cautious as the next man about meets, but not the kind of villain we are now talking about. Not the Krays or others involved in protection rackets. If they had a meet it would be in a club or at a house or pub. Certainly somewhere in public. This was how the Krays did their killings and inflicted grievous bodily harm: in public, confident that the silence of witnesses could be assured. Such actions were displays of their strength and invincibility. They didn't shoot people where no one could see them. Moreover, blackmailers and enforcers as a body do not send messages saying 'watch this space in a couple of weeks' time'. They arrive in force, smash up a club and administer public beatings. That is the proven way they establish the fear necessary to be successful.

It is suggested that, fearing some action by people of this kind, Freddie took the gun to protect himself, but I do not really regard this as feasible. Would he have chosen a cumbersome, single shot, old fairground rifle as a weapon and then restricted himself even more by hoping to use it inside the limited space of a car? I cannot believe it. I do not think for a moment he was being threatened. I cannot see him as the sort of person to be intimidated. And if he had been, despite his troubles, he had more than enough friends and admirers in the police who would have come to his rescue.

Perhaps Freddie just took the opportunity of going outside when his wife was not there.

Great play was made in Bavin's book that Gavin Thurston, the experienced Coroner, sat without a jury. This is quite normal unless the coroner believes there is some doubt about the evidence requiring the intervention of a jury. Then Bavin also suggests as an argument against suicide that the bullet actually entered Mills's eye. No one, he declares, would choose the eye as a suitable location. It could also be argued with equal vehemence that the eye is not the usual target of an assailant. There is no doubt that the eye as the site of injury is most unusual. There is something repugnant, in most people's minds, about putting a bullet through one's eye. Certainly the temple or mouth is the more usual target.

I am sure, however, that the eye was not chosen as the site. I believe he chose to shoot himself in the forehead and, at the moment of pulling the trigger, jerked the weapon, causing the bullet to be deflected into the eye. Keith Simpson, the very senior Home Office pathologist who was also an expert in the use of firearms, was quite satisfied the wound was self-inflicted.

One more thing was suggested as being peculiar, and that was there was no suicide note. In my experience, and I have dealt with scores of similar cases, the majority of suicides do not leave notes.

Freddie's death occurred at around the time the killings known as the Jack the Stripper murders ceased. I was never involved in the investigation into these murders of six prostitutes in the Hammersmith area, most of whom had had oral sex at the time of their death. All were found naked and this led to the nickname for the murderer. John du Rose, who led the investigation, suggested that the man responsible must have had considerable strength and have been in his forties. The investigation closed when, after the discovery of the last body in January 1965, a man committed suicide. The man, who was never named, had been a boxer. Quite wrongly two and two were put together to make five and the rumour grew that the boxer had been Freddie Mills. When I first heard this outrageous rumour I was lecturing at the Police Academy in Wakefield and I was horrified. These rumours were outrageous for there is no justification for any suggestion that Freddie was, in any way, a suspect in the investigation. I said then as I do now, with as much force as I can, that Freddie Mills was never, in any way, involved in this investigation.

When I told Chrissie that my enquiries had come to nothing she was clearly disappointed. Chrissie Mills is not alone in believing that her husband was murdered. Even today many people, including some of my colleagues on the Boxing Board of Control, are unwilling to accept that their and my great hero could have killed himself 'Whatever, you say, Nipper,' Bill Martin, a sportswriter and great friend of Freddie's told me only recently, 'I was with him just a few days before he died and he just did not give me the impression of a man who would commit suicide. I'll never believe he wasn't murdered.' However, I have to look at it on the evidence and, based on that, I am sadly forced to the inescapable conclusion that he did, in fact, take his own life.

But, as his daughter Susan said, 'It is irrelevant now whether it was suicide or he was killed as some people think. Whatever happened it will never bring him back. I am so happy I was able to have that sort of person as a father.'

I agree. So far as I am concerned Freddie Mills is still a great champion.

CHAPTER TEN

WHILST ALL THIS WAS going on the lawyers for the defendants, led by Ralph Haeems, the articled clerk from Sampson & Co., were, quite properly, on the attack. Apart from making regular demands for bail which were repeatedly refused by Kenneth Barraclough and his colleagues at Bow Street, Geraint Rees and Frank Milton,[1] they were clamouring to know exactly who were the victims not named in the charge of conspiracy to murder. The first of the committals was to start by the end of June and they would have to know then. There were sound reasons, however, why I had left out their names. First, I was afraid that had they been named they would have been approached to persuade them to change their minds about giving evidence, and one of the persuading techniques would have been physical violence. I also have to say that it was a good tactical move. The very fact that the defence appeared so concerned satisfied me they were worried.

Prior to 1967 all remand hearings and committal proceedings could be reported in full by the press and it was the daily bread and butter of court reporters who were then a fixture in the magistrates' courts. Many lawyers felt that this was unfair and the defendant suffered by having the allegations against him or her reported week by week in quite a sensational way. After all, at this stage, the defendant had no real chance of calling

[1] In turn he too became Chief Magistrate.

evidence and all he could do was to say he totally denied the charges. He was, it was thought, having his trial prejudiced. The Criminal Justice Act 1967 had changed things just in time to protect the Krays from weeks of adverse publicity. Now reporting restrictions were in force, all the press could tell the public were the names and addresses of the defendants, details of the charges they faced and the result of bail applications and committal proceedings. The reporting restrictions could only be lifted at the request of the defendants – or any one of them. It was something I hoped, but doubted, would happen, but it was just what Paul Wrightson did on behalf of Reggie Kray.

I could hardly believe it when on 17 May, before the charges for the murders of Cornell, Mitchell and McVitie were brought, he applied to the magistrate of the day, Geraint Rees, for the restrictions to be lifted. For what reason had this very experienced counsel lifted the veil?

This now meant that the press could report all the cut and thrust of the bail applications and hear the reasons David Hopkin, for the DPP, and I gave when we opposed bail. It was a brave, if risky, move and one which, had the Krays realised actual murder charges were in the pipeline, he probably would not have made. After all, at that stage things were still fairly nebulous. There were two conspiracies to murder with, quite frankly, not the best of evidence to support them, and a series of fraud charges. I think the Krays still believed in the strength of their organisation and that no more serious charges would be brought. Certainly Paul Wrightson later admitted before the Court of Appeal that he had been wrong when unsuccessfully applying for the reporting restrictions to be re-imposed.[2] I have always thought it was one of the worst tactical mistakes made by the defence in the whole case.

But for the moment he had a public platform from which to work. His next step was to tackle the vexed subject of the

---

2 The rule has now been changed and all defendants must agree to the reporting restrictions being lifted.

withholding of the name of the potential murder victim. Here now was a chance to obtain some sympathy. After all, what would the public think when they knew the prosecution was withholding vital information about their cases? 'We wanted the public to see what diabolical liberties the law's been taking,' Reggie is quoted as saying.[3]

Paul Wrightson said he made no application for bail, but that he had a question he would like to ask me. 'There is one charge of conspiring in 1968 to murder a male person. What is the name of that male person?'

Before I could reply David Hopkin was on his feet objecting. 'I don't quite see how my learned friend is entitled at this stage to ask these questions of this officer.'

'The reason for asking for this information is the basis of all justice. A man is entitled to know what is levelled against him. To say that he conspires to murder gives him no information at all. Either the answer is that it is a person unknown or, for various reasons, the officer refrains from telling, so that my clients and others shall not know,' replied Wrightson.

Mr Rees put an end to that for the day. 'I don't think any injustice will be done – I am not going to direct the Superintendent to answer your question today.'

The application to name the man became a regular feature of the remand hearings and a month later, on 14 June, Ivan Lawrence was still trying: 'For the sixth time I rise to my feet to ask the court to allow the officer in the case to answer the question, "What are the names of the two persons in the conspiracy-to-murder charges?"'

This time Frank Milton would have none of it, ruling it an inappropriate question to be put on an application for a remand.

Of course the defendants knew the whole time who the men were. They just wanted it out in the open. If they had waited a little longer they would have heard the evidence from the

---

3 *The Profession of Violence*, p. 304.

witnesses at the committal proceedings, and in any event Ivan Lawrence had been told some ten days earlier in a telephone conversation with Kenneth Jones.

But they were still not satisfied and eventually, on a hearing for *mandamus* to force us to name the victim, the Divisional Court indicated that it saw no reason why the man should not be named openly.

'No doubt,' said Lord Parker to Ivan Lawrence, 'you have considered the matter with your clients: if it serves your purpose and is in their interests, the court sees no reason why you should not give the name here and now.'

'Then I do,' said Mr Lawrence, 'it is George Caruana.'

By that time it was no longer important as far as I was concerned. There were other, far more pressing matters to occupy me.

Meanwhile still more of the lesser fry amongst the defendants were asking to see me, and I went to see each one when he asked. I had also established that members of the Firm had regularly been visiting the unfortunate Mitchell, and at one remand hearing I charged the Kray brothers, Tommy Cowley, Wally Garelick, 'Scotch' John Dickson and Cornelius Whitehead with being involved in the escape of Mitchell.

When all the 28 defendants appeared at Bow Street again on 31 May, I decided there was now sufficient evidence to charge Reggie and Albert Donaghue with the murder of Mitchell. So now, only three weeks after their arrest, the first murder charge was laid.

The committals started in the middle of June, but before then there had been a considerable amount of sparring between counsel who appeared for some of the defendants and me. The Krays watched this aspect of the proceedings with interest, smiling and grimacing when I appeared to lose a point and displaying complete indifference when I seemed to score.

On 19 June I charged Ronnie, Charlie and Cornelius Whitehead with the murder of Mitchell. It was now, I think, that the Krays began to realise the predicament they were in. Until then I am sure they felt the matter would not get beyond the magistrates' court and they would once again be discharged in a blaze of public sympathy. The twins were still convinced they could walk on water, and the murder charge against all three was the first sign that I had drained the pond.

They knew there would be no prospect of bail for them, but the others tried their damnedest; not the least of them was Joey Kaufman who faced three charges relating to the dealings in stolen bonds. Unlike the present time, when a defendant is effectively limited to two applications unless there is a substantial change in the circumstances of the case, in the 1960s an accused could make repeated applications on precisely the same grounds as the previous week, in the hope that one time he would find a sympathetic magistrate and strike lucky. Typical was that day, 19 June, when Robin Simpson, appearing for Kaufman, had a real run at me.

Giving my objections to bail I said, 'He is not resident in this country and I am perfectly satisfied from my enquiries that if he is given bail he will abscond and not appear to stand his trial.' I also said rather formally, 'It is suggested by the prosecution and it will be supported by evidence that this man is in fact the main conspirator in all the dealings involving securities. It is from this source that these securities came.' I went on to say I had been in touch with the FBI through the legal attaché to the American Embassy and said that I was not prepared to disclose at this stage what had been told me. 'It would be prejudicial to your client if I do so,' I added. The restrictions on the reporting of the committal proceedings had already been lifted and Robin Simpson was therefore in a bit of a bind. He did not want prejudicial stories printed freely about his client, but at the same time if he left things as they were his bail application was doomed. He knew also Kaufman had a drug conviction in America and did not want it reported.

'Let us have it out. One is sure the gentlemen of the press will be circumspect,' he said looking round at the dozen reporters. The day's magistrate, Frank Milton, was his usual amiable self and was quite clearly enjoying things.

'That is difficult,' he interjected, 'You or some of your colleagues have asked for publicity. One cannot be selective.'

Simpson plunged on and I agreed with him that the amount of drugs involved was very small but I persisted that I had other information which would be even worse if it came out.

'That puts me in a position,' he protested. 'You are suggesting that if I ask you everything then something very unhappy may come out.'

'That is why I have tried to avoid answering the question,' I replied.

'Well, what is it? Let us have it out. Let us be honest, let us have the truth,' he said.

That is exactly what he heard a few moments later: 'The suggestion made by my colleagues in America is that he is a member of an organisation known as the Mafia and that he is already suspected of offences in America, and if he is granted bail will be arrested when he arrives in America,' I told the Court. That was the end of the application. There was such a buzz in the courtroom that it was difficult to hear Mr Milton refuse bail.

I am not so sure that the 'Gentlemen of the Press' were circumspect that day, for the headline in the final night extra edition of the *Evening Standard* for that day read: '"Man from the Mafia" in the Kray Case. Yard Tell Court of FBI Tip'. 'Kray Case Man is a Member of the Mafia,' screamed the headline of the *Evening News*.

Even if the Director of Public Prosecutions was represented, and usually David Hopkin did appear on a remand hearing, it was then the practice for the police officer in the case to stand up, make his objections and be cross-examined. That was the time for the defence to try and whittle down the objections so that a successful application could be made for bail, or simply to throw as much mud as possible in the hope some might stick and be useful at some future time in the proceedings. One regular suggestion was that I was trying to intimidate defence witnesses. On the day the twins were charged with helping

Mitchell escape I had to object to bail for Tommy Cowley, Wallace Garelick, John Dickson and Connie Whitehead. Colin Cunningham, appearing for Whitehead, had some allegations to make.

'He was warned that if he helped in another case – and we all know which case that is – he would be arrested and kept in custody on remand for a year,' he said, addressing Mr Barraclough in a bail application.

I replied that I had no knowledge of the alleged threat.

Cunningham went on to suggest that I was 'virtually trying to intimidate witnesses who might be used in the defence of another case,' something I again denied. He was now joined in the attack by Ronald Stewart for Wally Garelick: 'I understand that similar intimidating words were said to Garelick as were said to Whitehead.'

It did neither of them any good. 'This makes no difference,' said Mr Barraclough, 'I am still not prepared to allow any of these men bail.'

The atmosphere in the courtroom during these hearings was always tense. Doors were locked and guarded by police on both sides. During one hour-long bail application one of the officers fainted and had to be carried out.

There was a suggestion that the convoy I had arranged to bring the defendants from prison to the weekly hearing at Bow Street was unfairly prejudicing them. I had to consider the very real possibility that the Krays were so influential that they might arrange for the prison van to be hijacked and so escape. I had arranged for the van to be escorted from the prison by police motorcycle outriders who made sure a path was cleared, allowing the van to get through the traffic at unusually high speeds. It was then unorthodox, but it cut down the risk of an ambush. Now it is considered commonplace. Once the committal proceedings started it became a daily spectacle with people waving at the van calling out, 'Mornin' Ronnie, mornin' Reggie' as they sped past.

I was rather surprised when Brian McConnell wrote in the *Daily Mirror* of the 'ever continuing story of Krayton Place' and describing the run through Brixton, Kennington and Lambeth to Covent Garden, questioning whether it was necessary. It was taken up and became another line of questioning for the defence lawyers.

'I am personally responsible for bringing them here in that way,' I told the Court, 'I am not doing it to ensure a maximum amount of publicity. My consideration is purely to transfer these men from the prison to the court.' I was asked if I thought a future jury at a future trial might be prejudiced with all the attention and publicity given to the method of escorting the prisoners. 'Unfortunately, it can't be avoided,' I replied. After all I had not lifted the reporting restrictions, nor had I written up the story of the prison-to-court run in the newspapers.[4]

The committal proceedings started on 25 June with the case relating to Frank Mitchell. Earlier in the day the packed Court had heard the discharge of Charles Mitchell and Billy Exley who had been charged with conspiracy to defraud in relation to six different Long Firms, and the granting of bail to the Krays' old running mate, Dickie Morgan. Various dates were set throughout July for the hearing of the different cases. Kenneth Jones outlined the prosecution's case and then the first witness was called in relation to the escape and death of Frank Mitchell. Described in the *Evening Standard* as 'sallow-faced, plumpish with long dark hair', 'Miss A' had been taken from her address in North London by Pat Allen who told her, 'Don't worry, you'll be back home in an hour or two.' In the end she never, ever returned. Now as she went through her evidence with John Leonard, she began the long story with how she had been invited for a car ride which went all the way from the Regency Club to Dartmoor to see Mitchell. We were off and running.

---

[4] My fears were not so fanciful. On 10 March 1969 two prisoners charged with robbing a Securicor van were 'sprung' in an ambush on their way from Wandsworth to the Old Bailey.

One of the greatest problems associated with police work is the reliability of witnesses. To take a statement is a relatively simple matter. What is important is that the defendant will come up to proof in the witness box. In other words will he or she say with conviction what they have said in their statements? Sometimes witnesses are got at, but all too often they change their minds about what they have seen and heard, with disastrous consequences for the prosecution. My witnesses were marvellous. From the day the committals started until the last of them was called at the Old Bailey, almost without exception, they gave their evidence perfectly and faced proper but relentless cross-examination with courage. Some of them were not the nicest of people. They were not the sort you would necessarily bring home for tea. Some of them were out-and-out crooks but, in the end, they did a great service by speaking out against a regime and individuals who were far more unscrupulous than they were. I admire them for it.

In particular poor Billy Exley, now a sick man with a chronic heart condition and with a doctor in court to assist him, gave evidence of the escape and harbouring of Mitchell. It was difficult. He was tested keenly by all the defending counsel who suggested he had done a deal with the police and was 'as guilty and involved as anyone'. Billy stuck to it and came through it well. We had jumped another hurdle.

Then there was the witness whose evidence and appearance caused the greatest sensation of all – the girl from Winston's Club, Liza. On the day she was due to give evidence there was a rail strike and, as she was hidden away in Surrey, with heavy traffic in the centre of London causing major delays, there was a problem about getting her to court. The ingenious Sergeant Bert Trevette came up with the solution. He called up Thames Division and asked for a launch to collect her and deliver her at Westminister Pier. With all this, however, by the time she arrived at Bow Street, Liza was in something of a state. At first when she was called she did not appear and for an instant I wondered if something major had gone wrong. No, she appeared in her dark glasses, smiled at Frank Milton and was forgiven. What had happened was that in her panic she had dropped her dark glasses down the lavatory bowl and had had trouble fishing them out.

On 5 July the defendants were committed for trial. Frank Milton said, 'I am satisfied on the evidence that Mitchell is dead and that he was murdered.' He did, however, uphold submissions by Desmond Vowden for Charles Kray and Sir Lionel Thompson for Connie Whitehead that there was no case to answer for their clients on the Mitchell murder charge. Whitehead was committed as being an accessory after the fact. So, even without a body, we now had the case before a jury.

It made up for some of the disappointments that were to come with the evidence of Paul Elvey and Alan Cooper in the committals for conspiracy to murder. Back in the 1960s their evidence seemed so fantastic as to be unbelievable. They too gave their evidence well and stood up well to skilled cross-examination. The problem was that the whole story was just so unbelievable. Who would have thought in 1968 it would be decided to kill someone by injecting them with poison from a hypodermic syringe contained in an innocent-looking suitcase? As Mary Holland wrote in the *Observer*, the week of 15 July had been 'the sensation of sitting right inside a superior thriller'.

> We have seen extraordinary contraptions in court. A neat hide attaché case was fitted up with clips and springs to hold a hypodermic needle that could be released by a cord to inject a lethal dose of hydrogen cyanide through a hole in the side when swung against someone's leg.
>
> There was the crossbow, a clumsy weapon of mahogany and steel with telescopic sights bought at Lillywhites. . . . We did not see the gelignite though we were shown a cheap sky-blue suitcase in which it was said to have been found.
>
> The evidence grew more bizarre as the week progressed. With Alan Cooper there were discussions of plans to kidnap the Pope and to release Tshombe, as well as the more immediate matter of killing someone involved in a case at the Old Bailey.

All this evidence led up to Eugene (Paul) Elvey. He was a young man with a high domed forehead, and sandy coloured hair. His eyes behind spectacles were sandy and his voice was pale and colourless to match.

'Is James Bond going to give evidence in the case?' asked Reggie on the Wednesday. It was, reported Ms Holland, the 'most apt comment of the week'.

Kenneth Barraclough was the stipendiary magistrate who heard this part of the committal proceedings and he, too, could not make head nor tail of it all. 'I have gone through the evidence with a fine toothcomb. To me it is so confused and therefore too slim to commit before a jury,' he said as on 23 July he discharged the defendants on the charges of conspiracy to murder.

By then it didn't matter to me so much. There were the other more substantive charges preferred and, as the days went by, my team was collecting more and more evidence.

And once more things were moving behind the scenes. On 16 July I had the biggest break of all. Whilst I was at Bow Street dealing with the Cornell committal proceedings I received a note. It read, 'You must talk to Supt Read say you've just been to see Donaghue and he wants to see you as soon as possible but not at the solicitors rooms at Brixton prison.'

It was handed to me by Donaghue's mother. She had been surreptitiously handed the note when she had visited her son. When I spoke to her she pleaded with me to see her son, saying it was a matter of life and death. I telephoned the Assistant Governor and made an appointment for Frank Cater and me to see Donaghue later that evening in an annexe to the prison hospital. Physically Donaghue was a big man. Known as Big Albert, he was a trusted member of the Firm, very close to the twins. He had undergone a unique initiation ceremony. One of his friends was little Lennie Hamilton who had been branded at Esmeralda's Barn in Knightsbridge. When he heard of the outrage Donaghue went to Reggie to demand recompense for his friend. Instead of receiving any money he had been shot in the foot. Donaghue had been obliged to go to hospital but, when he had been seen by the police, had said the shot had come from a passing car. He had, of course, no idea of the identity of the gunman. Naturally, this endeared him to the twins and he was co-opted onto the Firm. Now he was charged with Mitchell's escape and murder.

When he had been charged I had found him to be a sullen defiant man from whom I had decided no information would ever be forthcoming. Now a very frightened man, once the door closed behind us he came straight out and said, 'It's been put to me to volunteer for the Mitchell business and, if I do, my wife and kids will be all right.'

This was a sensation and I remember wondering just what he was going to say next. What he wanted was a deal. If the murder charge against him was dropped, in return he would tell me the lot. 'Mitchell – who done it. McVitie, Cornell, Marks. But,' he added, 'it can't be proved.'

I told him that it was impossible for me to do any kind of deal with him but if he wished to make a statement then, of course, I would take it down and send it to the DPP.

He agreed. 'Do you know,' he said, 'I had a meal sent in for the first time today because I know what can happen. This is how I'm thinking at the moment.'

Over the next three days he made a cold clinical statement in which he admitted he had collected Mitchell from Dartmoor. 'We was waiting in the car outside the phone box at Peter Tavy when Frank came running round the corner, large as life.'

He had driven him directly to Dunn's flat where arrangements were made for him to be guarded. He went on to describe the letters written on Mitchell's behalf, how he, Donaghue, had taken turns with Billy Exley and another to guard him, of the semi-kidnapping of Liza and of Mitchell's refusal to surrender himself to the police and his threats to the Krays. Finally he told me in chilling tones of Mitchell's death. He told me he had walked Mitchell out of the flat around the corner where they both climbed into a waiting van in which a man, Alf Gerard, was sitting. Almost immediately shots were fired and Mitchell was murdered. At the bottom of the road the van was stopped and Donaghue went back to the flat where he arranged to clean up all traces of Mitchell.

Then he said, 'I did make that phone call, but I didn't say "the dog is dead" like the girl said. What I said was, "That dog won".' This was a code, he explained, in case the phone was tapped. No one would be able to make anything out of an innocent remark like that. Quite apart from that, he gave me enormously detailed information regarding the Cornell shooting and the protection rackets run by the Firm. He also admitted his own part in the McVitie murder which consisted of completely redecorating Blonde Carol's flat in Evering Road and putting in new carpets and curtains. He added that the plan was that if he would wear the Mitchell murder, Ronnie would accept the Cornell killing and leave Ian Barrie and Reggie free of the most serious charges.

I had now what I believed to be the true story of the Mitchell escape and killing. The problem for me would be to persuade the lawyers that it was the truth and that Donaghue should become a prosecution witness. The difficulties were obvious. He had been committed for trial charged with murder and, without doubt, this would be said to be a despairing effort to save his own skin. On 19 July I had a conference with Kenneth Jones and David Hopkin to decide what to do about Donaghue. John du Rose wanted to see the immediate arrest of the men implicated by Donaghue, but counsel advised us to wait. For the time being Donaghue would be left charged with the murder of Mitchell. Later consideration could be given to its withdrawal and using him as a prosecution witness.

Donaghue's position in Brixton Prison was now untenable and so the next day saw the 'Operation Big Albert' to remove Donaghue to Winson Green Prison, and the mounting of a guard for his wife and family. As a cover story I let it be known he was being sent to Birmingham, thereby causing inconvenience to his wife for whom visits would be difficult, as a punishment for his non-co-operation. The story seems to have been accepted at least temporarily because Reggie's girlfriend at that time approached Donaghue's mother, urging her to write to her MP complaining about the move. She also told her that Reggie had authorised the payment of £5 a day and given instructions she was to be taken to Birmingham to see her son whenever she wanted.

Now I turned my full attention to the McVitie murder. Another meeting with my lady friend in the Sir Christopher Wren had proved most informative and I now had the names of the three brothers said to be involved – the Lambrianous.

I always believed that of them, Chrissie Lambrianou, would be the weakest link in the chain, and on 8 August, the day after his arrest in Birmingham, I had a long interview with him. Although he made certain admissions which were to prove fatal to his defence at the trial, he still emphatically denied any responsibility in the murder or any complicity with the Krays or their henchmen. At the end of the interview I recorded a note: 'He cannot make up his mind which side to play on. We shall hear more from CL.'

So it was back to Blonde Carol. The next day I had her brought to my office and again we had a long talk about the use of her flat for the killing of Jack the Hat. At first she was defiant as ever, and then she broke down in tears; quite suddenly it was a different story. As the tears began to flow she asked if I could make sure she was protected, and once I had made my promise she told me how Ronald and his party including Reggie, Ronnie Hart and Ronnie Bender had arrived unannounced late one evening, and ordered her out, telling her to go across to a friend's house. Although at first she had protested, she knew better really than to argue. When she returned in the early hours of the following day she had been prevented by Ronald Bender from going downstairs 'because there has been a bit of a bother'. She spoke of seeing Chrissie Lambrianou pour a bowl full of blood down the toilet and noticing that Bender was wearing a pair of her son's socks over his hands and the socks were now bloodstained. She had finally been allowed downstairs where she had found her carpet, along with her candlewick bedspread, had gone, and the carpet underlay, covered in blood, was being cut up and burned. The flat was later completely redecorated for her, she said.

This now confirmed what I had already suspected and what I knew from Albert Donaghue. McVitie had been killed in some fashion in this basement flat. I now knew the names of the men who were there, but it was no use arresting them. As Chrissie Lambrianou had done, they would simply deny all knowledge. Much of Donaghue's statement was hearsay; what I needed was someone to turn Queen's Evidence. In any conspiracy of this sort if five or six people are involved and there is insufficient outside evidence to prefer a charge the only hope is that one of the number will crack. If they all keep silent then it is hopeless, and this was the problem I faced.

We could make peripheral progress. We had previously scoured the flat for bloodstains without success. Now I knew that the wallpaper had been replaced, another search was indicated. I sent Frank Cater along with a man from the Met laboratory to Evering Road, and this time they found what they were looking for.

I had also been desperately searching for a man known as 'Ersh'. I did not know if this was his first or surname and it was some time before I learned that it was the Jewish diminutive of Harry. That made tracing him easier. Mooney's mob had been scouring the East End for him and at 6 p.m. on 20 August Harry Hopwood, who had been named by Donaghue as being at the McVitie party, was brought to see me at Tintagel House. He was a long-time friend of the Krays and was said to be related in some way. At first he was defiant, as I had expected, but when I told him that I knew he was involved in the murder and the only way of protecting himself was to tell me exactly what he knew, out came the story.

In the early hours of the morning the twins had come to his home covered in blood. Nodding at his brother, Ronnie said by way of explanation, 'He's just killed Jack the Hat.' They both bathed and changed into fresh clothes brought from Vallance Road. They washed their jewellery and coins and threw away their paper money. Hopwood had telephoned Charlie Kray and Tommy Cowley, telling them to come round. Ronnie Hart and Ronnie Bender had also come to his flat with a gun and a knife and he, Hopwood, had gone with Hart to the local canal and pitched them in. The twins' clothing had been put in a suitcase and given to one of Hopwood's relatives for its disposal.

By halfway through the interview Hopwood, who had been a trusted friend, realised he had completely committed himself and began to shake and blubber, saying he had been ordered to keep his mouth shut and since that time he had been living in fear. I told him that he would now be under police protection and asked if he wanted to make a statement. 'You've saved my life,' he said taking my hand.

Three hours later I saw Percy Merricks, Hopwood's relative. At first he too was unco-operative, and I told him I had enough evidence to charge him with being an accessory. He paled and asked, 'Will you look after me? What will happen to my wife and children? It's them I'm worried about, not me. These people are murderers, you know that. I never saw what was in the case. I was drunk at the time or I would never have done it.'

He too made a statement describing how he had been summoned to Hopwood's flat where he had seen both the twins, Hart and Bender. Hopwood had handed him a suitcase telling him to get rid of it and he had driven to his smallholding at East Fairleigh near Maidstone where he had put the case on a bonfire, poured two gallons of petrol over it, and set it alight.

The next day's task was going to the smallholding and sorting through the rubbish tip. Frank Cater and I went down and met up with a team of local officers. Every ounce of debris from the remains of the bonfire was sieved and, sure enough, there were hasps from a suitcase and some suit buttons.

I hoped we might find even more traces of McVitie and, with Merricks in tears, I began to question him about the disposal of the body and we searched all the outhouses, the cesspit and the surrounding area. Nothing was found and he had no more to say.

Three days later, however, there was success for the Underwater Search Unit when they found the gun in the canal exactly where Hopwood said he and Hart had thrown it. It had clearly been in the water and mud for some time and was in poor condition, but it was taken to John McCafferty, the ballistics expert at the Yard, for examination. He ran a series of tests and later was able to give evidence that there was a defect in the mechanism which would cause it to misfire.

Through Harry Mooney I was now putting as much pressure as possible on all known associates of the Krays, and I continued to interview anyone who I thought might be able to give any information. I particularly wanted to see Ronnie Hart, whom I knew to be deeply involved in the McVitie murder. I was desperate to discover what his attitude would be. The destabilising game was also working well. Without naming names Jock Ions and I had let it be known that some of the defendants in custody were working with me and that caused something amounting to panic amongst others. Whitehead, Cowley, Dickson and others demanded to see me to try and straighten out their positions. My visits to the prison were all in strict secrecy and although I assured each of them that what they might tell me would be in confidence, not one of them would yet have the courage to commit himself.

Eventually it was Dickson who decided to throw in his lot with the prosecution. He made a statement to Harry Mooney saying how he had driven Ronnie and Ian Barrie to the Blind Beggar on the night Cornell was shot. On the return journey to the Widow's pub in Tapp Street, Ronnie had said, 'I hope the bastard is dead.' Dickson had also given further information about the harbouring of Frank Mitchell, and it was time to consider whether he too should become a prosecution witness. Certainly he was no longer safe in the prison system and was given bail with sureties.

By the end of August Ronnie Hart was one of the few people

I still wished to interview who was still missing. Then came the final and biggest breakthrough. On the afternoon of Saturday 31 August his brother Terence came to me to say he had been paying protection money to the Krays since Ronnie had been on the run from prison. The money had been paid over in the lavatories at Charing Cross Station and at a pub near Vallance Road. I explained I wanted to see Ronnie more than anyone else and that it was only a matter of time before he was arrested and I did so. Terence promised to try to persuade his brother to come to see me, and three days later at 4.45 a.m. I had a call from Ronald saying he would come to Tintagel House in an hour's time.

I met him with Trevor Lloyd-Hughes, but Hart wanted to talk to me alone, saying he knew what he was doing (talking to me) was against his nature, as indeed it was, but that he knew he could not run for ever and he had heard he was being plotted up to get done. When I put his position clearly to him, explaining what the consequences of his co-operation would be, he merely nodded. He then began to tell me of the horrifying details of McVitie's death. The idea to kill McVitie was nothing more than a whim, he said. Ronnie had been elated when he had killed Cornell and had chided his brother urging him to 'do one' as well. 'I felt fucking marvellous. I have never felt so good, so bloody alive, before or since. Twenty years on and I can recall every second of the killing of George Cornell. I have replayed it in my mind millions of times. I had killed a man. I had got my button, as the Yanks say. I was a man to be feared. I was now the Colonel.'[5]

McVitie had therefore been selected as a victim, not because he posed a threat to the Krays, nor because of the botched shooting of Leslie Payne, but simply because he was available. Once the decision had been taken and they had stiffened themselves up with a few drinks, the twins and the gang

---

[5] Kray, Reggie and Ronnie with Fred Dineage, *Our Story*, Sidgwick & Jackson (1988), p. 73.

had walked into the Regency Club where they saw one of the owners, Anthony Barry. He agreed that McVitie was in the club, and when they told him they intended to kill McVitie on the spot, he protested to such effect that they decided to find an alternative venue. As they left Reggie put a gun on Barry's desk and told him to 'look after it'.

Two of the Lambrianou brothers were left at the club to make sure that McVitie did not leave, and the party moved towards Blonde Carol's Evering Road flat.

Once there they started drinking again, and Hart was sent to tell Barry to bring the gun to the flat. Barry complained, asking Hart to take it himself, but the instructions were specific. This was a cunning move by Reggie. Barry was now totally compromised and his silence ensured.

About 1.30 a.m. the Lambrianous were told to bring McVitie to the flat. As soon as he walked in Reggie put the gun to his head and pulled the trigger, but it did not fire. McVitie thought this was some kind of a joke, but when the gun was pointed at him a second time and again failed to go off he began to struggle desperately and to try to escape through a window.

The window was broken as McVitie fought to escape. As he was dragged back Ronnie goaded him: 'Come on Jack, stand up and take it like a man.'

Poor McVitie, by now convinced he was a dead man, could only reply, 'But I don't want to die like a man.' Ronnie then grabbed him from behind in a bearhug and Reggie, who had been given a large knife, plunged it deep into his face and stomach. When Jack finally collapsed on the floor Reggie stood astride him and drove the knife into McVitie's neck, twisting it as he did so.

Afterwards the body was placed in the candlewick bedspread I had heard about and, along with the blood-covered carpet, taken to South London where Charlie Kray later arranged for its disposal. This was finally undertaken by Freddie Foreman, a publican friend of the Krays. He also agreed to clean up the car in which they had made their frantic ride to Hopwood's home.

So at last I knew the full grisly details of McVitie's death, which would turn most people's stomachs. Even so, apparently, Reggie was later to admit: 'I did not regret it at the time and I don't regret it now. I have never felt a moment's remorse.'[6]

Hart also described the clean-up operation, confirming he had taken the twins to Hopwood's flat where they had scrubbed up and how their rings and jewellery along with the knife and gun had been carefully washed to remove fingerprints and powder traces.

By this time I had made up my mind that Hart was to be a prosecution witness. Without him there would be no case against Reggie or the others. It was a decision for which I was severely criticised at the trial, when the defence counsel asked why I had failed to charge Hart when he had admitted the murder to me. My reply was that my object was to get at the principal participants in the crime.

I told Hart I wanted what he had said taken down as a statement under caution and so just after 7 a.m. I called in Frank Cater and we began the long and laborious taking of the formal statement, breaking only for a lunch which Frank and I ate. We tried to persuade Hart to have some food but he was simply too nervous to eat. By the time he finished the statement late in the afternoon all three of us were exhausted.

Two days later I heard from Harry Hopwood again. He had forgotten to tell me that Reggie had cut his hand badly during the incident and he, Hopwood, had bandaged the wound. I decided it was time to see the doctor who had supplied the Krays with drugs and treated their victims for gunshot wounds. He called to see me at Tintagel House two days later. Yes, he had treated Reggie for a cut, but it was on the nose. No, he didn't think he had been used by them, although he admitted probing and treating gunshot wounds. No, he did not feel obliged to inform the authorities: his first loyalty was

6 *Our Story*, pp. 85–91.

to the family who were private clients. For the moment I put him down as a rather foolish old man and sent him away, but as the months went on I was to see him again.

By this time there were a considerable number of witnesses, not least Ronnie Hart and his wife Vicky, to be protected. Fortunately, I put Sergeant Bert Trevette in charge of this aspect of the case. He was a wise choice. Bert was one of those people who could have played the part of the master sergeant in an American war film, who can acquire anything under the most adverse conditions. He could find accommodation at a moment's notice, arrange the right kind of escorts, sort out the many domestic problems which arose from this kind of close-guarding relationship and, most importantly, keep them happy. Throughout this he could still appear in the morning with a smile on his face. He would always be happy to go along to the pub with the lads, but he never had anything stronger than orange juice. Bert was teetotal.

By far the most troublesome of the witnesses was Liza. As a night club hostess she had been used to freedom and the close attendance of her escort unnerved her.

One night she was so difficult that she was placed in a cell at the local police station. After this her escort was changed but this did not improve things. When she was holed up in a house in Surrey she and the officers went to the cinema together. Back home they were having a cup of coffee when the skirt of the WDC rode up over her knees – short skirts were in fashion at the time – as she sat on the low settee. For some reason Liza thought this attracted the attention of the male detective and stormed off upstairs, reappearing moments later wearing only a flimsy house coat.

'If that's what you want to look at, George, look at this,' she said as she opened it.

Fortunately he was a sensible married man and merely commented, 'Cover yourself up for goodness sake, Liza, I've seen that kind of thing before.'

Another day in a fit of temper she threw a vacuum cleaner at the WDC and a few days later it was a tray of glasses.

This time she cut her own hand, ran into the bathroom and locked the door, screaming she was dying.

As a rule, protecting officers with problems would not approach me directly. They had to go through Bert, but this time there was a personal delegation from the WDCs saying things were getting a bit heavy. The guards were changed again, this time for all male escorts. There were no problems with Liza after that.

There were other problems elsewhere. The 50-year-old wife of a 60-year-old witness alleged he was having sex with one of the female escorts, a very good-looking 22-year-old. The poor girl was removed with the assurance that I was satisfied the allegation was completely unfounded, but it was typical of the kind of silly difficulties that arose because of the unreal domestic situations in which people now found themselves. The only solution appeared to be to change the guards at regular and frequent intervals.

Of course it cannot have been any fun for any witness, let alone a high-spirited young woman, to be cooped up with people he or she did not know or necessarily like, for what turned out to be months on end. Despite the fear that occupied their minds at the beginning, the very presence of their guards soon began to play on their minds to such an extent that frustration began to replace fear.

Diversions had to be provided and, for example, I encouraged Hart to write a detailed life story. I said, 'You'll be sitting there with Vicky and you won't be allowed too much rein because my blokes'll be watching you, so write it all down.' He made extensive notes about pensions and clubs from which money was taken. I think a lot was truth and much of it we already knew, but it was the kind of thing that was virtually impossible to corroborate and we couldn't take any real action on it.

At this time there was also trouble with one of the guards assigned to protect another witness. He failed to come on duty on time and left the witness with a telephone number to contact if there was trouble. I went with Cater to keep observation and watched the officer arrive three hours later. The man was dismissed from the squad and made the subject of an internal disciplinary inquiry. It has been said that one of the reasons the investigation was successful was because I had refused to have officers who had served in the East End on my squad. This is nonsense. Although, of course, they were all screened this was not a primary consideration, indeed it was important that some officers brought with them a knowledge and experience of the East End and its criminals. Trevor Lloyd-Hughes, who had been on my first Kray team, was a case in point, and there were others who at some stage in their service had worked in the East End.

I was delighted with the final selection and I found members of my squad were both conscientious and completely loyal. There was only one other incident of misbehaviour during the whole inquiry. An officer leaked the news of an imminent arrest to the press. He too was immediately dismissed from the squad and was referred to an internal disciplinary board.

Prosecuting counsel had by now approved my decision to use Hart as a witness and so I was prepared to move against the other participants in McVitie's murder.

Harry Mooney's team organized another dawn raid and on 11 September Chrissie Lambrianou was brought in again. Thanks to Hart, I now knew much more about the part he had played and could question him more thoroughly. The allegations put to him were that he had brought McVitie from the Regency Club on 28 October to 97 Evering Road and that he was a party to the killing. I also put it to him that he had assisted in removing all traces of crime from the flat but, well within his rights, he declined to answer the questions except to say he had not set McVitie up. He was followed by his brother Tony who denied all knowledge of McVitie's killing and said he had in fact seen him about Christmas time in the Balls Pond Road. The next in was Ronnie Bender. He too denied being at the Evering Road party. I had them all transferred to West End Central Police

Station where they were charged with McVitie's murder. Off they went to Brixton to join other members of the Firm.

Meanwhile Kaufman was having a rough time. On Monday 9 September an application for bail had been refused. On the Thursday of that week he was belted by Reggie Kray, who dislodged a few of his teeth. Later he underwent an operation and was transferred to Winson Green.

By the time of the next court appearance it must have been apparent that there would be further charges against the twins. Ronnie had obviously been practising his reply: 'Your sarcastic insinuations are far too obnoxious to be appreciated.' As I wrote it down I looked across at Ralph Haeems and for the first time saw him smile, even if it was only a watery one.

Reggie replied, 'Not Guilty.' I noticed a scar on the palm of his left hand between thumb and forefinger and asked him how he had got it. 'I've got plenty more,' he replied, adding that he would speak to his solicitor.

There were now only two more people to be seen and charged in connection with the McVitie murder. The first was the owner of the Regency Club, Tony Barry, whom I saw on 1 October. Although the worst that could be said about him was that he was only a minor player in the murder, he was still an accessory before the fact. Barry denied the allegation, saying that whilst he accepted he knew Jack he knew nothing of his death. He too was charged with murder. The final man in the jigsaw was a very different kettle of fish: Frederick Foreman, the long-time friend of the Krays and the man who was said to have disposed of McVitie's body. When the allegations were put to him he said, 'It's just ridiculous.'

It is a measure of the speed at which things were happening that Foreman was charged with being an accessory after the fact to McVitie's murder on 9 October and the committal proceedings ended on 22 October.

In the meantime, soon after his arrival in Brixton prison, Tony Barry from the Regency Club had asked to see me. At this stage I was up to my eyes in it and sent Harry Mooney to talk with him. He took a detailed statement setting out the part Barry had played and confirming what Hart had told us. There was no doubt he expected to be asked to be a witness for the prosecution. Later that day I had a meeting with David Hopkin when we discussed the matter and he supported my decision that the case against Barry should proceed. As it turned out the part he played in the trial was of far more significance that I could ever have dreamed.

CHAPTER ELEVEN

EVEN THOUGH THE COMMITTAL proceedings were coming to an end, and did so in October, there was still an enormous amount of work to be done. In the late 1960s a trial before a judge and jury would be heard a month or so after the committal, possibly even less. A trial of this complexity would start within three months. Decisions had to be made about which witnesses would, in the end, be called to give evidence, as well as what charges each defendant would actually face. The decision as to which counts would be on the indictment was, in the final analysis, for counsel leading the prosecution, but before it was taken both David Hopkin and I had the chance to make our views known. Throughout late September, October and November, conferences with counsel, sometimes attended by the Director of Public Prosecutions, Sir Norman Skelhorne, were held in the Temple two or three times a week, lasting well into the evening. The main consideration, however, was the question of whether we could join the murders of Cornell, McVitie and Mitchell in the same indictment. The matter was tossed back and forth because we knew the defence would argue that the indictment should be split into three counts of murder to be heard separately. After hours of discussion it was also decided that the Mitchell case should be totally separate from the Cornell and McVitie murders, which should be heard together. We were all conscious that counsel for the defence would argue strongly that the indictment should be split into three so that each of the murder charges would be heard separately.[1]

In a case of this complexity it is inevitable that rumours fly around like bats in a belfry. Many of them concerned the whereabouts of the bodies of McVitie and Mitchell, others were directed as efforts to compromise members of my squad, some referred to attempts by those charged to escape when they next appeared at court, and others to naming associates of the Firm who had mysteriously disappeared. The latest was a tip from a national newspaper's crime reporter that the Krays were to be killed. Why, by whom, and by what method was not suggested and this limited my course of action. Nevertheless it was something to be taken seriously but the most I could do was to warn the prison authorities and hope they would take the necessary precautions.

I also had another message from Whitehead that he was desperate to see me. He had spoken to me earlier about the disappearance of a man, Billy Jack Frost, known as 'Frostie', from his home in the East End, and there were rumours that he had been attacked by members of the Firm. But I had long decided that there was no percentage in him and that I didn't trust his motives. My reply was that I would only visit him if he sent a letter to the Yard saying he wanted to see me without his solicitor present. At that time he was represented by Ralph Haeems and I was unwilling to have a conversation with Whitehead in front of Haeems which would clearly have put the lawyer in an invidious position.

The letter came and I went to see Whitehead once more. He was a fence-sitter, afraid to commit himself and afraid that he would miss the boat. He was both terrified of the Krays and

---

[1] This procedure was most unusual. Normally where a defendant was accused of two or more murders the Crown elected to proceed just on one case: so, for example, Neville Heath was never tried for the murder of Doreen Marshall but only for that of Margery Gardner.

afraid to go down with them. I took a long rambling statement from him in which he minimized his part in the Mitchell saga and the McVitie murder and was disparaging in his references to the twins. At the time it took me no further but, when it was read in court, Whitehead turned a pale shade of green.

Every minute of my days seemed to be taken up with interviews, court appearances, and placating witnesses and their relatives. It was something of a holiday when I was called before a selection board.

On 22 October I appeared before a local panel consisting of the Deputy Commissioner, the Assistant Commissioner (Crime) and the Assistant Commissioner ('B' Department) for approval to go forward to the extended interviews which had to be passed before being given a place on the Senior Staff Course at Bramshill National Police College. I thought it went well, and anyway it must have been a very swift interview because by 10.30 I was at Bow Street to give evidence in the McVitie committal on the day all the defendants were sent for trial.

Despite all the talk of McVitie's body being taken down to the country I always fancied it ended up nearer home. It would have been an incredible breakthrough to discover both it and that of Mitchell and I was always willing to listen to anyone who suggested they had information. Indeed I spent more time pursuing this line of investigation than any other. I always went to see anyone – members of the Firm or other prisoners – who might be able to give me a lead. Very often they hinted they could 'come up with something big' if only they could have bail. But when it came to it they were never either able or prepared to produce solid information.

At the back of my mind however there was always a thought that the bodies could easily have been disposed of right on the Krays' doorstep.

Just opposite their home on Vallance Road was the Cheshire Street Baths which were run by a man named Harry Granshaw. He had known the twins since they were boys and consequently was very friendly with them. He had allowed the baths to be used by them as an unofficial *poste restante* and I wondered whether he might have allowed them to be used for a more sinister purpose. First I checked to find that the boilers serving the baths would be large enough to consume a human body and then I had Mr Granshaw brought in.

He was patently loyal to the Krays and defended them vigorously. He agreed that it would be possible for a body to be consumed in the furnace but denied that it have ever been used for this purpose. It was not a matter I could pursue much further. There would be no possibility of remains being found in the ash cans after all this time and I bade Mr Granshaw good day. It was something that had teased my mind for some time. I always thought how convenient it would be to have a disposal unit so handy.

My days were full and there was little time to stop and consider. I remember seeing Marie Kaufman one morning at Scotland Yard when she again appealed for me to allow Joey to have bail; dashing from there to see the mother of one of my witnesses who wanted to be assured that her daughter was being well protected; next to see Ralph Haeems at Bow Street over some vital matter concerning one of his numerous clients; next to resolve the problem regarding two of the witnesses' escorts; then off again to Wandsworth Prison for yet another interview with one of the defendants and later that night travelling to Ronnie Hart's hideout to take a further statement from him.

This was not an untypical day and I knew what it was like being a juggler trying to keep all the plates spinning.

Friday 1 November provided something a bit out of the run of seeing defendants, organising security and the general preparation of the case. I had a call from a man called Joe Stafford, the father of Dennis Stafford who was serving life imprisonment for the murder of one Angus Stuart Sibbet in Newcastle. He asked to see me. Dennis had been born in the East End and knew the Krays well. Joe had been pestering me since his son's trial, in which I had not been in any way involved, saying his son was innocent and that he was convinced the Krays had something to do with the murder. Now, he said, Dennis and the other man involved in the murder wanted to speak to me. They didn't want to do this in Parkhurst on the Isle of Wight – could I get them transferred? Joe was by now an old man and I was sure this was a ploy to have his son sent to Leicester to cut down the long and tiring journey on visiting days. I said this was impossible in view of their then prison categories, and asked why this had never been mentioned either at the trial or at any time subsequently. Nevertheless I suggested he ask Dennis to write asking me to go and see him. I never heard another word.[2]

But on 3 December I was at a conference with Kenneth Jones and John Leonard when we received a much more interesting offer of help. We were discussing what parts of Donaghue's statement should be served on the defence and whether the addresses of witnesses should be disclosed to the defence,[3] when a quite unexpected offer came from Paul Wrightson, who represented Reggie, that the twins would plead guilty to certain charges if Charlie was allowed to go free. When I was asked my opinion I said, 'Let's fight all the way,' and this was agreed.

Early in December I had a break from the case. It was hardly a get-away break because I went to Eastbourne for three days of appraisals to see whether I was a suitable student to be sent on the Senior Command Course at Bramshill. It was called 'extended interviews' but to me it was three days of purgatory. I could ill afford the time to be away from the case, and I was fretting to get back to have things organised for the trial. After the hectic schedule I had been following I found it difficult suddenly to switch off and discuss methods of policing, relationships with

---

2 Dennis Stafford's case was eventually taken up by a number of people who became convinced he was not guilty. Books were written and there were two television programmes made, showing he could not possibly have committed the crime. Petitions were made to the Home Office and eventually he was released. Immediately he came to London he wrote a piece in a newspaper saying he was guilty of the crime. He then left the country.

3 A 1990 Home Office directive now prohibits the prosecution from disclosing the addresses of prosecution witnesses on statements served on the defence.

local government and what seemed at the time other mundane matters.

After Christmas I had an urgent meeting at the Home Office to discuss the arrangements for the production of the defendants at the Old Bailey. By now they were scattered throughout the country – Wandsworth, Brixton, Maidstone and Birmingham were some of the prisons housing them. Some had made statements of confession and so had to be segregated from those who had not.

There was also the question of preparing the security in the courtroom itself, of arranging for all the documents – there were four filing cabinets which had to be taken to the court and removed each day – the safe custody of the hundreds of exhibits and, most importantly, the transportation of witnesses. Another point which had to be dealt with was the protection of the jury. This was going to require a considerable number of officers who would be providing round-the-clock protection, and I was obliged to look for further help from the Yard. I was not really surprised at the response I had from my team – they had shown their worth time and again – but I was delighted by it. I was confident that administratively we should have a smooth and safe hearing.

And suddenly Wednesday 8 January came and we made our way to the Old Bailey. The No. 1 Court there is the most famous in the world. It has an air about it like no other I've been in. It has something to do with the fact that many of the world's most famous murderers have stood in the dock there – but it's not just that. I've watched dignitaries from other countries, judges and lawyers, let alone policemen, enter, catch their breath and almost instinctively bow. It is a special place, and now it was to see the Krays, at the pinnacle of their career. Win, lose or draw, they were going to make the most of it.

No bedraggled and defeated looking defendants they. Every day they wore immaculate suits, freshly laundered shirts and neat ties. Their hair was brushed and combed and they looked for all the world like their self-descriptions on their charge sheets – company directors. The other defendants had responded to the twins' sartorial lead. They too wore sober suits, shirts and ties.

The twins particularly revelled in the continuing limelight. When the Clerk called, 'Put up Ronald Kray, Reginald Kray . . .' they would come up the stairs, look first at the public gallery and nod and smile to their mother, Violet, who unfailingly attended the trial, and to any other friends and family who were present that day. Then there was a half bow to the judge and a respectful nod to counsel. They showed everyone *they* knew how to behave, and for a time it worried me. It was early days, but I was afraid the jury would get the wrong impression from their appearance.

Kenneth Jones QC, large and rubicund, John Leonard, neat, dapper and precise, and James Crespi, enormous and untidy, prosecuted. Crespi was a huge man who was later injured in the IRA attack on the Old Bailey. Gossip at the Bar had it that he could eat 18 Wimpys at a sitting, but during lunchtime, when we would invariably have a working lunch holding conferences, he would eat just one slice of white bread and one Kit-Kat or Dairy Milk. 'It keeps me going, Mr Read, it keeps me going,' he said when I commented, rather rudely, that it did not seem much. Later when I dined with him I was to find that his appetite was no larger than mine.

The defendants were represented by the heavies of the Criminal Bar, some but not all of whom had been at the committal proceedings and many of whom were to go on to take some form of judicial appointment. Paul Wrightson appeared with Monty Sherbourne for Reggie Kray; Desmond Vowden and Ronald Stewart for Charles Kray; Sir Lionel Thompson, in smart suits and gold jewellery, was back in action for Connie Whitehead; Petre Crowder with Patrick Pakenham, son of Lord Longford, represented Christopher Lambrianou; the saturnine Barry Hudson QC and Clive, one of the identical Nicholls twins, represented Anthony Barry; Ivan Lawrence, a man who had had a meteoric career at the Criminal Bar, was the junior barrister for Ronnie Kray. He was led by John Platts-Mills QC who, although he defended regularly, was not really one of the Old Bailey regular heavies. He had, of course, represented Ronnie at the Hideaway Club trial and now he would lead the attack on the prosecution witnesses. He was a tall, distinguished-looking, gentle scholarly man, given to long rambling sentences and explanations which confused the witness, with the result that he was never quite able to get the answer he wanted. A typical example is his discussion with a witness about the Grave Maurice.

Q. The Grave Maurice was one of his well-known drinking places.
A. Yes.
Q. The Grave Maurice . . . The Graf . . . meaning Prince . . . Prince Maurice . . . the brother of Prince Rupert. . .
A. The Grave Maurice as I know it.

By the time he had finished with a witness, he or she had thoroughly settled into the routine of cross-examination and, as a result, counsel following him had their weapon of surprise blunted. I have often wondered whether, from a defence point of view, it would have been better for the twins to have switched leading counsel and had the altogether more penetrative Paul Wrightson lead off for the defence. But criminals believe in luck and John Platts-Mills was lucky for Ronnie, who had great faith in him. But dealing with the formidable array of witnesses we had this time was a very different proposition from dealing with Hew McCowan.

The judge, I had been delighted to hear, was Melford Stevenson. He was one of the old-fashioned judges who compelled respect and who would stand no nonsense from counsel, prisoner or witness. There was no doubt either that he was known as a prosecutor's judge. He had had a junior brief in the Bodkin Adams case, and indeed he had prosecuted numerous times, whilst his best-known defence brief had been for the unfortunate Ruth Ellis. In private life he lived in Winchelsea in a house he had named 'Truncheons' and was regarded as a man of charm and a good raconteur at his club, the Garrick. From the prosecution's point of view there could not have been a better choice.

With a dock full of 11 defendants and accompanying prison officers, it became apparent that there was going to be a problem for witnesses making identifications when a witness said, 'The third from the right, did that include or exclude one of the dock officers?' To solve this Melford Stevenson ordered the defendants to wear identification numbers around their necks. He had done this successfully in 1962 when he had the so-called Mussie Gang[4] wear placards.

Mr John Platts-Mills and Melford Stevenson were no strangers to each other. In one trial Stevenson had angrily ordered that part of Platts-Mills' fees be withheld because he had alleged that the police had lifted and planted a fingerprint of his client. He was clearly going to face an uphill struggle when he began with a string of applications. The first of these was to sever the indictments, and now he found counsel of a number of the other defendants were quite happy for the two murder charges to be heard together. The basis of Platts-Mills' argument was that prejudice would spill over from one case to the next if they were heard together. There was also the sop that for much of the time defendants would be listening to evidence which did not concern them, and a good deal of public money would be wasted. In reply Kenneth Jones said that instead of isolated incidents, of which the Cornell one depended to a large extent on identification evidence, here were two ruthless murders committed by members of the same family, one of whom was involved in both. The murders had many similarities, not the least that there was no apparent motive. The application failed, as did one to restrict the press reporting of the case. In this case the judge said he had no power to make such an order.[5]

---

[4] The 'Mussie' Gang was a gang of youths who had broken up a dancehall in Finchley and had generally conducted a reign of terror in the neighbourhood. They were clearly quite unable to stand up to Melford Stevenson who sentenced the ringleader to five years' imprisonment.

[5] The trial judge now has the power to make an order forbidding reporting of all or any part of a trial under the Contempt of Court Act 1981.

Platts-Mills then turned his attention to the matter of the defendants wearing identification numbers, and asked the judge to withdraw the order. 'I have known of many a factory on strike for less than that,' he said.

But Melford Stevenson was having none of it, nor did he have any interest in listening to representations made about what Platts-Mills called 'a convoy of armed machines travelling the road with enormous disturbance of traffic'.

'What has that got to do with me?' asked the judge, adding 'I am going neither to frown nor to smile or do anything about it. It has nothing to do with me.'

And so the arguments continued until the first day ended with John Dickson being sentenced to nine months' imprisonment for harbouring Frank Mitchell. Since he had served four and a half months on remand this effectively meant his immediate release. It had been finally decided that he should be called as a prosecution witness, and it was important that he should be sentenced first to avoid the suggestion that the quality of his evidence might lengthen or shorten any period of imprisonment.

It had been a day of flexing muscles and sparring between the prosecution, defence counsel and the judge who had all been manoeuvering, testing the ability and reactions of each other. It promised exciting days ahead.

The second day began, just before the jury was sworn, with a demonstration of will. Melford Stevenson adhered to his decision that the defendants were to wear their numbers. The defendants had decided they would not.

'It's not a cattle market,' protested Ronnie. He tore the offending label from his neck and threw it onto the floor of the dock. And off camc the labels.

'Keep them on, too,' ordered Stevenson, telling the defendants to leave the dock and put their numbers on properly.

Platts-Mills desperately tried to pour some oil on the waters: '. . . in many different parts it was the practice to label prisoners in various ways, but it has now been stopped and in the last of those jurisdictions in Hong Kong the learned judge finally ruled that such an indignity should not be imposed on the prisoners.'

'It is not a question of imposing an indignity upon anybody,' retorted Stevenson. 'On my direction take them down and put them on.'

Now came what the waiting jurors must have seen as the first split in the ranks of the main bunch of defendants. Barry Hudson had his client Anthony Barry firmly under control and was quick to dissociate him from the others.

'My client has his number on, my lord. May he remain?'

'Yes of course he can.' And to the others, 'Take them down.'

But in the end it was a minor triumph for the defendants. After further discussions it was agreed that there would be numbers at the front of the dock to help with identification, and I prepared a plan showing who was where.

'I have been asked by one of the accused – I understand on behalf of all of them – to say how very much they appreciate the dispensation the Court has allowed,' said Platts-Mills.

'That is a great relief to me,' replied Stevenson sardonically. And then the jury was brought into the box to be sworn. There were five objections to jurors by Ronald Kray, two by Reggie, three by Charles, and the Crown asked nine to 'stand by', the equivalent of a challenge.[6]

So at long last the real business began. Kenneth Jones began his opening speech to the jury explaining how the Crown put the case against each of the defendants. Ronnie Kray and Ian Barrie had shot Cornell in the Blind Beggar and Reggie was an accessory to that murder. Ronnie and Reggie had killed McVitie at Evering Road whilst the Lambrianous and Ronald Bender were present and participants. Foreman, Connie Whitehead and Charles Kray had been called in later to help with the clearing up and were accessories after the fact of murder. Anthony Barry was an accessory before the fact. Jones read Anthony Barry's statement to the jury. This was the one he had made almost

---

[6] At that time each defendant could make seven challenges without giving a reason. The number was reduced to three and then in 1990 the right of peremptory challenge was abolished.

immediately he had been remanded in custody and when he had seen a solicitor. In it Barry had told of how on the night of McVitie's murder he had been in his club, the Regency, when Reggie had pulled out a gun in his office and said, 'I'm going to do Jack.' He had been given the gun to mind; shortly after, Ronnie Hart had come in and told him to take the gun round to Reggie at Evering Road. He had asked Hart to take the gun but had been told that 'Reggie wanted me to take the gun'.

Knowing the consequences of refusal, he had done so and had later been told by either Hart or Bender to 'Forget what happened the other night'.

The statement concluded:

> I am completely innocent of being involved in the murder of Jack McVitie and I want to add that me and my family have never been involved in any violence. Whatever I did that night, I did because it was beyond my power to refuse to do what I was asked to do in the circumstances. It was more than my life was worth to refuse.

It had always been apparent that Barry was going to raise the defence of duress. Jones went on to explain this to the jury:

> There are certain restricted circumstances in which, when a man is acting under a threat of violence, and in that sense has no alternative but to do what he did, that that constitutes a defence for him. It is, however, difficult at the moment to see how this can apply here because, of course, what Barry did involved getting into his car after leaving the club and driving up the road to take the weapon into the flat where Reginald Kray was; so obviously that was a journey which he carried out when he could have been under no immediate threat of violence.

What he meant was that once the Kray party had left the Regency, Barry could have telephoned the police or taken the gun in to the local police station. It was not as if a gun or knife was being held to his back all that evening. As for the account itself, Jones conceded, 'the view of the Crown is that it certainly contains a large part of the truth'. In the end it was going to be for Melford Stevenson to direct the jury whether the violence or its threat could constitute a defence in law.

So at last the jury was to hear the evidence. It was therefore a bit of a let-down to find the first witness was the rather prosaic Frederick Luger, the plan-drawer, followed by Howard Jones, a senior photographer, but we all held our breath when the third witness was called. Mrs X, the barmaid from the Blind Beggar so patiently courted by Harry Mooney and Pat Allen, came into the box. In a manner of speaking the trial had at last begun. Kenneth Jones patiently took her through her evidence and then asked her to make an identification. She was nervous. Of course she was. . . For two years this had been hanging over her head and now she was standing in the full glare of publicity telling the world how she had seen George Cornell shot to death. Mr Jones coaxed her patiently until he finally reached the telling question. Would she look around the court and point out the man who shot Cornell? Without hesitation she raised her hand.

'Number One over there, Ronald Kray.' And a few moments later she went on to pick out Ian Barrie.

In the book *Our Story*, Ronnie Kray says, 'The moment the blonde barmaid began to give evidence against us a smile appeared on Nipper Read's face, a gleam of triumph. He knew he'd got us bang to rights.'[7] In fact it was at this moment that I believed justice was going to be done. This frail little woman, who had been so terrified she had lost all reason, now had so much confidence in both the police and in herself that she could point to Ronnie across the short distance separating the witness box and the dock and say very clearly, 'Number One over there, Ronnie Kray', and go on to recount how, after the shooting, the record on the pub's gramophone had somehow stuck and was playing over and over again the Walker Brothers singing, 'The sun ain't gonna shine anymore'.

Platts-Mills, before he began to cross-examine, asked for the jury to be allowed to go and see the Blind Beggar. He was

---

[7] p. 98.

supported by Petre Crowder and the end of the morning and the first part of the afternoon was taken up with a discussion as to whether this should be permitted. It was plain from the start that Stevenson was against him, but Platts-Mills would not give up without a struggle.

'This case depends upon a single witness. There are thirty witnesses appropriate to this particular section, but the barmaid stands alone, and it all depends on where she was, and what she saw.'

'Of course it does.'

And there on Day Three was the crux of the whole case. If the barmaid stood up to cross-examination and the jury found that Cornell had been shot by Ronnie in cold blood, it would not be too difficult a step for them to find that McVitie had been killed in cold blood too, even though most of the witnesses to the second killing were themselves involved. Finally Melford Stevenson ruled that, for the time being at least, there was no need for a visit to the Blind Beggar and so Platts-Mills rose to cross-examine.

This was the moment Mrs X was dreading. She looked like a little sparrow clinging desperately to the protection of the witness box whilst Platts-Mills, standing six foot four in his black gown and wig and with his pince-nez perched precariously on the end of his nose, seemed like a great black hawk hovering over its prey.

The main weakness in her evidence was that she had told the jury at the inquest on Cornell that she had not seen the killing, and it was something onto which the hawk swooped.

Q. You remember swearing on oath?
A. Yes.
Q. That does not matter to you a scrap?
A. It matters a lot.
Q. What matters?
A. Having to tell lies. I was so terrified what might happen to me or my children, I had to tell lies.

That put an end to complaints about her reasons for lying at the Coroner's Court, particularly as she added, 'I was terrified I would get shot like George Cornell did if I told the truth.'

She stood up magnificently to this long and rightly persistent cross-examination and I felt proud of her. It was late in the afternoon when Platts-Mills sat down and by this time she was showing signs of feeling unwell.

'Do you feel well enough to continue?' asked Mr William Howard for Ian Barrie. Howard was a stickler for professional manners. He once roasted a younger member of the Bar for wearing a purple shirt beneath his white collar and tabs. Melford Stevenson asked if she would rather come back on Monday.

'No, I would rather get it over with now,' she replied.

Answering questions from Mr Howard, she explained she had refused to attend an identification parade immediately after the shooting. At the one held in June 1968, when asked if she could identify the second man, she had replied, 'I think that is the man, I am not absolutely sure.' Now she had the chance to elaborate on her reply.

> I was in such a state that day. Once I recognised him on the ID parade I can remember all I wanted to do was to get out of the room, and I'm not absolutely sure what I said, but I knew it was him.

Howard tried to show that, surrounded as she was by police officers, there had been no need to be frightened.

'I have been surrounded by policemen all through this, and I'm still frightened,' was her reply.

A few more questions and it appeared her ordeal was over. She was allowed to go. I had been in enough courts to know she had stood up well to the attacks on her credibility and I believed she had been an excellent witness who obviously had made a big impression on the jury as she did on all counsel. Now I felt more confident that the other witnesses would be believed.

Mrs X might have finished for the week but I had not. There was an epidemic of Hong Kong flu about and Melford Stevenson told the jury he had had an inoculation and asked them to have one as well. One juror had already been done, one wanted to talk to his doctor, and I had to arrange for the remaining ten to have theirs. In the end David Hopkin helped out by asking Adrian Whiteson, the doctor to the British Boxing Board of Control, to jab the jurors.

Melford Stevenson then told the jury that if anyone was intending to be absent overnight or over a weekend he should tell the jury bailiff where he was going. Each member was given an emergency number for the police and, with that, the first week of the trial ended.

Once a major trial has begun and the first two or three days are over, it settles down into something of a set routine. It is the same for both jury and the actors. As people become more familiar with the place and the faces it almost becomes a nine-to-five job or, in this case, a ten-thirty to four-thirty. Often the high points are fairly well spaced out over a matter of days and, for those involved, whilst it is not in any way dreary, there is nevertheless a good deal of repetition, particularly if there are a number of defendants.

Personally I have always found it fascinating. When I left the police service I would often go to the Bailey to listen to any case that was being heard. Perhaps I just needed to wean myself from being a detective.

Clients like to see their 'brief' earning his money – even though they are on legal aid – and even though the better policy may be to sit tight and say nothing. Consequently counsel will sometimes ask a few fairly innocuous questions just to keep his client happy and show he is earning his corn. It does, however, tend to drag things out. Some counsel are more long-winded than others and, in this trial at any rate, John Platts-Mills was one of those. As Ronnie's counsel he had to go first, and so he had to take the strain of the cross-examination for all. It was also clear from the start that he would get no help from Melford Stevenson who was impatient with his tactics. He knew this, ignored it, and even seemed to welcome the fencing with the judge as he fought back. No client could complain he did not give value for money in terms of endeavour.

The second week's hearings had barely started when there was a discussion with another witness about Mrs X, the barmaid. Platts-Mills now wanted her recalled.

STEVENSON: I think she did say something about feeling ill, but I think referring to feeling ill, and I have no doubt she did.

PLATTS-MILLS: I thought your lordship had further information. I asked whether she wouldn't prefer to stand up, the better to be heard. I think my lord said apparently she is suffering from something that makes it inconvenient.

STEVENSON: When I permitted her to sit down, I was indulging in no more than common courtesy.

PLATTS-MILLS: I accept that at once. One has that at all times from my lord – but what I was suggesting was that the lady really was faint in the box. My lord, of course we all saw when she came down, she couldn't stand up.

STEVENSON: She was obviously very distressed. I felt no surprise about that – perhaps you didn't.

In the end, however, the poor woman's ordeal was not over. She was brought back to the court and subjected to even more cross-examination, which seemed to me at least to take matters no further at all.

There were certainly very few dull patches. Hardly had the barmaid left the witness box on the Monday afternoon than John 'Scotch Jack' Dickson gave evidence that he had driven Ronnie and Barrie to the Blind Beggar the night Cornell was killed and then on to the Lion in Tapp Street. On the way Kray had started coughing and had said, 'I hope the bastard is dead'. Dickson, as a former member of the Firm, was fair game for counsel for the defence and it was put to him that he had turned Queen's Evidence to save his own skin. This allegation was put to one prosecution witness after another throughout the trial and most of them denied it. Dickson certainly did.

Although a number of witnesses gave evidence about different matters it had been decided that it would make things simpler for the jury if their evidence was compartmentalised so that each piece of the puzzle was dealt with separately. Normally as the officer in the case I would be called to give evidence last of all. In this trial, on day eight I found myself in the witness box giving evidence about the identification parade when Ian Barrie had been picked out by Mrs X.[8] There had been a complication on the parade because Barrie had scarring down one side of his face and all the parade had been covered in sticking-plaster. I was sure Mrs X had made her identification without any hesitation, but Ralph Haeems had been present and was convinced she had been hesitant and had only said, 'I think that's the man.'

Platts-Mills took the opportunity to question me over the arrangements I had made for the protection of the witnesses and, as I expected, the subject of the El Morocco party held after the acquittal in the McCowan case came up as well.

Platts-Mills put it to me that before leaving I had said to Ronnie Kray, 'Here's to the next time.' A veiled threat if ever I heard one. In reply I pointed out that the only person to whom I had spoken was Gilbert France and he left the matter there. There was no mention of the photograph or of my drinking the twins' health.

When Platts-Mills questioned me further about the Cornell murder itself I was at a distinct disadvantage. Now the gaping hole in the Yard's file on the investigation was exposed. Platts-Mills put to me the names of a number of people who had been seen after Cornell's murder and long before I took on the enquiry. I was obliged to answer that there were no notes or records of any interviews.

It was then that Platts-Mills, with a Freudian slip, turned to the question of what he called 'better terms' for the witnesses 'that would help the police to harm – I mean to prosecute – the Krays.'

I said I could not accept that. 'Some people who made

---

[8] The rules concerning the conduct of identification parades have now been changed and the officer in the investigation takes no part at all. The process is organised by a senior uniformed officer who is completely independent of the investigation. This is much fairer for all and it has largely stopped argument over what was said by a witness.

statements to the police at an early stage in fact had the charges against them withdrawn,' I replied.

Platts-Mills was keen to know the position regarding the ailing Billy Exley, an important witness in both the current trial and the one relating to Frank Mitchell still to come. 'He was, as far as you can see, in his own statement, plainly guilty of harbouring Mitchell and probably of helping him get away?'

But I wasn't going to be drawn on that particular issue. 'Well, I wouldn't agree to that, sir. He did make a statement in which he admitted some part in it, but the degree of his responsibility is something which would have to be debated.'

It was the standard skirmishing between counsel and police witnesses which goes on in a case where witnesses on the fringe of the crime give evidence for the Crown. Rarely does a knock-out occur with a witness. Platts-Mills was not really expecting me to agree with him, merely to score some points in front of the jury. But this time he took it so far and not far enough. Down came the wrath of Stevenson and Jones on his head. When cross-examining Mrs X, Platts-Mills had made an allegation of bribery, saying that the police were paying for her story, and asked if the police had given her a new house. Clearly he should have put this to me to give me an opportunity to explain.

'You made an accusation of corruption by the police in the clearest terms when you were cross-examining Mrs X. Here is the officer in charge of the case. You ought either to ask him about that allegation or you ought to abandon it,' said Melford Stevenson.

Platts-Mills protested he had been misunderstood, but Stevenson said he should either withdraw or pursue the allegation and he chose the latter course. I then explained that she had been moved from her flat to a house in Essex by the local authority at my request. I told him also that there were no facilities for the police to advance money in these circumstances to buy a house for a witness. Now Platts-Mills tried to have it both ways. He withdrew the allegation about the money and stood by the allegation relating to the new house.

Jones was furious: 'But my learned friend ought to put that

this officer has acted corruptly in so doing.'

'Of course he should,' said Melford Stevenson.

Platts-Mills defended himself valiantly. 'My lord, it is nonsense. I never suggested it for one moment and I deny ever hinting it.'

For once the judge backed down. 'However, that is probably as far as we shall get with it,' adding, 'If that is your view of proper behaviour I have nothing more to say.'

It is difficult to know what a jury makes of exchanges like these. For those of us familiar with this kind of sparring it is an accepted part of court procedure. But I wonder what the jurors, strangers to this cut and thrust between counsel and the judge, make of it? Sometimes I fancy they side with the authoritarian figure, the judge, as the person controlling the proceedings who should therefore have their respect. But on other occasions I am sure they tend to support counsel if they think he or she has been unfairly bullied and browbeaten by the judge. But Melford Stevenson, as a judge, was a master of assessing a jury and bending it to his will. He rarely miscalculated his approach and, watching the jury, it was clear he had their support, particularly in his clashes with Platts-Mills.

After only five days the Cornell case was over. It had not been expected to last so long but much of the time had been taken up with legal argument. I thought the witnesses had stood up well, giving their evidence on the lines of their proofs, and I thought things were going well. But now we were entering a second and, from the viewpoint of the prosecution, more dangerous phase of the trial. From now on, all the crucial witnesses for the Crown could be described as 'tainted'. They were almost all, in one form or another, accomplices to McVitie's murder, and there was no doubt the defence would make a meal out of at least some of them. Indeed I could see counsel metaphorically rubbing their hands in anticipation. However, before the witnesses were called, Desmond Vowden, on behalf of Charles Kray, applied for a separate trial, arguing the prejudice from the Cornell trial would make it impossible for his client to receive a fair trial. Little had been said of him in the previous week, but he feared that what had been said would colour the minds of the jury against him. Charles had been mentioned by Billy Exley as visiting Frank Mitchell in Dartmoor and being in various public houses but, along with Whitehead and Frederick Foreman who had not really been mentioned so far, the Cornell part of the case really had nothing to do with him. Kenneth Jones in reply remarked that, 'I took great care in my opening speech to underline that these men must be tried separately[9] and that sort of matter must not be allowed to influence the jury's mind.'

'I shall hope to exercise equal care when and if I come to sum up the case,' replied the judge suavely, as he rejected Vowden's submission.

So off we went again. Mrs McVitie denied that her husband was a quarrelsome man, and admitted that he had once had a row in South London with Freddie Foreman but nothing of any significance came out of it. The formal witnesses came and went. What we were all waiting for was the appearance of Ronnie Hart. How he managed would be crucial to this part of the case.

When he was called he walked quickly into the witness box and confidently took the oath. A big, good-looking young man with a florid face, neatly brushed dark hair, wearing a dark suit and plain tie, it was apparent he could have been No. 15 in the dock instead of facing it.

Mr Jones patiently took him through the evidence: of how Tony Barry tried to get the Kray party out of the Regency Club, pleading there should be no killing there, how they went back to Blonde Carol's flat and stood around watching the boxing on the television. He described how Barry brought the gun to Reggie and how he had been told to be the look-out for when McVitie came down the steps.

'And then he (Ronnie) was going to turn the record player up to drown the noise of the shot.'

He described how McVitie had his arm trapped under

---

9 That is, their cases considered individually.

Reggie's and how the gun had failed to go off. 'Reggie gave it to Bender, and he pulled the thing on top backwards and forwards to try and make it go.' And later he told the Court: 'The next thing I remember was they was up against the wall again, Reggie and McVitie, and this time Reggie has his back to the wall and Ronald Kray had the carving knife and he was trying to push it into McVitie's back.' He went on to describe how Ronnie held McVitie while Reggie had repeatedly stabbed the man and had finished him off by plunging the knife into his throat.

After the murder, said Hart, Bender was told to throw the body over the railway lines in Cazenove Road. Bender gave him, Hart, the knife and gun and he took it, wrapped in a towel, to Hopwood's flat where he washed it for a second time along with the twins' jewellery. Later he had thrown the gun and knife into the canal.

In the case of witnesses like Hart the only thing counsel for the defence can do is discredit them totally. Here was an eye-witness account to a murder committed not by strangers but people whom Hart knew well. It was put to him time and again he was giving the evidence to save his skin and he replied that he was – from the Kray twins. And after three days in the witness box Hart came out of it with his story intact. Some years later, in an effort to have the case against Freddie Foreman reopened, he gave a story to the *Sunday Times* that his evidence in respect of Freddie Foreman had been false and that the only reason he had been able to go through with his evidence was because I had been supplying him with pills before he went into court. It was a story which was utter rubbish. Peter Pringle, who wrote it, telephoned me on the Saturday before the issue, to ask for my comments. I told him that since the matter would be likely to be the subject of a disciplinary report I could and would not do so. In fact it was treated contemptuously by the authorities and no questions were ever asked of me.

What I had done, after the trial was over, was personally to lend Hart some money when he wrote, broke and begging for help whilst trying to sell his story to the newspapers.

'In my opinion,' he wrote in one letter thanking me, 'you have saved my life and I will never forget that as long as I live.'

But he did. He never repaid me.

Throughout the trial there was never one day when the end of the hearing meant I could relax. Apart from the fact that we had a conference at the end of each session discussing the progress of the case and tactics for the next day's hearing, there were constant rumours of what might or might not happen. All but the most outrageous had to be followed up.

A Detective Constable employed on witness protection reported that a publican had approached him saying a girl, representing herself as being from a television company, wanted an appointment with him. That had to be looked into very smartly indeed. Then some newshound said his photographer had a picture of one of the policemen in the case talking to a juror – dynamite if it was correct. For his own sake I had the officer taken off the enquiry and the matter investigated by a senior police officer. It came to nothing, but that was the sort of thing which could have blown the case right out of the water.

Next I began to hear stories that 'something would happen' after the hearing one Friday. But I could not find out what the 'something' was. It could have been a mass break-out, a concerted effort to free all the prisoners, a demonstration, almost anything. It wasn't a situation I could simply ignore and so I arranged for members of the Special Patrol Group to watch the 'cage' where the defendants were held prior to being put on prison vans. Nothing happened, but you never know.

On 18 January there was a report that a witness had been got at by a defendant. This turned out to be completely untrue – the witness gave evidence perfectly well a few days later – but it still had to be investigated, taking up valuable time. Then there was a rumour that 'something of importance' would be found under the bar at the Regency Club. I sent off a team to have a good search but there was nothing of interest. Of more importance was the arrival at Scotland Yard of a man who wished to confess to the murders of Mitchell and McVitie. I had him interviewed by DCI Robertson and Trevor Lloyd-Hughes and he turned out to be a 'nutter'.

Meanwhile Liza, the nightclub hostess, was getting into a panic again. The waiting was getting to her. I had an urgent message that the Mitchell case must come on soon or 'she would never make it'. A quiet, comforting chat and she was back to normal, but that had meant a long car ride to Surrey and back, and two and a half hours of my best Claire Rayner technique.

A juror said that he had been told by a friend, 'Don't forget to find them guilty.' I reported this to Kenneth Jones, and Melford Stevenson was informed, but it was decided no further action should be taken. Then a rival gang was said to have put together another contract to snuff out Leslie Payne who had still to give evidence. I had to call in the escorts, warn them about the problem and tell them to make sure Payne wasn't seen around.

A constant rumour was that a prosecution witness had been to see the defence lawyers to say his evidence had been false and his statement had been taken under threats from me and other officers. This is, however, a fairly common rumour during any big trial and it was one which, in the absence of any details, I came to ignore.

Next there was a suggestion that one of the defendants, whilst giving evidence, would throw a tumbler at the judge and then try to assault me. Additional precautions had to be taken, but again it was one of those rumours. Jock Ions, the faithful prison officer, reported that he had heard I was to be 'stitched up', but again this was an on-going threat and I knew that the precautions I normally took should be sufficient to take care of that one. Very few of these stories could simply be dismissed and it meant, once again, time and resources were used up. In the end they all came to nothing. So did the suggestion that McVitie had been buried in the disused Barnes cemetery.

Then the judge received a letter from Scotland, suggesting he needed some life insurance. We were not sure what to make of it. It could easily have been a threat, and as a precaution his house was watched for some days and he was given a bodyguard until we discovered it was a genuine, if ill-timed, version of junk mail.

Later in the trial one of the defence counsel approached me with a problem and his home was kept under observation for several days.

Meanwhile the prosecution witnesses had followed each other into the witness box, each standing up well to his or her cross-examination, and as they did so the veneer which had masked the true identities of the twins was dashed away. I had been concerned the jury would see the defendants as well-behaved gentlemen who could not possibly have committed these atrocious crimes, but now there were more and more outbursts from the dock. As Mrs McVitie gave evidence that 'it took ten of you to kill my Jack', there were calls of 'Liar'. Kenneth Jones was called a 'Fat Slob'. There were interruptions during the evidence of other witnesses. The defendants had at last begun to shed their company director suits.

By now the split amongst the defendants was clearly visible and widening, with Barry Hudson for Tony Barry, the Regency Club owner, successfully driving a wedge between his client and the others as he set out to show the domination the Firm had over the East End in general and Barry and the Regency Club in particular. Try as he might, Platts-Mills could not stop Hudson putting questions to the witnesses which, whilst they did not necessarily pin either of the murders on the twins, showed the hold they had over people. And when Platts-Mills objected, he found Melford Stevenson unsympathetic.

'What are you objecting to? What is sometimes referred to as a cut-throat defence is no novelty.'

After Harry Mooney read Barry's statement to the Court he was questioned by Platts-Mills, and told him that of all the witness statements we had taken about the case and which we had, of course, investigated, only one, from a man of low intelligence in Blackpool, had been demonstrably false. Finally I gave evidence once more. First Sir Lionel Thompson challenged the admissibility of the statement I had taken from Whitehead at what was euphemistically referred to as a 'house in Wandsworth'. It was the nick, of course, but the jury was not supposed to know whether any of the defendants had been in custody before the trial. Silly really – if any one of them had read a morning or evening paper about my 'convoy of armed machines travelling the road with enormous disturbance of traffic' it must have been crystal clear.

Sir Lionel had been intending to challenge not only the statement's admissibility but also the contents. It contained a number of disparaging remarks about the Krays, and he did not want them read out in court. He had also been given a very different version of what had occurred when the statement had been taken. I had, however, forseen that something of this nature might occur and, when I had seen defendants in prison, I had secretly tape-recorded the interviews, carrying the machine in a box file intended to look as though it contained only papers. However, I spoke to Sir Lionel during an adjournment and played him the part of the interview which showed that Whitehead had said precisely what I was giving in evidence. After that he confined his cross-examination to an interpretation of what had been said. It was left to Whitehead to convince the Krays he had been 'verballed'.

Then Barry Hudson made further progress in separating his client from the main body of defendants, pointing out that not only was he sitting in the dock away from the others but that he was in a prison well away from London.

'Would it be right to say that in all your dealings with the defendant Anthony Barry you got the impression that he was in great fear?'

'Yes, I did, sir,' was my reply.

Hudson had scored again.

So, shortly after lunch on 30 January, the 17th day of the trial, the prosecution evidence came to a close. It is often said by both police and lawyers that the high water mark of the defence case is the close of the prosecution and I certainly think it was true in this one. Some inroads had been made into the evidence of the witnesses in the McVitie case. Memories had been tested and, not surprisingly, found wanting. Some had admitted lying about certain aspects of the case. It had been forcefully pointed out that many of the witnesses were accomplices and had something to gain by giving false evidence. All good jury points.

But now the defendants had to decide which amongst them, if any, would go into the witness box and face what would undoubtedly be a severe cross-examination by Kenneth Jones or John Leonard. There was also the likelihood of an intervention or two from Melford Stevenson. It was a difficult decision both for the individual defendant and his counsel. In the end, whatever advice is offered, it has to be for the defendant to make up his own mind. If he is told not to give evidence and is still found guilty, then he is in a position to blame his advisers. 'You told me not to give evidence. I wanted to and if I had I'd have been acquitted,' is a common complaint.

It was quite clear that Ronnie had not committed himself by the time Platts-Mills made his opening speech. It was also apparent that counsel was trying to give himself sufficient room for manoeuvre, so that whichever decision was taken it would not look that odd. Halfway through he made an incautious comment and was trapped by Melford Stevenson. It resulted in a fiery exchange.

'. . . he will tell you . . .,' said Platts-Mills, and immediately Stevenson pounced.

'Do you mean your client is going to give evidence or do you mean he is not?'

'I would have preferred your lordship had not asked me that question.'

'I apprehend if he does not give evidence on oath he will give evidence from the dock.'[10]

'He cannot give evidence from the dock; he can make a statement. That is a very different thing from giving evidence.'

Later towards the end of his address Platts-Mills admitted that no decision had yet been made as to whether Ronnie would give

---

10 The law has now been changed. Either a defendant gives evidence on oath or he must remain silent.

evidence, and he was about to be allowed five minutes to take further instructions when his client shouted from the dock.

'Sir, I will go in the box.'

Whilst I hoped he would, I certainly had not thought he would do so. I could not believe he would expose himself to the probing and persistent questioning of Kenneth Jones. From the way Platts-Mills had opened his case he must have advised against it, but suddenly Ronnie made up his mind.

As he climbed the steps of the witness box the jury had an even closer look at him. They must have noticed that he looked bigger than when he was seated in the dock and they probably felt, as most people did, that he carried an air of menace with him.

Platts-Mills took him carefully though his evidence. He had not killed Cornell, with whom he was on friendly terms – indeed, he had only a few days before his death sent his little boy who was in hospital some chocolates. He had also tried to get him a job. There was a hint that Exley had a grudge against him. Nor had he been a party to the McVitie killing. The gist of the defence was that there was mistaken identity so far as the Cornell killing was concerned and that it was really Hart who had murdered McVitie. Blonde Carol was in love with him and was lying to protect him, and Hopwood, who had also given evidence, was a receiver and giving evidence to protect himself. Anything else was a police conspiracy to get the Krays and their friends.

When there are co-accused, a defendant giving evidence is cross-examined on their behalf before the Crown takes up the reins. Very often the cross-examination is a friendly one, but here he was going to get a double handful of hostile questions. Barry Hudson for Tony Barry was keen to press him on his reputation, asking why some years earlier he had carried a loaded revolver. Platts-Mills was soon on his feet objecting to the admissibility of the line of questioning.

'. . . he is perfectly entitled on instructions to raise the matter, if he thinks they have a purpose to the defence. Of course they are proper questions,' said the judge.

'I was a bit silly,' explained Ronnie.

Hudson then went on to suggest the Krays had been collecting a £50-a-week pension from the Regency, something Ronnie dismissed as a figment of the imagination. It was all a wicked conspiracy against him.

But if he felt he had a bad time with Barry Hudson, far worse was to come when Kenneth Jones rose to question him.

He was forced to admit that on the occasion he had behaved 'a bit silly' as a 22-year-old, a man had been stabbed in the back with a bayonet. He was being persecuted by the police, he said, to get him convicted of murder. Naturally he brought up the El Morocco party once more. I had gone there uninvited and threatened I would catch up with him later, he said. Then in an unexpected outburst he rattled off lots of people who, he said, were his 'influential and distinguished friends', something which prompted a JAK cartoon in the *Evening Standard*. 'If I wasn't here now I would probably be drinking with Judy Garland,' he boasted. Throughout the long cross-examination he became excited and abusive. It was impossible for him to control his temper, and when asked if he was known as the Colonel he replied, 'Yes, and you're known as Taffy Jones.' He was demolished by Melford Stevenson, but so far as he was concerned the damage was done. The jury was seeing, at first hand, the kind of irrational flare-ups of which Ronnie was capable.

Nor was he really helped by the fact that his first witness was Frankie Fraser, sentenced for his attack on Jack Spot and a member of the Richardson gang, then serving a total of 15 years' imprisonment. Now he was here as a character witness. He did manage to get out that whilst in prison he had heard a man he named had killed Cornell. Ronnie was 'a good bloke'. Jones lovingly put his list of convictions to him, including the fact that he had been twice certified as insane. When he left the witness box he waved and called out, 'Good luck, Ron.' Even the recipient of his wishes must have realised the harm he had done himself by calling 'Mad Frankie'.

Ian Barrie, who was said to be the second man in the Blind Beggar, made a two-line statement from the dock saying he was innocent, and denying a conversation he had with Harry

Mooney. After seeing Ronnie's débâcle he was not going to make the same mistake. Reggie Kray, too, restrained himself. He said the evidence was a pack of lies and in particular I had lied on two instances. He was also allowed to show the jury the scar on his hand, something I thought he would have been better advised to conceal. The worst thing said about him, he believed, was that Whitehead and his wife were afraid of him, and he produced both a letter from Mrs Whitehead and a poem he had written about 'Little Connie, bright and bonnie', their child. After some argument he was allowed to read the poem and he did this in a soft hesitating voice, much to the surprise of the rest of the members of the dock who squirmed with embarrassment.

Finally, he said, 'What I'd like to say to the jury, sir – to try this case on the merits of the evidence and not on the prejudice. Thanks very much,' he concluded and sat down, clearly pleased with his performance. Petre Crowder was taken by surprise. Chrissie Lambrianou sent him a message from the dock saying he wished to give evidence to deny the allegations against him. But it was always the intention of Barry Hudson to call Tony Barry and he did so on Friday 7 February, the 22nd day of the trial, following a long legal argument about whether the statement he made in prison after his arrest should be shown to the jury. Now it was all out in the open. Barry gave evidence that he and his brothers had been terrified by the Krays and their friends. He had thought the revolver he had taken to Evering Road was not in working condition – as it proved – and in any event he was in fear of his life and felt he could not refuse. He was never really shaken in his evidence by any of the counsel for the co-accused, giving his replies in a most convincing manner. Kenneth Jones was delighted to be in a position to cross-examine Barry. He was, after all, giving the most damning evidence against the Krays. It was almost like having another witness for the prosecution. As much as anything went to convict the others, it was his evidence.

On Thursday 27 February, the 36th day of the trial, Melford Stevenson began summing-up. We were all waiting to see how he dealt with Barry's case. So far as the the others were concerned it really was a question of 'you did' – 'I didn't, it was you', but

Barry was in a different position.

He pointed out it was for the prosecution to prove the case against Barry and to disprove his defence of duress.

> So you have to face the questions: what was Barry's intention when he took the gun to Reginald Kray? And: was he acting under duress? Those questions require you to consider whether Barry was, by reason of the threat of which he has given evidence, so terrified that he ceased to be an independent actor. . . . In other words, that he had no independent will of his own. Is that plain to you? I hope it is.

Now it was in the hands of the jury. Whilst I felt reasonably confident, one can never be sure with a jury. It merely wanted one of them to be influenced by a particular witness or a piece of evidence and he could start to bring it all down like a pack of cards. As they filed from their box I began to go over in my mind how we might have improved the investigation and presented a better picture. Then I realized how ridiculous that thinking was. We were committed. It was now up to the twelve men. All we could do was wait.

Jones and Leonard hurried away to the sanctuary of the Bar Mess and Frank Cater and I walked across to Matron's room to start drinking seemingly endless cups of tea.

In the event the evidence was plain enough. On Tuesday 4 March, the 39th day of the trial, Tony Barry was the only one acquitted and discharged. I didn't mind that. Indeed, I was glad to see him leave the dock. All the others were remanded until the next day for sentence. Ronald Kray and Ian Barrie were convicted of Cornell's murder, with Reggie being convicted as an accessory. Both the twins, the Lambrianou brothers and Ronald Bender were convicted of the murder of Jack McVitie whilst Charles Kray, Frederick Foreman, and Cornelius Whitehead were all convicted of being accessories after the fact. Albert Donaghue pleaded guilty to being an accessory. Once the immediate emotion of the verdicts had passed I was keen to get away from the court and buy my lads the drinks they so richly deserved.

The next day Melford Stevenson was at his most perky. I didn't feel that bright. The wine had flowed freely and I was not at my best.

There had been tremendous press coverage overnight and the Old Bailey was once again packed with reporters and the public. The jury too had returned to hear the sentences. Once again the judge dealt with the defendants individually, to avoid demonstrations.

I was about to be recalled to the witness box to give the antecedents in each of their cases when Platts-Mills made one final submission that because of the second trial and the immense publicity the case had generated there should be no minimum term to be imposed in the case of the obligatory life sentence his client faced.

'I reject that submission,' said the judge, and listened patiently whilst I gave Ronnie Kray's antecedents. There was also a final outburst from the dock. In answer to a question from the judge I said I had been unable to trace any Kray assets except for a house, The Brooks, at Bildeston, Suffolk.

'That's my mother's house,' shouted Ronnie. But it was no longer important.

> Ronald Kray, I am not going to waste words on you. The sentence upon you is that you will go to life imprisonment. In my view society has earned a rest from your activities and I recommend that you be detained for thirty years. Put him down.

Next up was Barrie. The minimum of his life term to be served was 20 years. Reginald Kray followed him and also had a 30-year recommendation imposed. Christopher and Anthony Lambrianou had 15 years' minimum whilst Bender received a 20-year minimum. Charles Kray was next.

> It may well be that you are not a member of what has been called in this case 'the Firm', but I am satisfied that you were an active and ready helper in the dreadful enterprise of concealing the traces of murder that your brother committed and that you were called in and consulted for

that purpose, and that you were energetic in carrying out that purpose. The sentence upon you is that you go to prison for ten years.

Frederick Foreman received exactly the same sentence, whilst Whitehead received seven years.

When the last of the defendants had gone down Melford Stevenson called me into the witness box. 'I can't let this case pass without saying that the debt the public owes Superintendent Read and his officers cannot be overstated and can never be discharged.' It only remained for him to thank the jury and to decline to order Anthony Barry to pay a contribution of £138 to his legal aid costs. As he did so I wondered about the sentences.

Thirty years was a long time. The example had been set with the sentences handed out to the train robbers, but this was different. This was the break-up of an organised gang who had brought terror to the East End, where the leaders were so confident of their authority they could kill in the presence of witnesses, knowing that the silence of those witnesses could be guaranteed. I had no doubt Melford Stevenson had this in mind when he passed the sentences. To many of us the length of them was no surprise.

Now there were handshakes all round. Frank Cater and I grinned a lot. At last Harry Mooney looked as though he was pleased with the way things had gone. David Hopkin wiped his forehead to indicate what a slog it had all been.

The jury went off for a drink together. Now after forty-odd days under surveillance from my team they could get back to some semblance of normality. It wasn't over for me by any means. Kenneth Jones, as business-like as usual, barked 'Conference' and I trooped after him and John Leonard to his room.

There was a lot to be done with the Mitchell trial in the offing. Decisions had to be made about Donaghue and the part he was to play. Finally it was decided he would be used as a prosecution witness and the murder charge against him would be dropped. Next was the question of what to do about Frederick Foreman and Charles Kray. It was decided that they should be charged – Charles for the second time – and I was sent down to the cells to tell them that a charge would be put to them soon.

Now a Bill of Indictment would be applied for. This would save any committal proceedings against Foreman. So far as Charles Kray was concerned, the charge against him would merely be put into the indictment. It was a legal procedure which overruled the magistrate's decision to find he had no case to answer.

Alf Gerard, named as the killer of Mitchell by Donaghue, was long gone. I had been looking for him for months but all indications were that he had fled the country and there was no evidence just where he was. The trial would have to start without him.

The conference over, my lads could relax a little, and Frank Cater and I were swept off to a lunch at the Press Club. The reporters had laid on a dish of the day especially for us – 'Krayfish'. We were delighted.

Over the next few days the newspapers had a fine time. There were headlines in every issue showing pictures of the twins and containing the details of their lives from birth to conviction. The reporters had been gathering copy for months. Everyone who had ever spoken to the Krays seemed to have been interviewed and squeezed dry of their recollection of the experience. 'End of a Reign of Terror', 'The Firm that ruled the East End by Fear', 'The nearest we came to Al Capone'. It was sensational stuff.

The coverage did, however, present a problem. How in the Mitchell case could the defendants get a fair trial when their names had been plastered all over the papers saying they had just received 30 years? It was something we were going to have to face in the coming weeks.

Just a week after the sentencing I was called to another conference. There had been a sensational development. Manny Fryde, still working for Sampsons and overseeing Ralph Haeems, was offering certain pleas on behalf of his clients, one of whom was, he said, prepared to make a statement. Of course, this was initially attractive. It could cut down the time and expense of a trial. There was a sting in the tail. The murder charge against one of them would have to be dropped. Nevertheless, it was discussed and very carefully thought over by Jones, Leonard, David Hopkin and myself in conference, along with Frank Cater. I was all for going to see the man at once, but the lawyers advised we should proceed with care. Finally we agreed we could not come to a real conclusion until we knew what the person would say. It was decided as a first step to approach counsel for that defendant to see if he would agree to a visit from me and to make a statement under caution. In the end no statement was forthcoming. If it had gone through it would have been a sensational end to the trial.

Between the trials I arranged a party for the jurors in the first case and their escorts. It took place at the Mount Pleasant Hotel in King's Cross. There were no speeches, no presentations, simply a bit of food and a few drinks together with a cabaret act by a pop group. It was simply a thank-you to the jurors who had been guarded for so long and who had co-operated so well in what must have been very difficult circumstances for them. They could, after all, have led my men a merry dance if they had wished. Unfortunately some people did not see the gathering as a simple get-together and, in particular, Kenneth Jones and John Leonard were less than pleased, saying they thought it looked bad. In hindsight perhaps they were right.

Then on 23 March I received an urgent message to go to Wormwood Scrubs. Michael Kenrick, awaiting trial on the bonds charges, had committed suicide there. I went there and, as I identified the body, thought what a tragedy this was. In the whole affair Kenrick was one of the most decent. He had been inveigled into crime by Cooper who had persuaded him to smuggle a one-off consignment of gold. It had proved so easy that other runs had followed until he had been nicked. He simply could not face another long term added to the five-year sentence he was already serving, and so somehow got hold of some pills and ended it all. The irony was that those who were concerned with Kenrick in dealing in the bonds had the cases against them dropped. So poor Kenrick would not have received an additional sentence. What a waste of a life!

Matron's room at the Old Bailey wasn't just available for tea. On the day of Kenrick's death I was approached by one of the counsel in the second trial who told me his client was absolutely terrified and that he had advised him to 'tell the absolute truth'. What could I do?

I said that there would be no problem in moving him to another prison and, if he wanted, I would go and see him. The barrister suggested he, the client, would prepare a proof of evidence to be given to the firm of solicitors acting for him which would be absolutely false and at the last minute would request to see him (counsel) and give another version. But although I went to see him, nothing came of it. It was just one more instance of the bluff and double bluff which was going on.

Two of the defendants in the Mitchell trial had served notices of alibi[11] and so enquiries were necessary to test the validity of these. By now the case was two years old, and tracing people who had been around at the time was difficult. One had gone to Australia and another to South Africa. Others had just disappeared. There was one witness still around to support one of the alibis. The old doctor whom I had seen earlier confirmed that he had been treating one of the defendants, who was confined to bed. For the moment it looked as though the alibi was sound, but I was to see the good doctor yet again. Three days into the trial he came to the Old Bailey to tell me he now realised the seriousness of the position and that all he had been treating the defendant for was a cold. There was no question of the man being confined to bed!

As far as I was concerned the Mitchell case was by far the most interesting of the three. There was the contention that he was still alive. After all, sightings had been received from all parts of the

---

11 An alibi is a complete answer to a charge. It establishes that the suspect was in another place at the time of the offence. Merely because an alibi is broken does not mean that the defendant committed the offence. Alibis are given for all sorts of reasons. A broken alibi does not actually help a defendant, however. A good example is the case of Steinie Morrison. His alibi was broken and, although the judge told the jury they must not regard this as proof of guilt, they did so.

world, and I prepared a list of all the ones I could trace. But even setting that on one side the case had everything: his history, his unfortunate upbringing, his convictions, his assaults on prison staff, spells in solitary, his apparent reformation, the spectacular escape, his time in Dunn's flat – 'changing one prison cell for another' said Kenneth Jones – Liza, and finally his sudden death. This was the stuff of which films were made and, in my mind, I was already running through the dramatic impact I was sure it would have on the jury. If the McVitie case had been successful, just wait for this tale.

On 14 April I had the final meeting with counsel when we discussed the order of witnesses and the progress made checking out the alibis. I was confident we were all prepared. My witnesses were now composed and confident. Even Liza was actually looking forward to her day in the spotlight. For security reasons it had been decided the case should be heard in Court No. 2. Eight of the ten defendants had already been convicted and it was feared that there might be some attempt at an escape. Although bigger, Court No. 2 was easier to protect.

And so the second trial began on 15 April with Mr Justice Lawton, a tough but much more accessible and jovial judge, presiding. He was the son of a prison governor and had had a substantial civil as well as criminal practice at the Bar. One of his earliest cases had been the defence of Harry Dobkin.[12] He had also defended Gunther Podola.[13]

The proceedings opened with another unusual but this time successful submission by John Platts-Mills regarding the publicity which the previous case had attracted. He wanted the opportunity to examine the potential jurors to see if they had been prejudiced against Ronnie Kray by what they had

---

12 In 1942 workmen clearing a bombed chapel in Lambeth had found the partly mummified body of a female. As a result of brilliant forensic work it was possible to match the teeth with the dental history of Dobkin's wife who had disappeared some 18 months earlier. Separated from him, she had been pestering Dobkin for maintenance payments. He was hanged on 27 January 1943.

13 See Chapter 4.

read in the popular press. If he could establish this he was then in a position to challenge the juror for cause and so not waste his peremptory challenges. He called Ralph Haeems to produce a bundle of the most lurid of the newspaper cuttings, arguing that their headlines were bound to have affected the minds of potential jurors. At first the judge was not helpful. He agreed that it was the practice in America, where days are spent testing the religious beliefs and political views of jurors, but he felt the practice was foreign to the administration of justice here. He also pointed out that there was no one in the United Kingdom who had read a newspaper and not heard of Ronald Kray. However, he agreed there should be cross-examination to see what newspapers the jurors had read. So, for the first time in this country, we had the spectacle of jurors *en bloc* being questioned regarding their capability to try a case.[14]

Apart from challenges made by other counsel to get all women off the jury, Mr Platts-Mills challenged each juror for cause and, after a short cross-examination, established bias in a number of the cases. Those jurors were stood down. So instead of taking a few minutes to empanel a jury it was not until the third day that we were able to get under way. Even then there was a hiatus. Two of the defendants changed their pleas to harbouring Mitchell, and were each sentenced to a term of nine months' imprisonment.

When, at last, we were under way, Mr Justice Lawton, with his knowledge of how prisons should be conducted, had a hard time believing the stories of Mitchell's activities on the Moor. He just could not believe that a prisoner would be in a position where he could buy scotch and vodka almost wholesale to take back to prison, let alone be able to hire a taxi to go to Tavistock to buy a budgie.

'Did it ever enter your head that inmates of Dartmoor nearly eleven miles away would be having a mid-morning drink in your bar?' he asked the landlord of the Elephant's Nest, adding,

---

[14] Mr Justice Lawton did not really approve of the process. 'I found the whole procedure very unsatisfactory,' he said in an interview in the *New Law Journal*, 30 January 1987, p 98.

'It just sounds like Cloud Cuckoo Land.' When he heard the evidence of a fellow prisoner that it was Mitchell who ran the prison, he raised his eyebrows in a mixture of disbelief and horror.

When it came to her turn, despite all her fears, Liza was magnificent. She gave her evidence in a clear concise way, enduring a gruelling cross-examination without faltering.

In fact when the trial began it was something of a mirror of the first. However, this time instead of Hart, a man with some personality, as the principal witness, there was Albert Donaghue in his role.

I had been wrong about Donaghue. When I first saw him, the time he was nicked at West End Central, I gave him the usual spiel: 'This is the time to make up your mind and decide whose side you want to be on.' He was a big cold person, the sort of guy of whom you would think 'That's a waste of time'. In fact he offered to become an informer but even then he confessed without emotion. It was the same at the trial: he was cold, absolutely cold.

Of course there was Liza; there was Billy Exley, still alive but a dying man; there were dozens of witnesses but, when it came to it, only Albert Donaghue who could deal with what happened outside Lennie Dunn's flat when Mitchell was being moved. And the defence, just as they had done with Hart, had a field day putting the blame on the uncharismatic Donaghue. So far as they were concerned he was the last person to see Mitchell alive. And besides, where was Alf Gerard?

At the close of the prosecution case, a submission that there was no case to answer made on behalf of Ronald and Charles Kray on the murder count was successful. It was the second time Charles Kray had been acquitted of the same charge.

On Friday 16 May at 10.40 a.m. the jury retired to consider their verdicts on Ronnie, Reggie and the remaining defendants. They were back in an hour and a half to ask a question, and came back again at half past three when they were told to try a little while longer to reach a unanimous verdict. Just before 5 p.m. they were told they could bring in a majority verdict of at least

10–2. This time they were gone just under the hour.

When the jury returned a verdict of guilty on the first count that Reggie had conspired to effect the escape of Mitchell, I thought 'Here we go again', but so far as all the others were concerned the jury returned verdicts of not guilty.

When Reggie was sentenced to a total of five years' imprisonment he simply said, 'God bless you all. Thank you,' as he left the dock. I doubt he included me.

Without doubt we would have been better off pursuing Manny Fryde's offer more vigorously.

CHAPTER TWELVE

THE APPEALS OF THE Kray brothers, Whitehead, the Lambrianous, Bender, Foreman, and Barrie were heard in the High Court in the Strand in July. There were numerous grounds of appeal lodged, but the two main ones boiled down to the refusal by Melford Stevenson to allow separate trials for the murders of Cornell and McVitie, because Barry, in the latter case, had run the defence of duress, and the fact that in Reggie's case his defence had not been adequately put to the jury during the summing-up. Although the appeals lasted six days, Lord Widgery, the Lord Chief Justice, made short work of them in the Court's decision given on 22 July. As to the first ground he said:

> These two cases exhibit unusual features in common; each was committed in cold blood and without obvious motivation. Each bore the stamp of a gang leader asserting his authority by killing in the presence of witnesses, whose silence could be assured by that authority. Neither murder could be committed except on the basis that members of the Firm would rally round and clear up the traces and secure the silence of those who may be inclined to give the offenders away. All these factors make it important and desirable in the public interest for these two unusual cases to be tried together. Also the interest of the press in this affair was so great that if the two murders had been tried separately the publicity attending the first trial would have made a fair trial on the remaining charge impossible.

He went on to say:

> Duress is not available to a murderer but it is to an accessory, but he must show that he could take no alternative course. In this case we are satisfied that by reason of threats Barry was so terrified that he ceased to be an independent actor and that the evidence of violence by the Krays which Barry put before the court was accordingly relevant and admissible.

As for the second ground:

> When the defence call evidence, a failure to put the case derived from that defence will almost always be fatal to the conviction but it is well established that the judge need not repeat all the argument of counsel, and, when no evidence is called, the defence necessarily consists of argument.

Because a conviction for murder carries a mandatory life sentence there was no possible appeal by the twins against sentence, but again the others had short shrift from the judges.

> Above all, this case tells a deplorable story of the activities of a gang in which the accessories sought to cover up the vicious and brutal conduct of the gang leaders. When such cases are brought to justice it is not sufficient to pass exemplary sentences on the leaders alone.

As I turned to leave court I saw the clerk to one of the Appeal judges signal to me. I went over and he told me that I was wanted in the judge's private rooms. I felt some trepidation as I walked along the corridor but when I met them I felt an arm around my shoulders.

'Now Mr Read,' said one, 'come and have a glass of sherry and tell us if they really were as bad as they seemed.'

Although the Krays sought leave to appeal to the House of Lords again on the question of joining two different cases in the indictment, that, so far as the criminal proceedings were concerned, was nearly that. In dismissing the application, their Lordships said the test to apply was whether the two or more offences exhibited such similar features as to make it appropriate and convenient to try them together. In this instance they did.

After the Mitchell trial there had been long conferences as to the desirability of proceeding with all the fraud trials, something which would necessarily have meant the brothers facing further long and costly hearings which, even had they been convicted, would not have added a single day to their sentences. Other defendants had been in custody for periods which meant that had they too been convicted they would surely have been released immediately. Personally I felt that in view of the hard work which my squad had put into the case and the strength of the evidence, the cases should have been heard, even if on conviction no further punishment was imposed. Apart from anything else it would have been something on the defendants' records if they had decided to commit further offences in the future. Despite my arguments I was overruled and on 25 May a number of fringe defendants pleaded guilty or had no evidence offered against them.

I then had to arrange the dispersal of the members of the Firm around the country. For security reasons it was vital they went to different prisons so, for example, Freddie Foreman went to Leicester, Whitehead to Hull, Charlie and Ronnie Kray to Durham. Reggie went to Parkhurst. Later Mrs Kray was to complain to the Home Office that it was bad for the twins to be separated like this and they were moved to be together.

Before they were delivered, I went to Durham on a test run to see how long it would take and to make arrangements with the Chief Constables of the various forces through which the route passed for escorts from their forces to meet us and drop us off at their boundaries. On Wednesday 28 May everything went like clockwork. We had a convoy of seven Jaguars and each escort picked us up precisely as we entered their Constabulary area and handed us over to the next. By the time we reached Durham, and delivered our charges to the prison authorities, we were 30 minutes ahead of schedule.

On a number of occasions John du Rose had asked me what we were going to do when the case was completed, and I told him we should let the squad continue. I pointed out there was plenty of work to justify its retention and, at his request, submitted a report to this effect. This he minuted and passed to the Home Office. As a result the Serious Crime Squad was established as a unit and the *ad hoc* arrangement of my squad was no longer necessary.

The work done by Harry Mooney to put the lid on the East End had been so effective that no one was daring to occupy the vacuum left by the dismemberment of the Kray Firm. However, I was now to look at target criminals, and one North London gang fell neatly into my catchment area. They were the obvious first choice and we looked at them intently for a period of time, but they certainly weren't doing the things you would expect them to be doing if they had taken over from the Krays. They had one or two clubs in the West End who were paying them money but it was being done in a very different way from the Krays' reign of terror. It was really rather a friendly business with this gang – almost a two-way operation with benefits to both sides. We thought they would jump in and occupy the vacuum, but it never happened. I think they sensed that if they had done that they would have let themselves in for a major investigation and consequently all sorts of troubles. It was a good example of preventive policing.

As the record of the Serious Crime Squad suggests however, it was only a temporary lull and, as I forecast, the squad more than justified its formation.

Now for a time came the plaudits. John du Rose had come to see me at Tintagel House and had taken me onto the staircase where we were assured of complete privacy. 'The Commissioner has told me your future is assured. You will be the next Commander and there will be a medal in it for you.' Of course I was delighted and it never occurred to me to question his word. There was even a suggestion in the *Sunday Express* that I should receive a knighthood. Later, along with my original team, I was invited to the Yard for a celebratory drink at which both the Commissioner and Peter Brodie were present. Each took me aside and confirmed just what du Rose had told me. I was to be the next person promoted Commander in the CID. It was then I was sent to Bramshill on the seventh Senior Command Course.

This was not a reward for the work done on the Kray case. I had earned my place on the course by surviving a strenuous sifting process, comprising an area selection and then a three-day extended interview system. I had got that far before, but the last time I had upset the officer in charge, Sir Arthur Young, by questioning the value of the whole procedure. What had happened was that one of the civilian invigilators had suggested I was not the right sort of material. The type of officers being sought were those who could converse with members of police committees, etc. I had laughed at this and asked Sir Arthur whether he had ever listened to what such people talked about. 'The most intelligent level of conversation with them,' I said, 'is usually about last Saturday's game and "'ow much can we get for that pratt of a winger 'oo can't cross t' ball to save 'is bleedin' life."'

I had already attended the first Intermediate Command Course and I now saw the Senior Course as qualifying me for very senior rank. Competition for places on the course is very keen, as only 24 applicants are accepted annually. Curiously there are few from the Met, and of those that are successful the majority leave to serve in provincial forces. Perversely it seems that, contrary to Home Office policy, the Yard selects its senior officers from those who are not so highly qualified.

I was delighted to be joining the course, but I was not really concerned to prove myself. I was content in the knowledge I would continue my career in the Met's CID and I was not looking for posts in provincial forces. For this reason I freewheeled much of the time and enjoyed the companionship and relaxation rather than seeing it as an intellectual challenge. Indeed, at the end of the course, the Commandant, Colin Wood, said he hoped I had enjoyed it and that he had seen it as a therapeutic exercise for me.

Obviously during the course the subject of the Kray trial came up and several of the members expressed surprise that there had been no official recognition of the part I had played. They felt that this could usefully have been exploited by the Met for political and publicity reasons.

As part of the course I was sent to do a project with the Lancashire Constabulary and whilst there I had lunch with one of the legendary characters of the police service, Bill Palfrey, the Chief Constable who had amalgamated 14 forces to create the new Lancashire Constabulary. We were talking about the inquiry over lunch when he asked, 'What did you get out of it, Nipper?' and when I replied, 'Nothing so far,' he said, 'Do you mean to tell me they never even gave you a bloody gong? They don't appreciate a good man. I'll tell you what, Nipper, any time you want to come to Lancashire, there's a job here for you.'

As for the gong, I was to wait until January 1976 when I received the Queen's Police Medal for distinguished service, and that was nothing at all to do with my work on the Kray inquiry.

Back at Bramshill at the end of the course I was disturbed to find I was not told where I was to serve on my return to the Met. I thought it significant that prior to the final week of the course the Deputy Commissioner came to the college and told all my uniformed colleagues from the Met on the course where they would be posted. For the moment, so far as I was concerned, I was still on the strength of the Murder Squad, although obviously I had been replaced during my absence. So, to try to find out where I was going, I asked one of my colleagues on the course, an Assistant Chief from Thames Valley, who was visiting the Yard, to see what he could discover from one of the Deputy Assistant Commissioners with whom he was friendly.

When he returned I was astounded to hear that he had been told I needed more Divisional experience. I really could not believe this. I was the most experienced Divisional senior CID officer in the force. Apart from my time with the Murder

Squad and the secondment to the Train Robbery inquiry I had never been off a Division. I saw it as an indication of the ineptitude of those in charge and of how little they really knew of the men under their command.

Finally, on the Friday I left the college, I telephoned the Yard and was told to report to 'Y' Division (Wood Green) on the following Monday. When I later complained about this to a senior CID officer I was brushed off with the excuse that it was 'an administrative breakdown'. But I knew that the Commissioner would have to assert himself to see that my future was indeed 'assured'. It was clear that the Fifth Floor had taken a distinct dislike to me.

There were further disturbing signs when a newspaper article appeared, indicating that the Yard was launching a purge on the personality cult. Headed 'Yard takes Star Men out of Limelight', the report said that the Commissioner, Sir John Waldron, and Peter Brodie were worried about two recent cases which had resulted in publicity for the officers leading them. These were the Great Train Robbery and Tommy Butler and the Kray case and me. The Home Secretary James Callaghan, it continued, had decided not to set up a permanent gang-busting squad at the Yard.

The information had been leaked by the Fifth Floor to the newspapers to discredit me. It could not affect Tommy. He was much too near the end of his career for it to make any difference to him and I know he shrugged it off. I thought it to be another mistake on the part of Brodie, who would have advised the Commissioner, in failing to react, and another indication of the way he was so easily manipulated by 'the faceless ones'.

The whole mystique of the CID and Scotland Yard had been created by individuals who achieved publicity for their success in particular cases. It probably began with Chief Inspector Walter Dew and his chase across the Atlantic to capture Crippen and Ethel Le Neve, but it had been carried on, over the years, by such great names as Fred Wensley, Reggie Spooner, Bill 'Cherub' Chapman, Jack 'Charlie Artful' Capstick, Ted Greeno, Peter Beveridge and Robert Fabian. All achieved the sort of publicity which resulted in Scotland Yard becoming world famous, not for traffic management, public order control, or new policing methods but for the quality and resulting success of its detectives in the field. In my view this latest move was an entirely misconceived decision on the part of the Commissioner, and resulted in a blanket of anonymity being laid over the work of extremely good detectives who could have carried the torch and furthered the name of Scotland Yard.

Indeed, the reaction by the top brass to the Kray inquiry had been mixed all along. My appointment to the inquiry had been treated with some disdain by the favoured ones on the Fifth Floor, the men who flitted from one department of the Yard to another and who were never involved in anything other than carefully selected inquiries. They received rapid promotion and were always in high profile at functions, chumming it with senior officers.

My association with Fred Gerrard from way back in 1964 had resulted in my being dubbed as one of his protégés, and therefore my face did not fit. From the beginning of the inquiry most of these people thought the job could not be done and were not averse to leaking information to the press and their favoured reporters. There had been a leakage – at best unfortunate and potentially very dangerous – to Norman Lucas of the *Sunday Mirror* at a crucial time in the investigation.[1] By the time of the committal proceedings which had resulted in two cases being discharged I was being avoided as if I had a dose of the clap. It was only when we reached the Old Bailey and things were starting to look better that the Commissioner and Peter Brodie put in an appearance.

As the success of the operation became more apparent, feeling on the Fifth Floor changed to one of positive resentment that it was unable to share the glory. This was not unusual. The

---

[1] 'Mafia Launch Forged Fivers Plan', 3 March 1968. The article went on to say that I was checking on a team of London gangsters.

same thing had happened in the Richardson case when every effort had been made to steer the limelight away from Gerry McArthur, the real author of its success. It was apparent that success in a major investigation such as his and mine is not the best way to further a career. As I learned, it can be distinctly detrimental.

The small-mindedness of the people to whom I am referring can best be summed up by the tie incident. It was customary at the conclusion of a major inquiry to produce a tie with some form of motif to celebrate the case. So far as I was concerned, it was important in the Kray case because many of those employed on jury and witness protection had never been to my office and really didn't know too much about the case. Nevertheless, they had been vital in helping to achieve the result. I felt a tie would be some kind of reward and they could wear it with pride to show to their friends and colleagues that they had been part of the inquiry. I therefore designed one, combining the double initials K, the flagstaff of Tintagel House which featured a ball and crown, a chain-linked circle signifying protection and the logo *Noster Firmus* which, I assured everybody, meant Our Firm. The tie had been discussed briefly at a drink at the Yard. The Commissioner said he understood the men would be getting a tie and asked WDC Pat Allen what she and the other women would be getting. She replied flippantly, 'Well, we would like to have a garter. I think it will be a scarf.'

I had had a sample made up, but before I could order production to begin I received a direction that the idea was to be abandoned. I just could not believe it and protested strongly. Although I pressed for a reason I was only told that it would not be in the best interests of the CID and the Force. This was indeed hard news for the men and women who had worked so tirelessly. It might not have been much but it would have been some recognition of the part they had played, and I was disappointed for them. Many of them complained to me that they had worked on far less significant inquiries and had been given a memorial tie. It was difficult for me to explain that the reason was not them or the inquiry but probably the fact that I had been in charge. Some time previously Arthur Lewis, the MP for West Ham North, had suggested that there should be special recognition for all my squad; the idea was clearly being firmly stamped upon.

And so I went to Wood Green and North London where my investigations into one case made it clear that the promises made to me by du Rose, Waldron and Brodie after the Kray case would never be fulfilled and I had no real future in the Met other than as a timeserver. For obvious reasons it became known as the 'Babes in the Wood' case.

The inquiry concerned the disappearance and deaths of two young children in the Ponders End area of Enfield. Gary Hanlon, then aged 13, and Susan Blatchford, 11, left their homes on the afternoon of 31 March 1970, and were last seen together about 4.30 p.m. When they failed to return home their parents reported it to the police at Ponders End, and details were recorded in the missing persons book, as kept at each police station. As the Chief Superintendent in charge of the CID on 'Y' Division, when I went to a station there were certain books, such as the charge book, prisoners' book and so on I checked as a routine matter. The missing persons book was one of these. I saw and initialled the report and spoke to the officer dealing with the inquiry, WPC Josie Lowbridge. She said she was unusually concerned about the disappearance of the children and I said that unless they had been found or returned the next day I would take up the enquiry. There can be a number of reasons why kids go missing – quarrels with their parents or brothers and sisters, or they have simply gone to spend the night with friends and have not told anybody.

The next day when I returned they still had not been found and I set up a murder headquarters at Ponders End. Of course it wasn't that yet and I hoped it wouldn't be, but I wasn't going to take a chance and so I started the thing off as a serious investigation from Day One.

In a police career some things stick in your mind and you say, 'This won't ever happen to me.' I remembered back to my early days at Paddington: three young children went missing on the Harrow Road section. It was nothing to do with me – I wasn't remotely involved – but I remembered every detail of it and always said to myself that if I was in charge of such a search I would do things differently. The police searched for them unsuccessfully for days, then a workman heard noises from a metal coal bunker, opened the lid and there were the children. They had climbed in it to play, and when the lid came down they were unable to open it again. They had been in there for seven days and only survived because it had rained and they were able to drink rainwater as it had leaked into the bin.

The police had rightly been severely criticised for not finding the children. They had searched all right but not systematically. Probably a dozen officers had looked at the bunker and thought somebody had searched inside. I was damned sure this was not going to happen in my case.

I drew up orders for the searching of houses (the final total was 4,356). This included sheds, outhouses, cars, boats, lofts and any other area where a child could have gone by itself or been taken. I insisted each should be marked with a white cross to indicate it had been examined and that the officer would then return to me a form signed to this effect. Everyone was warned that, if later it was discovered that the search had not been completely properly, he or she would be out of a job.

I had the walls of the operations room covered with maps of the area, with each section marked off after it had been searched. I could trace Susan and Gary up to the Sewardstone Road, the busy B194 road leading from Waltham Abbey to Harlow. In my first report I wrote that once they reached the road they could have gone either left or right or, if they had been picked up by car, almost anywhere. On the other side of this road was another police area, 'J' Division, and here there were open fields and woods.

It was necessary to use the dog section, and this is where the operation went wrong. In charge was Sergeant Burnell, an experienced and competent officer who mustered every dog-handler in the district to begin a systematic search of this vast area. The dog searches were scored off each day on the map as he reported in, and I was satisfied he was conducting the operation in a careful and proficient manner.

During that search we used 250 men, 28 dogs, a helicopter and frogmen – there were two sewage farms and two enormous reservoirs in the area. A team of women police was also employed and we were helped by hundreds of members of the public searching open fields and other areas.

One theory was that they might have run off with a fairground show which had been in the area, or even been abducted by a traveller with them. I deputed a team to track down every single caravan and sideshow from that fair, but the officers came back with no lead at all. So I sent my DI Peter Darke to talk to the fairground people again. He drew a blank and so I went myself. Nothing was any use. This end of the enquiry was dead.

In the first month there were 218 sightings of the children and each of them was a bust. Four clairvoyants, including Gerard Croiset who had been so uncannily successful in the Boston Strangler case, were sent samples of the children's clothes by their parents and gave four separate explanations for the children's disappearance but all said they believed they were alive and still in the Enfield area. They all indicated various places where the children might be found, and these were followed up but they too came to nothing.

Then in a rather vain hope that they might have run away voluntarily, gypsy camps throughout the country were simultaneously searched in a gigantic and complex operation. Again it came to naught.

After a month of determined searching and persistent enquiries I reported that, 'The awful truth is that we haven't been able to turn up a single fragment of evidence between the lot of us.' At this stage the only explanation seemed to be that the children had suffered some tragic accident. There were so many natural hazards in the area. Besides the reservoirs and sewage pits there was the River Lea, as well as acres of woodland. It was not the answer, however. Two months later the matter was resolved. On 17 June a farmer was out shooting with his dog which went into the wood just off the Sewardstone Road and would not come out. He went in after him and discovered a kind of a hide in which were the two bodies. It looked as though it had been made from branches and twigs into which the children had crept and had died.

I went over to the wood and found it was very difficult to penetrate the thick undergrowth. The children were found with her arm around him – although younger, the girl was a much bigger and better developed child than the boy – and this led to the belief that they had died of cold. This was when the newspapers headlined their stories as the 'Babes in the Wood' case. In fact, at one stage, after examinations had been made, some of the experts thought there was no possibility of a third party involvement. The pathologist Professor James Cameron was unable to give a cause of death owing to the absence of vital organs and so the mystery remained.

I did not, and still do not, agree that a third party was not involved. Susan had been wearing jeans. First of all a patch had been taken out which the pathologist said was by rats or other animals. That may be, but, more importantly to my mind, her jeans had been ripped completely down each side of the seam as though the trousers had been kippered. They had been pulled off as you strip the skin off a fish. It was impossible to ascribe any explanation for this other than that it had been done deliberately by a third party, and I was determined to find out how.

I obtained a dozen similar pairs of jeans, and had a young officer, David Veness, now a Commander, wear them. I then tried to tear them in the same fashion as Susan's and found there was only one way. If he was lying down and I grabbed hold of the waistband and gave a good pull the jeans then split at the seams. Doing that they came away easily. Another factor was that one of Susan's shoes was found outside the wood, and certain of her underclothes were missing.

Bearing in mind all the circumstances, I was convinced the two children had been murdered. There was no other possible satisfactory explanation.

In retrospect I should have acted differently at the beginning of the inquiry. Gary had an older brother who, when I saw him in the initial stages of the enquiry, was in shock. He was going off immediately to stay with relations in the country and, of course, I did not wish to delay that. Later when he returned and I had a longer chat with him he told me the children had been in the habit of going into the wood where the bodies were found. If I had known that from the beginning we would have found the bodies earlier and so been able to establish the cause of death.

It was a difficult choice. When I first saw him the boy was not really up to questioning and I took the sympathetic view which most people would have supported. Later, however, I felt that had I been more persistent he might have given me that vital piece of information which could have changed the whole complexion of the case. In my final report I emphasised that in situations like this the gathering of information is paramount, and any feeling of sympathy must be sacrificed to this end.

Of course there had to be an inquiry. Why did the dog searchers not find the bodies – which had clearly been in the hide for some time – when they searched the wood? The day after they were found a Police Constable came to me and said, 'Guv'nor, they weren't in that wood when we searched it.' I asked how he could say that. 'Because I can tell you I went in that hide and crouched in it until my dog found me.' I said, 'Look, if you're trying to suggest that the bodies were put in there after you searched forget it. I don't want excuses. I'm looking for reasons.'

The sergeant in charge of the dog section provided them. 'When they get to a situation like that,' he told me, 'the handler releases the dog and he goes into the wood. Then the handler walks round the end of the wood and whistles and the dog comes out.'

'What does the dog do if he finds something?'

'It depends entirely upon the dog. Some may bark, others back off, others whimper. There is no set pattern of behaviour and if the dog is called to heel by its handler it will go immediately.'

I therefore recommended that the training of dogs should be revised so that in a similar situation they would either bark or remain stationary, so the handler knew his dog had made a 'find'.

Now we stripped the Little Wood where the bodies were found, and there was a great deal of debris – panties, bras, condoms. It was clearly a place where courting couples went and therefore frequented by the usual Peeping Toms and sexual perverts. My theory was that the children had wandered up there to play when a man of this type inveigled them into the wood and attacked them.

We had a suspect – a man who had just been released from prison and who had a long history of sexual assaults. He had been seen on Day One and although he was not entirely ruled out of the enquiry he was able to account for his movements. Then, later, when he was found to be out and about almost every night, I put two officers on his tail. One night they found him in Enfield with a large knife. That was enough. We plundered him. When we searched his bedroom I could not believe it. In wardrobes, in suitcases, underneath his bed, everywhere, were hundreds of bits of gear – panties, bras, and slips. He stole them from clothes-lines and what he did with them afterwards was his business. There was also other property which was identified as coming from a housebreaking in the Enfield area. All the linen was removed and sifted to see if anything could be traced back to Susan, but it could not.

Once he was lodged in the police station I questioned him again about the children for some time but he would not admit anything. We had no witnesses with whom to confront him, so I could not pursue the matter any further. He was, however, charged with 17 counts of burglary and housebreaking for which he received five years' imprisonment.

Faced with all the evidence, the Coroner returned an open verdict. He could not do otherwise, but my report concluded that the children had been murdered. In my view it was the only theory which supported the facts. The problem was proving it. I hoped to be able to continue with the enquiry but I was told in no uncertain terms that it would be a waste of time and manpower and I was obliged to close the case.

My birthday is 31 March and since 1970 not one has gone past when I do not think of Susan Blatchford and Gary Hanlon. I still hope that – somehow – the case may be resolved, but now I doubt it.

By the end of that inquiry two new Commanders had been appointed and it was obvious that Brodie's thinking had been affected by lobbying from the hierarchy. I seemed to be going nowhere in the Met, and so I successfully applied for the position of Assistant Chief Constable of my native Nottinghamshire.

When my appointment was announced Brodie asked to see me in his offices at the Yard. 'Well, Nipper,' he said, 'so you've decided that your future lies in the provinces. It's a good decision, I'm sure.'

But he raised his eyebrows when I replied, 'No, I didn't decide. You decided. I was always satisfied that my future was here in the Met CID as I told you before, but it appears that you had other ideas.'

He was staggered. 'But, my dear chap, I had no idea you felt like this.' And I'm sure he meant what he said, but by this time I was in full flow and I couldn't give a damn. I was going to another Force and all the bitterness and resentment I felt at the perfidious chicanery from the Fifth Floor burst out. I reminded Brodie that I had been promised that my future was assured and that I was to have been the next Commander, as he himself had told me.

He blustered momentarily and then said, 'Yes, but that's right. No one has gone in front of you.' I pointed out that there had been two fresh appointments since the promise had been made, something he tried to explain away by saying they were merely inconsequential postings. He went on to make further excuses and it infuriated me when he said, 'You must realise I can only act on the advice I am given.'

I exploded at this and told him in that event he was the most ill-advised senior officer I had ever met.

He was obviously embarrassed at my outburst, but his reaction has always seemed to me to be a most extraordinary one. He got up from his desk, walked over to the window and gestured to the street outside. 'Nothing is certain in this world,' he said. 'I could walk out of this building today and be knocked over by a bus.' He returned and sat down. 'I want to assure you, Nipper, I don't belong to any secret society or anything like that.'

He was obviously referring to Freemasonry which had a very strong membership on the Fifth Floor. I had never even considered his involvement, and his introduction of the subject was completely unnecessary. I was glad to be going and he was clearly glad to end the interview. He wished me luck with all the grace he could muster and I left the Yard for what I then thought would be the last time.

Some little time later, in casual conversation with one of my fellow CID officers, I learned that Brodie had been at the initiation ceremony into a Masonic Lodge of one of the men who had been appointed Commander before me.

Had du Rose still been serving I would not have had to apply for jobs outside the Met. John was strong enough to have made Brodie keep his promise but, once he left, lesser people dripped into his ear until they left the impression they wanted. Although I had always like Brodie, my assessment of him as being ill-advised was borne out later at the corruption trials when he gave evidence on behalf of convicted officers. His misguided loyalty to the wrong people made him the implacable foe of Sir Robert Mark, who destroyed him with the observation that the CID was 'the most routinely corrupt organisation in London', and who removed the command of the CID from Brodie and placed it in the hands of the Divisional Commanders. Perhaps it is to Brodie's credit that he still tried to defend his 'chaps', saying they were a straight bunch of guys, but with *The Times* inquiry and the Porn Squad investigation his position was becoming intolerable.

From that point on, he almost relinquished his command to the 'mandarins' who relished the situation.

Robert Mark had come to the Met from Leicestershire, following his inquiry into prison escapes which included George Blake, Ronnie Biggs and Frank Mitchell. He had been appointed Assistant Commissioner and had had a very bad reception from senior officers. A typical instance came on his first day when the Commissioner dropped a letter on his desk in which it was suggested he apply for the position of Chief Constable of Lancashire which had just become vacant. 'I suggest you give it some thought,' he said.

Brodie was one of the 'old school' of officers who tried to freeze Mark out, but it was Mark who was offered the position of Commissioner on the death of Joseph Simpson. He turned it down, suggesting the caretaker appointment of Waldron, hoping that by Waldron's retirement he, Mark, would have learned sufficient about the Met to know how to deal with it when he took over. When Mark was appointed Deputy Commissioner, Brodie knew his chance had gone.

I didn't see Brodie again until 1972 when I went to the Home Office where I had been called for interview for the post of National Co-ordinator of the Regional Crime Squads. Brodie was one of the members of the panel. He greeted me warmly when we met outside, shook my hand said how nice it was to see me again and wished me all the best. 'I'm sorry to tell you the competition against you is very strong,' he said. 'I don't think you're going to get it this time. I've got three Commanders in for it and one is first favourite for the job. Never mind. . . . Good luck anyway.'

The first favourite was Commander Ken Drury, who in July 1977 was sentenced to eight years' imprisonment after he had been found guilty of corruption.

CHAPTER THIRTEEN

I CANNOT SAY THAT I enjoyed my time in Nottingham. In October 1970 I was appointed as Assistant Chief Constable (Operations) when Stuart Whitely was upgraded to Deputy Chief. Directly answerable to the Chief Constable Rex Fletcher, a local man who had served all his time in the Nottingham City force, my duties consisted of supervising the entire operational work of the Nottinghamshire Combined Constabulary – six territorial Divisions, traffic, the CID, and the Regional Crime Squad. I looked forward to the challenge of a completely different responsibility, and I wanted to make a success of the appointment.

It should have been like coming home – I was back on my native heath – but it did not seem that way. I found that working relationships were very different from those in the Met and, worse, the Chief and I did not get along at all well from the beginning. For some reason we just didn't see eye to eye.

One early incident occurred when I visited the Force Driving School at Newark. It was, in fact, a District Driving School, which was then fashionable under a Home Office scheme. This meant that other, less well-equipped Forces sent their drivers to the school. There were district schools up and down the country including ones in the Met, and at Wakefield and Chelmsford. I was appalled when I saw our 'school'. Situated at the back of Newark Police Station in some old stables, it was short of equipment and it lacked almost every other facility which would qualify it as a District Training School. I told the Chief Inspector in charge of the school that I would do something to improve the equipment problem and would try to get some new quarters, but when I returned to Nottingham and told Rex Fletcher that I was horrified at the lack of facilities he was surprised because he had always been so proud of his old driving school.

The Chief Inspector from the school came to see me soon afterwards to ask if I could get him a sectionalised engine. This is the kind of aid essential to an instructor lecturing on the component parts of an engine and the way they integrate to enable it to function. Despite the fact that the school had been in operation for some years, they did not have one. I asked whether he knew where he could obtain one. Of course he did, so I ordered him to go and purchase it at a cost of around £400, and get the firm to bill the Force.

The explosion came soon afterwards, when the force accountant (strictly the Force Administration Officer) burst into my office and demanded to know by what right I had authorised this purchase. I told him it was none of his business, but that it was a valuable piece of equipment essential for the work of the driving school.

In reply he said I should realise that the Force was working on an annual budget and there had been no provision for the purchase of such equipment. I told him that the Force must surely have some kind of contingency fund to cover for eventualities of this kind. He was not pleased and so I took out my cheque book and said, 'Look, if the Notts Combined Constabulary don't have the money, I'll pay for it and you can pay me back when you're in funds.' That settled it, of course, but it did not make for a good beginning.

I was never very happy during my first few months and so it was a relief when in the spring of 1971 I was asked by another Chief Constable, Sandy Willison, to undertake an investigation into allegations against the head of the CID of the West Mercia Force. Rex Fletcher had never done one himself and I suppose he thought it meant merely a couple of weeks away. He seemed delighted I had been asked.

The inquiry was the result of a total of 114 individual complaints against members of the Force and the Home Office Forensic Laboratory by the headmaster and staff of a private school in the Black Country. A man with no academic qualifications, he had set up a school taking mentally retarded children from the local authorities. Over a period of time there had been allegations that he had sexually assaulted a number of the boys. These had been dismissed as the fantasies of the complainants, but eventually he had been prosecuted and acquitted. Now he was alleging, amongst other things, that the evidence against him had been fabricated.

I thought the only way to make a proper investigation into his complaints was to go back to the start and re-investigate every one of the 27 charges which had been levelled against the headmaster. It was a formidable task. The 56 complainants had now been removed, and to see each and every one of the young people involved now they were away from the disturbing atmosphere of the school was quite an undertaking. Some had been placed in other institutions and some had returned to their homes. This meant I had to travel up and down the country to take the statements. To help me, I enlisted a Chief Inspector from the Nottingham force.

Rex Fletcher had no grasp of the enormity of the inquiry and, at first, thought it would be possible for me to continue my duties in Nottingham alongside the investigations in Shropshire. Of course this was impossible because of the scope of the inquiry, and indeed to get anything done in a reasonable time the Chief Inspector and I were obliged to make our headquarters near the school itself.

On the occasions when I did see Fletcher he persisted in asking when I was coming back to work. It seemed he believed that I was swanning off down the country. When I did complete the inquiry in the August, the report itself was 281 pages long, and with statements I had taken and other appendices the bundle of documents totalled 948 pages. Once

I had completed it, I plonked it on Rex Fletcher's desk in the hope that he would at last appreciate just how big an inquiry it had been. Two minutes later he returned it to me without comment. Clearly he had not even read the conclusions. Later I received a letter from Sandy Willison thanking me for my assistance and commenting, 'I don't think any of us had any idea of the extent of this inquiry. . .' Rex Fletcher had marked it 'NOTED'.

In fact the inquiry exonerated the CID from the allegations of malpractice, but pointed out certain minor infringements of the discipline code. What did concern me about the affair was the ease with which schools of this kind could be set up and run without any restriction, by unqualified people. I made a considerable number of comments in the hope that changes would be made to the law governing such schools.

One incident whilst I was at Nottingham reminded me of the enquiry into the Babes in the Wood case. A murder occurred near the M29 when a girl had left London to pick up her boyfriend's car. She had hitchhiked and had been traced as far as that road where she had been given a lift in an Austin Countryman. Then she vanished and was later found dead. Charlie Palmer from the Murder Squad came up and he wanted help from me. It was a matter of checking out all known Austin Countrymen and again I devised a scheme so that every officer put his signature to a report saying such-and-such a car had been checked. There was one officer detailed to carry out one particular check, a very well-thought-of Detective Constable who had everything going for him. In fact I had recommended him to go on an accelerated promotion course. His duty was to check on a particular Austin Countryman. He was given a sheet to sign and came back to say he had done the check. Later the woman owner of the car rang up to say that she had heard we were looking at all Austin Countrymans; she had one and did we want to come and see it? I sacked him. He could never be trusted again in an inquiry – ever.

The Nottinghamshire Force had a wonderful record of murder clear-ups, of which they were justly proud. The only blot on their sheet concerned the landlord of a pub known locally as The Pretty Windows because of the attractive lace curtains which hung there. He had been stabbed one night whilst taking his dog for a walk after closing time. Scotland Yard had been called in with Fred Gerrard in the frame. Rex Fletcher was then the Detective Superintendent and he and Fred had given it their best shot, but no one was ever caught. The local officers believed this was because the Yard had been called in. They felt they would have coped better if they had been left on their own.

During my time there were a number of murders, all of which were cleared up by the hard-working Detective Superintendent Larry Readwin. But one looked hopeless. An old man had been found dead on some waste ground adjoining a partly demolished gasworks. He had been battered to death and, as he was a down and out, it was unlikely that robbery was a motive.

I went to the scene with Larry and after looking at the bare landscape remarked, 'Well, this looks like your 100 per cent record is going.'

'Wait on, Boss, you never know,' was his reply.

The only buildings overlooking the site were about three-quarters of a mile away, and more in hope than expectation Larry sent officers to do a house-to-house inquiry. But his luck held – or was it the fact that, like a good copper, he decided to send in his men despite there being only a remote possibility of any help? At the second house a woman said, 'Thanks for calling. Matter of fact my husband was going to ring you people.' The man had had an accident and, being off work, sat most days looking out of his bedroom window with a pair of binoculars. He gave the officer a perfect description of the attacker, who had hit the old man with a brick, adding the interesting feature that the attacker 'had a white Alsatian dog on a lead with him'. From then on it was a matter of elimination, and Larry's record survived intact.

When the appointment as National Co-ordinator of the Regional Crime Squads was advertised at the end of 1971

I jumped at it. This time I was convinced I would get it. I had applied before when the appointment had gone to Jock Forbes, and my disappointment had been lessened when the Chief Inspector of Her Majesty's Constabulary had said, 'Don't worry, your time will come.'

Now, hearing of my application, some of my old crime reporter friends were taking bets that I would succeed, and Peter Burden, who had reported the closure of my crime squad, now headlined, 'Gangbuster Read may get Top Job'.

I did – on 10 March 1972. The appointment was mine, despite Peter Brodie's conviction that his candidate Commander Drury would get the job. Afterwards Brodie wrote me a handsome letter saying that I had done 'extremely well at the interview' and assuring me of the 'backing and support of "C" department' at Scotland Yard. I wrote in reply, thanking him for his good wishes and offers of help, but I also reminded him that 'as I told you before I left, I was convinced that I was embroiled in petty jealousies and intrigues which were not of my making'.

I was delighted to be leaving Nottinghamshire and, I suspect, Rex Fletcher was none too sorry to see me go. My replacement was a young man named Geoffrey Dear.[1] When I welcomed him to the post he asked me what the Chief was like. I replied I felt it would be unfair of me to comment, but when I returned to see him in a month's time we could talk about it. When I did see him next we didn't need to discuss the Chief. He didn't get on with him either.

It was great to be going back to Tintagel House as the first Assistant Chief to be appointed to the post. I retained that rank but I was paid as a Deputy Assistant Commissioner (£5,466–£6,270 p.a.). Technically I was on loan to the Home Office who were my new masters, but the post in Nottingham

[1] He later went on to become as Assistant Commissioner in the Met and the Chief Constable of West Midlands before taking his present appointment as one of Her Majesty's Inspectorate.

was kept open for me. My office in Tintagel House, which had originally been designed for the Receiver of the Metropolitan Police, was a corner suite on the sixth floor with a panoramic view over the Thames towards the Tate Gallery. Far larger than any offices in Scotland Yard, it was the envy of all senior officers in the Met who visited me from time to time.

Regional Crime Squads (RCS),[2] which had been set up five years earlier, had been modelled on the Birmingham City Crime Squads established by their one-time Chief Constable Edward Dodd, who later, as Sir Edward, became Her Majesty's Chief Inspector of Constabulary.

Announcing my appointment, the Home Office sent out a press notice describing the work of the Regional Crime Squads.

> Regional Crime Squads are mobile groups of experienced detectives operating across Force boundaries. They concentrate primarily on major criminals and their most notable recent success was the arrest and conviction of a highly professional lorry-hijacking gang at the end of 1971.
>
> The National Co-ordinator supervises the progress made by Regional Crime Squads and acts as a focal point for the collection of experience and the development of new ideas. He exercises a co-ordinating function when squads from more than one region are required to take part in a particular operation. He is available to advise and help in any way required of him by chief constables or by Regional Co-ordinators.

The sting was in the sentence about helping when required by Chief Constables. When the RCS were first introduced, many Chief Constables were reluctant to accept them and others were openly hostile. Later, when the scheme received the blessing

---

2 There are 47 autonomous police forces in the country and superimposed on them is the Crime Squad organisation. The country is divided into nine regions, each of which has a squad of differing strength under the command of a Detective Chief Superintendent.

of the Home Office, some Chief Constables showed their contempt by unloading some of their poorest material into the squads. This meant they had little chance of success and it was only because of the persistence and enthusiasm of the first National Co-ordinator, John Bliss, that the squads survived.

Chief Constables in those days jealously guarded their autonomy and resented any encroachment into their police areas, often to a point approaching paranoia. The thought of a freebooting, no frontiers, uncontrolled band of marauding thief-takers, looting and plundering their patches, was anathema to them. Indeed, by the time I came to take charge the very existence of the squads was in question. Some Chief Constables considered the squads had been set up only as an experiment for a limited period which had now expired. They questioned whether the experiment had been successful.

Almost immediately upon my appointment I found myself at the National Police College at Bramshill defending the role of the Regional Crime Squads at a meeting of the Association of Chief Police Officers. My friend Sandy Willison from West Mercia had been chosen as 'Prosecuting Officer'. He was proposing the motion that the RCS were not a functional organisation but were a drain on Chief Constables and should therefore be disbanded. The Association had taken my appointment as the opportunity to question the validity of the squads, and it was my task to persuade them the RCS were an effective and necessary organisation. After a lengthy debate I was successful in convincing the Association that there was a place in modern policing for them, and the RCS were given another lease of life. So began the happiest period of my police service.

John Bliss, my old DI from Albany Street, was the man who had really set up the Crime Squads and got them running, something for which he never received the credit he deserved. As soon as he heard of my appointment he got in touch with me and it was gratifying to find he was still as interested in the squads as when he was in charge. He still had the most innovative and far-seeing views about their development. Until I retired we never lost touch.

I became as passionate about the squads as John had been, and I was increasingly aware of the constraints under which they worked. In one of my first annual reports I pointed out the problems associated with investigating across-border crimes, and suggested that, from the outset, such crimes should become the responsibility of the squad. I went on to recommend that any crime of an unusually complex or time-consuming nature which would divert the local head of CID from his responsibility of overseeing his command should be delegated to the squad.

This was far too innovative to receive official approval, and it was only after many serious cases exposed the flaws in the multiple command system that the soundness of my recommendations was accepted.

The case of the Yorkshire Ripper is a typical example. In this case a number of independent investigators were appointed to separate murder enquiries when the similarity of the cases indicated the need for one senior officer to co-ordinate the whole inquiry. By the time this appointment was made the investigations were becoming stale.

Similarly, there was the case of a little girl who was abducted in Edinburgh and whose body was found in Stafford. Two seats of enquiry were being conducted with no one appointed as co-ordinator: a fact which could only detract from the success of the enquiry.

A third case, and one in which, in 1975, I was involved to a certain extent, was that of the Black Panther.[3] Here was a situation where a number of very experienced senior detectives

---

[3] Donald Neilson, known as the Black Panther because of the hood he wore, kidnapped 17-year-old Lesley Whittle, demanding £50,000 ransom from her relatives. He kept her in a drainage shaft where on 7 March 1975 her body was found hanging from a wire round her neck. Neilson, who was captured on 11 December of that year, had also killed three sub-post-office officials during a series of armed robberies. He received life imprisonment.

were busily engaged in investigating major crime in their own areas. There was Bob Booth, the DCS from West Mercia, investigating the kidnapping of Lesley Whittle. He was a most forthright man of enormous experience and one with a great deal of confidence. Another officer, Joe Mounsey, had an impeccable record in Lancashire where he too was a Detective Chief Superintendent. He later became Assistant Chief Constable of his Force. He was a tough, no-nonsense copper who was investigating the post office robberies which had resulted in murder. Then there were officers from North Yorkshire and Dudley who were also investigating murders committed by the same man. All were good experienced detectives, but what was needed was the appointment of a senior officer to co-ordinate all the enquiries.

When Arthur Rees, the Chief Constable of Staffordshire, called in the Yard for assistance in the murder of Lesley Whittle whose body had been found in his Force area, John Morrison, the head of the Murder Squad, was appointed. This was an unusual choice and was obviously made in an endeavour to overcome the conflict resulting from the characters involved. Unfortunately, even with toughness and diplomacy Morrison's appointment did little to fuse the investigation into a cohesive entity.

I went to Stafford to see the parties concerned, but lacking an overriding authority it was impossible to overcome the clash of personalities, and indeed the matter degenerated to the extent that the major combatants were not even speaking to each other. In all my experience there was never an occasion when a case more urgently demanded the appointment of a supremo to take complete charge of the various enquiries. It cried out for a single authority to co-ordinate and direct the progress of the investigation. This lack of communication was most frustrating. At one stage I called a meeting of senior officers in my office and told them: 'The stage has now been reached when the public realises we have a situation which is becoming fragmented because of clashes of personalities. Let's get one thing clear. It doesn't matter who nicks this bastard, whether it's you, a PC on the beat, the van driver or a WPC. The important thing is to nick him, and the way things are going we shall never do it.'

In the end Neilson was stopped by two bobbies in the small mining town of Mansfield Woodhouse, where he was acting suspiciously. After a fierce struggle, in which members of the public joined, he was detained.

Each year in my annual report I was able to say that the relationship between the Chief Constables and the RCS had improved. I had suggested to the Regional Co-ordinators that it really was a matter of showing each of the Chiefs that his commitment by way of manpower and resources to the squads was being repaid handsomely. Fortunately the quality of the men now being appointed to the squads had improved enormously since the early days, and they were both enjoying the work and having considerable success. I believed the actual number of arrests was unimportant. I insisted we tackle only the most prestigious cases and take them to a conclusion, irrespective of time or personnel. Nor were the squads to compete with the local CID or make arrests to produce attractive statistics.

All the members of the squads had training in both foot and mobile surveillance, and professional and travelling criminals were targeted and kept under constant surveillance. This meant that every region had teams of detectives prepared to undertake long-distance surveillance at a moment's notice. As a result I was obliged to reconsider the normal requests by Chief Constables in murder cases. My priority was the concentration on target criminals, and I made sure that if members of the squad were seconded to murder or other investigations they should be employed on aspects of the case which would not suffer if they were withdrawn after a week or two.

Every opportunity was taken by the squads to undertake the multi-regional operations for which they were so eminently suited, and some of them were concluded with spectacular success. In one, officers from 4, 5, and 7 Regions, covering the West Midlands, East Anglia, and the Western Counties, combined to break up a ring trafficking in illegal immigrants. In the end ten people were arrested in places as far apart as Wiltshire, Norwich and Coventry. In another, officers from Regions 5, 6 and 9 combined to undertake an enquiry into the theft of containers from Southampton. Under the command of Detective Superintendent Ian McGregor (now Assistant Chief Constable, British Transport Police) they arrested 61 people who were charged with stealing property valued at over £1 million. This was what the squads were designed to do and I revelled in their success.

By 1974, despite my discouragement of headcounting, I was able to report that Crime Squad personnel had made 8,036 arrests, assisted in 116 murder enquiries, and received 242 commendations during the year as well as over 300 letters of appreciation, many from Chief Constables and police authorities. I was delighted.

Their successes begat others and I was able to persuade the Chief Constables to extend the period of their men's secondment to the squads from two to three years, as well as approving promotion on the squad. Previously when a man was promoted he returned to his Force. Now I was able to retain him.

My appointment was for two years, but in the end I was fortunate and the appointment lasted for five years. When I went there the Chief HMI was Sir John Hill, a Met man, a lovely old-fashioned gentleman of the type you used to find in the police force at that time. He asked, 'How long are you here for, Nipper?' and I replied, 'As long as you want me, sir.'

'Well,' he said, 'we might as well see it out to the end.' In other words he meant until I had done my 30 years' service in 1977. Then in 1976, when Sir John retired, his replacement called me in to see him. 'I think it's time you left,' he said brusquely. I couldn't argue. I had been there far longer than I could have reasonably expected, and I had seen the squads reach new peaks of efficiency. I began to wonder what my next move would be. I was only 52 and my place at Nottingham was still open. I didn't in the least fancy going back there to an administrative job. I now realised that my failure to relate to Rex Fletcher could have been more my fault than I had been prepared to accept. I had just completed the Kray operation, during which I had been allowed to operate almost completely independently. The limitations imposed by my new job as Assistant Chief had been irksome, even if I had not admitted it.

Now I was in a similar position. For five years I had been my own boss. I had not been at anyone's beck and call, or subject to persistent scrutiny. I had been able to travel all over the country examining the work of the squads as and when I wanted, and the very thought of going back to that routine of morning meetings and checking reports filled me with apprehension. In fact I knew I wouldn't be able to do it. The freedom I had enjoyed over the previous five years had made it impossible to accept a post where I was tied down and fettered.

During my time in London I had met Sir Jack Hayward, a man with important business connections in the Bahamas. He had suggested that on my retirement I should go and work for him on the Islands, and with this in mind I left the police service. I was surprised to find that it was not the wrench I had thought it would be. After only a matter of a few weeks I found there was, after all, life outside The Job.

Sir Jack's intention was that I become an executive president in one of his companies which ran what was then the biggest casino on Grand Bahama Island. I was introduced by him to a number of very influential people including the Prime Minister, Mr (now Sir) Lyndon Pindling. He welcomed me cordially, saying he hoped I would enjoy the beauty and pleasure of the Islands and that he looked forward to my working there.

For anyone working in the Bahamas it was necessary to obtain both a resident's and a work permit – both renewed annually – and so I met the Gaming Board there, and was assured there would be no problems in obtaining the work permit, and the resident's permit would then be a formality.

I was shown the flat I was to have, taken to the Golf Club for lunch, and enjoyed a social round. Everything seemed to be settled. I returned to England and waited. Weeks turned into months and, if I had allowed it, months would have turned into years. Clearly there was a problem. When I spoke to Jack Hayward he told me there had been some problem, either with the Gaming Board or with immigration. I'm still not clear which, but they didn't seem to want me in the Bahamas. No one said anything officially but that was that.

I was very disappointed and so was Jack Hayward, but even he with his influence was impotent at the hands of the politicians. The prospect of living in that climate on the pay I had been offered really appealed to me. One of my referees had been Sir Ranulph 'Rasher' Bacon, who had conducted a Royal Commission into Gaming in the Bahamas. I met him again at a Chief Constable's dinner. 'You never got that job in the Bahamas, did you, old son?'

'Matter of fact I didn't, but how did you know?' I asked.

'Come on,' he laughed, 'You didn't really expect to get in there with your background and reputation did you? They couldn't afford to let a man like you in there with all that corruption going on.' From then on I was a little more philosophical about my failure to find a place in the sun.

So there I was out of work. For the first time in my life since my demob, I was sitting round doing nothing.

For twenty-odd years Alden McCray had been the European representative of the FBI stationed at the American Embassy. We had been involved in a number of criminal investigations together, and meeting on the lecture circuit when we travelled to the various Detective Training Schools we had become good friends. We decided to give it a try at setting up a private detective agency. Alden was very well known; I had a bit of a reputation and we thought it might take off. There was nothing permanent. No rushing in to start a company, Read & McCray. First we wanted to see how things would go. We got some nice contracts. I began vetting the people going out as croupiers to the Bahamas, and Alden had some work with

De Beers, the diamond merchants. He was sent by them to Venezuela and then on to America to discuss a whole range of ventures that might prove fruitful to us. He came back on a Tuesday and rang full of enthusiasm to tell me he thought there were enormous prospects.

We agreed to meet at his home in Willesden on the Thursday at 10 a.m. He died in bed on the Tuesday night. I was shattered. Alden was a man full of life and industry, and his sudden death made me realise just how fragile relationships are. It brought home to me the uncertainty of self-employment and the need to ensure a steady income. I gave up the thought of being a private detective immediately.

Some time afterwards I learned that one of my old colleagues, Trevor Williams, was leaving his post as Security Adviser to the National Museums and Galleries. I wasn't really keen to apply for the job. I suppose I was recovering from the let-down of the Bahamas and particularly the death of Alden. Also when I left the Yard I had promised myself I would not become involved in any kind of security work. Nevertheless, I went to see Trevor, whom I had known as a Deputy Assistant Commissioner at the Yard. We talked about it and he convinced me that this was a most unusual security job. I also spoke to another old mate, Jack Mannings, who had been the first National Security Adviser. 'Nipper,' he said, 'this is the best security job in the country, thc best.' What appealed to me from the start was that I was once again going to be my own boss. No overpowering supervision and plenty of freedom of choice. I decided to spend a couple of weeks with Trevor before making a decision, and when I found how pleasant the work was I applied for the post. The competition was keen, but I was fortunate enough to become the third National Security Adviser – a post created following the theft of Goya's 'Duke of Wellington' from the National Gallery.

My office was in the National Gallery itself and my responsibility was to advise all the forty-plus National Museums and Art Galleries on all matters of security, including the vetting of a borrowing institution. There is a continuing exchange of material between art galleries and museums throughout the world and, of course, security is a paramount feature of the arrangements.

Anyone in the world who wanted to borrow from any of the National collections had to have their security vetted by me. If, say, the Louvre in Paris, the National Gallery in Washington, or the Uffizi in Florence wanted to borrow a painting, I went over to check them out first. Sometimes it was I who physically took pieces when they were loaned to exhibitions. Then there was the actual security of premises in this country. I had to deal with everything from external security and the alarm systems to the level of manpower required. It was a most fascinating job with a great deal of travel involved. I was now in a position to visit centres of art which were previously closed to me. Imagine being able to say, 'I want to look over the whole of the Prado please,' and I would be conducted into galleries and cellars alike. It was to be my work for eight years and I loved it.

The last major operation in which I was involved was the transfer from this country of many millions of pounds worth of paintings, furniture, silverware, ceramics and armour which made up the Treasure Houses of Britain exhibition at the National Gallery, Washington. It was far too valuable to be sent in bulk – no insurance company would look at insuring it: the British and American governments had underwritten the project – and I arranged flights for small quantities of the artefacts, sometimes taking the very valuable jewellery personally in a suitcase placed in a specially booked seat next to me.

It was only when Pat, my wife, still a serving policewoman, was diagnosed as having multiple sclerosis and had to leave the Force after 28 years that I decided to retire with her.

My greatest interest outside work was always boxing, and so I felt honoured when I was invited to join the British Boxing Board of Control as a member of the Southern Area Council. I was later asked to become a Steward of the Board and, of course, I was delighted. This provided the equivalent of a third career, and just as fulfilling. To show how things keep turning in a circle, my dear friend David Hopkin is the Chairman.

Once again I was able to travel – Venezuela, Costa Rica, Las Vegas, New York, and of course all over Europe. I was able to meet my boyhood heroes – Jack Peterson, the President of the Board who sadly died in 1990, Cliff Curvis, now a Steward, Tommy Farr, Harry Mizler, Jack (Kid) Berg, Sugar Ray Robinson – and many of the modern-day fighters – Ali, Mike Tyson, Henry Cooper, Floyd Patterson, Evander Holyfield and many others.

I was always in regular attendance at the World Boxing Association meetings and I was surprised when in 1989 Jimmy Binns, the Association's legal adviser, told me I must be sure to attend the Convention to be held later that year in Philadelphia. It was during the meeting that I was appointed Vice-President. It was a proud moment because I was the first member of the British Board to be honoured in this way.

I can honestly look back and say I have had three careers, each of which has been vastly different from the previous one and each totally fulfilling. I realise I am a fortunate man.

EPILOGUE

Don't talk to me of his achievements. Is he lucky?
Napoleon Bonaparte

AFTER SUCH A long time it is difficult to know what has happened to some of the characters from my story. Some, such as Billy Exley, Limehouse Willey, and Tommy Cowley are dead, as are Melford Stevenson, Desmond Vowden who defended Charles Kray, Trevor Lloyd-Hughes, Ernie Millen, John du Rose, Peter Brodie and my old tutor Martin Walsh. Some, such as Ronnie and Reggie, are still in prison or hospital. Others, such as some members of the Train Robbery team, have served their sentences and are once more in prison or are dead. Liza went off round the world with her boyfriend. Others in the cases have just gone back to their ordinary lives.

Of my first two Sergeants in the second Kray inquiry, Algie Hemingway went on to become a Commander, whilst Alan Wright left the Force and qualified as a lawyer. Harry Mooney left the service after completing his full term and became a solicitor. Frank Cater went on to become the Commander of the Flying Squad. He has now retired and works for Securicor. Two of the most active men on the second Kray inquiry, Mick Richards and Georgie Ness, became respectively a Deputy Assistant Commissioner and a Commander. Bert Trevette retired after completing 30 years' service and became the Harbour Master at Dover.

Nowadays when I go to police functions I am approached by fellows who tell me they were on my squad, but I find it difficult to remember them. Of course I can easily recall the original team and most of those on the action squad, but those who were employed on the protection of the witnesses and the jury were so numerous I'm afraid I have to rely on their word.

Over the years Kenneth Jones, John Leonard, both appointed High Court judges, James Crespi QC and Sir David Hopkin, who made up the prosecution team, have had a dinner every couple of years with Frank Cater and me. At first we used to chat about the case and analyse it to see what mistakes we had made. Then Frank and I would disclose little bits of information which had never been passed to the lawyers and which amused them. Now when we meet we talk about mundane things, our health, politics, the world situation. Rarely do we mention the Krays although the next time we meet – if there is a next time – we can discuss the film about them and its proposed sequel.

From time to time I am asked to appear on television or do a broadcast, and over the years I have always expressed surprise that there has been such continued interest in the case. Now, looking back through the newspaper cuttings, I realise they have never been far out of the public's eye. Following the release of the film there has been even more interest shown in them, and the inevitable question I am asked is do I think the Krays should be released.

Ronnie, of course, is a special case. He is still in Broadmoor and relies on the care and medication provided there to keep him stable. As he was committed to a prison to serve his sentence and was then moved to Broadmoor, he would have to be reclassified as sane and then moved back to a normal prison before he could be considered for parole. For the moment this seems to be a remote possibility. Reggie, on the other hand, becomes eligible for parole this year. When the evidence about the butchery of the defenceless Jack McVitie came out in 1968 it seemed quite terrible. Now, nearly 25 years later, it seems we have heard tales which, if not worse, were at least as bad.

Unfortunately the book which the Krays wrote, attempting to justify their actions and offering no word of repentance, may not go down too well with members of the Parole Board. In describing the McVitie killing, Reggie writes: 'I did not regret it at the time and I do not regret it now.' Of course, this may be seen as Reggie wanting to re-establish himself in the eyes of his own society, in which any admission of guilt or show of remorse means a betrayal of that society, but it is a statement I am sure the Parole Board will consider.

Their lives have been so fictionalised that people think they have been hard done by. Last year I went to a reception at Scotland Yard and met some people from a film company. They were quite young and were technical people, directors, producers. Their view was quite incredible. They were convinced that the Krays had been railroaded and that any offence they had committed was minimised by the fact that it had been committed against a fellow gangster, and therefore they should not have received such a harsh sentence and were entitled to a deal of public sympathy. One of the film company was a young girl who said to me, 'You've got to remember all they did was kill their own. . .'

I asked in what way did that lessen the offence. 'If I killed you that would be awful, but if I killed a prostitute, someone on the fringe of criminality and someone whose lifestyle did not equate with yours, would that mitigate the offence?'

But, bearing in mind some of the examples I have given – the Train Robbers and Eddie Richardson for example – there is nothing to show that prison has a better chance of stopping people from committing crimes in the long term. In their case it is clear that long sentences did not the slightest good except, as Melford Stevenson said, in giving society a rest for a few years. The odd character like Jimmy Boyle or John McVicar may benefit, but they are certainly the exceptions. I have long held the view that the only real curb on an active criminal is old age. In other words when he is too old to climb a drainpipe, to have a battle or to run away from the cops, then he'll reform.

I appreciate that so far I have said little or nothing about my home life. The police force is a demanding mistress and, as is the case with so many other officers, both male and female, who have devoted much time to the job, my first marriage unfortunately broke up.

I had married Marion Millar in 1951 and our daughter Maralyn was born two years later. As I made my way in the job I spent less and less time at home and inevitably this soured the relationship between my wife and myself. The pressure exerted by the two lengthy Kray enquiries made matters between us almost intolerable, and indeed our relationship broke down irreparably. Marion and I were divorced in 1979 and the following year I married my present wife Pat. Sadly Marion died following a heart attack in 1986. Maralyn now lives in the North of England where she is the area supervisor for a commercial catering company. Pat and Maralyn get on famously and, together with Maralyn's friend Alan, we spend a lot of time together.

There is in fact a final postscript. In December 1989 Pat and I went to Bournemouth to meet with some friends for the weekend. Walking through the town in the late afternoon sunshine I went into a newsagent's to buy a paper, and there had a convulsive fit. It lasted only a few minutes, but I was taken to the local hospital and released an hour later. Pat drove me back to London where on the Monday I saw a specialist who referred me for a series of tests. During his examination he asked whether I had ever had an attack before. At first I said no, but then I remembered an incident back in 1958. Marion's father had died suddenly and I had driven her back to Fifeshire in heavy snow and what had been appalling road conditions. The next day I had been shovelling snow from the driveway of the house and had had a fainting attack which, I was told later, had been accompanied by convulsions. The doctor who came to see me was told and put it down to exhaustion. Now, the specialist realised immediately what it was, and diagnosed me as an epileptic. I had, he said, been suffering from this condition for 30 years. As he wrote to my GP, had this been diagnosed at the time I would have been out of the Force within weeks.

He was right of course. I would have been pensioned off for failing to meet the required medical standards. All I would have known about the Train Robbers, Jack Buggy, the Black Panther, the Krays or any of the others would have been what I read in the newspapers and somebody else's book. I am indeed a lucky man. Napoleon would have liked me.

INDEX